W9-AKK-325

Praise for *Learning from Catastrophes*

"What an extraordinary range of experiences and what an experienced array of authors! This book is actually exciting to read, whether or not you are professionally concerned with anticipating or coping with catastrophes or their aftermath. But if those are your concerns, this book will not only inform you but stimulate your own thinking."

—**Thomas Schelling**, Emeritus Distinguished University Professor at the School of Public Policy of the University of Maryland, and recipient of the 2005 Nobel Prize in Economic Science

"*Learning from Catastrophes* brings together the expertise of two distinguished academics, Howard Kunreuther and Michael Useem, and other prominent thought leaders to shed light on a provocative topic of our times—risk. Kunreuther is a leading expert on the economic impact of large scale catastrophes and brings a well-honed perspective to the risk sciences. Useem is a driving force in studying leadership attributes, incorporating leadership studies into business curriculum and applying them in business. Together, the two professors of The Wharton School, University of Pennsylvania have presented a thoughtful analysis of extreme events and recommendations for mitigating their impacts. Spawned by discussions at the 2009 World Economic Forum, this book is a must read for those whose careers touch on the prediction of and response to catastrophes."

—**Jay Fishman**, Chairman and Chief Executive Officer, The Travelers Companies, Inc.

"The first decade of this century has seen natural disasters, acts of mass violence, and a severe financial crisis; but also increasing global integration and growing prosperity in many areas. *Learning from Catastrophes* is a most timely look at how we can use the latter to be better prepared for the former. The richness of ideas in this book reflects the diversity and expertise of the contributors. There is, however, a single thread that runs through it—that the answer lies in communication and collaboration and that we have a shared global responsibility to harness technology, intellectual resources, and financial capital to prevent recurrence of these events and mitigate their impact."

—**K. V. Kamath**, Chairman, ICICI Bank, and former President, Confederation of Indian Industry

"In this volume, Howard Kunreuther and Michael Useem have gathered together a cast of brilliant thinkers to impart lifesaving knowledge for successfully navigating the hazards of the twenty-first century. This deeply optimistic book not only equips the reader with the intellectual tools for confronting our worst fears head-on, but teaches us that we can become a better, more compassionate, and prosperous global society in the process."

—**Stephen E. Flynn**, Senior Fellow for Counterterrorism and National Security Studies, Council on Foreign Relations

Learning from Catastrophes

Learning from Catastrophes

Strategies for Reaction and Response

Edited by Howard Kunreuther and Michael Useem

Alan Berger
Case Brown
Séan Cleary
Arnold Howitt
Bridget M. Hutter
Michel Jarraud
Carolyn Kousky
Herman "Dutch" Leonard
Geoff Love
Thomas Lovejoy
Michele McNabb
Erwann Michel-Kerjan
Suzanne Nora Johnson
Kristine Pearson
Harvey Rubin
Jiah-Shin Teh
Detlof von Winterfeldt
Lan Xue
Richard Zeckhauser
Kaibin Zhong

In Collaboration with
the World Economic Forum
Global Agenda Council on
the Mitigation of Natural Disasters

Vice President, Publisher: Tim Moore
Associate Publisher and Director of Marketing: Amy Neidlinger
Wharton Editor: Steve Kobrin
Executive Editor: Jeanne Glasser
Editorial Assistant: Myesha Graham
Operations Manager: Gina Kanouse
Senior Marketing Manager: Julie Phifer
Publicity Manager: Laura Czaja
Assistant Marketing Manager: Megan Colvin
Cover Designer: Chuti Prasertsith
Managing Editor: Kristy Hart
Project Editor: Jovana San Nicolas-Shirley
Copy Editor: Keith Cline
Proofreader: Apostrophe Editing Services
Indexer: Joy Dean Lee
Compositor: Jake McFarland
Manufacturing Buyer: Dan Uhrig

Publishing as Wharton School Publishing
Upper Saddle River, New Jersey 07458

Wharton School Publishing offers excellent discounts on this book when ordered in quantity for bulk purchases or special sales. For more information, please contact U.S. Corporate and Government Sales, 1-800-382-3419, corpsales@pearsontechgroup.com. For sales outside the U.S., please contact International Sales at international@pearson.com.

Printed in the United States of America

First Printing December 2009

ISBN-10: 0-13-704485-2
ISBN-13: 978-0-13-704485-6

Pearson Education LTD.
Pearson Education Australia PTY, Limited.
Pearson Education Singapore, Pte. Ltd.
Pearson Education North Asia, Ltd.
Pearson Education Canada, Ltd.
Pearson Educación de Mexico, S.A. de C.V.
Pearson Education—Japan
Pearson Education Malaysia, Pte. Ltd.

Library of Congress Cataloging-in-Publication Data

Kunreuther, Howard.

Learning from catastrophes : strategies for reaction and response / Howard Kunreuther, Michael Useem.

p. cm.

Includes bibliographical references and index.

ISBN-13: 978-0-13-704485-6 (hardcover : alk. paper)

ISBN-10: 0-13-704485-2

1. Risk management. 2. Emergency management. I. Useem, Michael. II. Title.

HD61.K86 2010

363.34—dc22

2009032585

Contents

Part II: Linking Risk Assessment, Risk Perception, and Risk Management

Part III: Applications to Catastrophic Risks

Foreword

In late autumn 2008, more than 700 experts gathered in Dubai for the inaugural meeting of the World Economic Forum's Global Agenda Councils. Initiated less than 12 months earlier, the idea behind the Councils was to bring together some of the best minds from business, academia, and government to focus on the most pressing questions of our times. From that gathering emerged fresh thinking, sometimes provocative, sometimes pragmatic, as to how to mobilize the combined forces of the public, private, and nongovernmental sectors around issues ranging from global economic imbalances to ecosystems and biodiversity. One of these councils, the Council on the Mitigation of Natural Disasters, under the chairmanship of Howard Kunreuther and Michael Useem, left Dubai with an even stronger vision of the need for a holistic approach to this issue, a vision they explore in this book.

The initial focus of the council members was on natural catastrophes, which wreak havoc on lives, communities, and economies. These events occur across countries, climates, and economic sectors, and only mitigating strategies, preparedness, and response readiness can make a difference. What emerged from the council's thinking was how much the principles and operational elements relevant for natural catastrophe mitigation and management can be applied to other incident-driven risks. In their discussions with experts and practitioners from fields as diverse as terrorism prevention, pandemic preparedness, and technical or even nuclear accident avoidance, the council's principles were unanimously deemed applicable.

Thus, the focus of *Learning from Catastrophes* is on improving our ability to identify and manage events that are perceived to be highly unlikely, but which, if they do occur, can have catastrophic impact at both the national and global levels. Left to our own devices, we tend to underappreciate such low-probability, high-consequence events. Our minds often turn them into "no likelihood"—although sometimes into the opposite and equally pernicious prescription of "near certainty." As a result, those who are responsible for leading major institutions have a special and specific calling to recognize and guard against these human shortcomings.

The empirical evidence presented in this book points to the value of building an effective forecasting capacity and persuasively communicating information on high-consequence risks to everybody potentially affected. The authors also recommend drawing upon economic and other incentives to encourage individuals, firms, and public agencies to work together in undertaking protective measures for reducing losses from disasters and in building a culture of resilience and sustainability.

To avoid and mitigate both natural and unnatural calamities in the future, you will want to incorporate this book's directives into your strategic and operational planning processes and leadership programs. Leaders from business and the public and nonprofit leaders could do a lot to protect their organizations and communities by putting the principles highlighted in *Learning from Catastrophes* into practice. This book provides a useful set of principles for guiding decision making and leadership so essential for averting and overcoming those future risks that are sure to threaten yet again our global prosperity.

—Klaus Schwab
Founder and Executive Chairman
World Economic Forum

Preface

According to the 2008 *World Disasters Report,* natural calamities in 2007 affected more than 200 million people. Their direct cost in 2007 totaled more than $60 billion; the financial impact of the Sichuan earthquake in 2008 alone has been estimated to exceed $70 billion. The cost of the 2008–09 global financial crisis reached hundreds of billions of dollars in many countries. A widespread outbreak of swine flu could wreak havoc on a comparable scale.

This book offers critical lessons for those who are most responsible for avoiding the worst, whether natural calamities or unnatural catastrophes ranging from financial crises to terrorist attacks.

All are low-probability but high-consequence events. By examining what worked and what did not in prior disasters, we can be better equipped to prevent and mitigate future disasters. One cannot fully learn to effectively manage extreme risk without looking to the lessons from both natural and unnatural disasters.

If New Orleans had well-maintained levees and evacuation plans, land-use management programs, and well-enforced building codes, and if insurers could charge premiums that reflected risk and could reward with price reductions those who adopted loss-reduction measures, the devastation from Hurricane Katrina would have been far less. But in fact, short-term savings trumped long-term safeguards.

If federal regulators had required transparency in credit-default swaps, if bank CEOs had insisted that quarterly windfalls be balanced against future earnings, and if loan officers had to live with the subprime risks they were foisting on others, we would be talking about market correction, not credit calamity. But in fact, private greed trumped collective good.

If we know that we will predictably underpredict—and thus underanticipate the next catastrophe—we can do something about it in advance. Now is the time for all of us to appreciate the importance of recognizing risks and preparing for them before they result in another Katrina washout or credit tsunami. Above all, leaders need to remember that *a low risk is not no risk*.

Drawing on the knowledge of a select set of leading experts on natural disasters and other extreme events, this book takes stock of what we know about decision making, risk reduction, and strategies for encouraging preventive actions. *Learning from Catastrophes* provides a framework and a core set of principles for designing strategies for managing risks that have a relatively small chance of occurring—but could create severe consequences if they do.

Learning from Catastrophes is intended for readers with a general or professional interest in understanding behavior and developing more effective strategies for reducing losses from low-probability, high-consequence events. These events include large-scale natural disasters, financial crises, industrial accidents, rogue trading, corporate bankruptcies, pandemics, and terrorist attacks. The book should be of interest to policy makers, risk managers, and business leaders; those directly engaged in preparation for, mitigation of, and recovery from catastrophes; and decision makers in organizations ranging from insurance firms and financial companies to emergency preparedness agencies and other governmental organizations concerned with the risks from disasters.

We owe a great debt of gratitude to World Economic Forum Executive Chairman Klaus Schwab for his leadership in creating and supporting the Global Agenda Councils. We are extremely grateful as well for the assistance of Matthias Caton, Martina Gmür, Stéphane Oertel, Fiona Paua, and Sheana Tambourgi of the World Economic Forum in supporting our Global Agenda Council on the Mitigation of Natural Disasters. It was through a number of wide-ranging discussions with members of this council and a meeting of all the councils in Dubai in November 2008 that this book took shape.

We also want to thank Carol Heller of the Wharton Risk Management and Decision Processes Center, for her careful and comprehensive guidance of this project from its inception to the completion of this book. Jeanne Glasser, Russ Hall, Steven Kobrin, Timothy C. Moore, Teresa Regan, and Jovana San Nicolas-Shirley of Wharton School Publishing provided unstinting support in bringing this book to completion so that it would be available in time for the Annual

Meeting of the World Economic Forum in Davos, Switzerland, in 2010. We hope, in time, that lessons from this book will help to reduce the potential impact of future catastrophes.

—Howard Kunreuther and Michael Useem
The Wharton School, University of Pennsylvania
October 2009

1

Principles and Challenges for Reducing Risks from Disasters

Howard Kunreuther and Michael Useem
The Wharton School, University of Pennsylvania

Overview

This chapter provides a framework and a set of guiding principles for designing alternative strategies for reducing losses from low-probability, high-consequence events. This framework highlights the importance of expert assessment of the risk, as well as the importance of understanding how the public perceives the risk. These two elements should serve as a basis for developing and evaluating strategies to manage risk. Seven principles provide guidance to leaders in designing measures that will reduce losses in advance of a disaster and in developing efficient and equitable means to aid the recovery process following a catastrophe.

The past decade has been particularly devastating on the natural disaster front, especially in developing countries. The tragic tsunami of December 2004 killed more than 280,000 people in Southeast Asia. Cyclone Nargis in May 2008 killed an estimated 140,000 in Myanmar. A 7.9-Richter-scale earthquake in the same month killed nearly 70,000 and left some 5 million homeless in China. Widespread flooding in Mozambique following a tropical storm in February and March 2000 displaced more than a million residents.

Even in a developed country like the United States, which has extensive experience with natural catastrophes and ample resources to prepare for them, the 2004 and 2005 hurricane seasons proved devastating. Hurricane Katrina, which hit Louisiana and Mississippi at the end of August 2005, killed 1,300 people and forced 1.5 million to evacuate—a record for the country. Economic damages were estimated at more than $150 billion.

The world experienced comparably catastrophic shocks in 2008. The subprime mortgage crisis of mid-2008 overwhelmed dozens of financial companies in the United States, from Fannie Mae and Freddie Mac to Lehman Brothers and AIG. The stock market crash in the autumn destroyed more than a trillion dollars in investor wealth worldwide. The great credit squeeze directly impacted Main Street in developed countries and "No Street" in emerging economies, leading to worldwide recession in 2009.

This book provides experience-based and research-informed insights into how individuals engaged in disaster mitigation can better manage the risk associated with both natural and unnatural calamities. Here we provide a framework that highlights the importance of linking risk assessment and risk perception in designing strategies for managing risks in our increasingly interconnected world. The framework also outlines a set of guiding principles for the role that leaders can take to mitigate those risks and effectively respond when the possibility of an extreme event turns into reality.

Framework for Analysis

Systematically investigating the impacts of natural and unnatural disasters requires input from many disciplines. Engineering and the natural sciences provide data on the nature of the risks associated with disasters of different magnitudes and the uncertainties surrounding them (*risk assessment*). Geography, organizational theory, psychology, sociology, and other social sciences provide insights into how individuals, groups, organizations, and nations perceive risks and make decisions (*risk perception and choice*). Economists and policy analysts examine various strategies for reducing future losses and for dealing with recovery problems (*risk management strategies*).

Risk Assessment

The science of estimating the chances of specific extreme events occurring and their potential consequences originates in the field of property insurance and the science of natural hazards. In the 1800s, residential insurers managed their risk by "mapping" the structures that they covered, pinning tacks onto a wall map to display the degree of physical concentration of exposure. Although crude, the technique served insurers well at the time and limited their risk. Widespread usage of such "mapping" ended in the 1960s when it finally became too cumbersome and time-consuming to execute. Now, Geographic Information Systems (GIS) software and other digital products achieve the same with much more extensive data and sophisticated technologies.[1]

Whatever the risk-assessment process method, four basic elements for assessing risk remain the same: hazard, inventory, vulnerability, and loss (see Figure 1.1). The first element focuses on the risk of a *hazard*. For example, an earthquake hazard is characterized by its likely epicenter location and magnitude, along with other significant parameters. A hurricane is distinguished by its projected path and wind speed. One could also describe the hazard associated with terrorism or a pandemic by characterizing the target of a violent attack or the spread rate of a potentially catastrophic disease such as swine flu or severe acute respiratory syndrome (SARS). The hazard can also be usefully characterized as a range of potential scenarios. For example, what is the likelihood that a hurricane of magnitude 3, 4, or 5 on the Saffir-Simpson scale might strike the Miami, Florida, area in 2010?

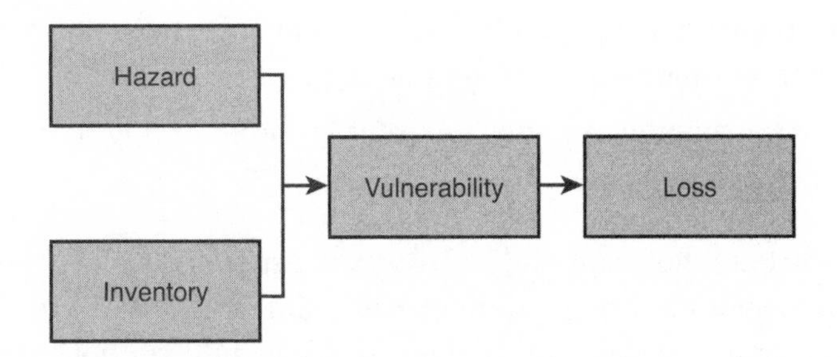

Figure 1.1 Elements of the risk-assessment process model

The risk-assessment process model's second element identifies the *inventory* of properties, humans, and the physical environment at risk. To fully inventory structures, for instance, requires evaluation of their location, physical dimensions, and construction quality. Taken together, the hazard and inventory elements enable calculation of the model's third element, the damage *vulnerability* of the structures or people at risk. And from the measure of vulnerability, the human and property *loss,* the fourth element, can be evaluated.

In working with catastrophes in this model, it is also useful to distinguish between *direct* and *indirect* losses. Direct losses include injuries, fatalities, financial losses, and the cost to repair or replace a structure, restore a service, or rescue a company. Indirect losses include future foregone income, slower growth, and other longer-term consequences of evacuation costs, disrupted schooling, and company bankruptcies.

Scientists and engineers develop reasonably accurate models for assessing risk with this model and specifying the degree of uncertainty in each of the components. In doing so, analysts take special care to minimize the role of subjective assessments and personal biases in building their estimates. But because such factors still sometimes intrude, it is not uncommon for the public to learn from one expert that there is little about which to be concerned related to a given risk, and from another expert that the alarm bells should be sounding.

Not surprisingly, the public responds in disparate ways to the added uncertainty resulting from conflicting expert forecasts. Some may simply decide to ignore the expert judgments. Others may be drawn to the expert prediction most compatible with the individual's own predispositions. Still others may seek out a host of expert opinions and then draw independent assessments of where the preponderance of informed forecasts are pointing.

Consider the uncertainties inherent in the following natural and unnatural disasters:

- What are the chances that Tokyo will experience an earthquake of magnitude 7 or greater next year, and what will be the resulting property damage, human loss, and interruption of commerce in Japan, East Asia, and beyond?

- What is the prospect of a major terrorist attack in Europe, and what would be the resulting human casualties and economic impacts?
- What is the probability of an African pandemic in the next five years, what type of disease is most likely to spread, where will it start, and how soon will it reach other continents?
- What is the probability that 5 of the 20 largest financial institutions worldwide will fail within the next 24 months and either go bankrupt, as did Lehman Brothers, or enter government receivership, as in the case of the Royal Bank of Scotland?
- What is the chance that the top ten insurance companies and commercial banks will have their credit rating dropped four tiers—say from AAA (almost no credit risk) to A1 or A+ (safe unless unforeseen events arise)—in the coming year?

When expert analysts attempt to answer these questions, they usually ask for more precise information to define the event for their model. Take the question related to the chances of an earthquake of magnitude 7 or greater in Tokyo next year. Experts will want to know how to define Tokyo (the city proper or the entire metropolitan region), whether *next year* means the calendar or fiscal year, and what should be included among the indirect losses. Because experts often take variant responses to these kinds of questions into account, divergent forecasts for even relatively specific events can leave people and their leaders unclear whether and how to prepare and respond.

For many years, the focus of hazard-loss estimation for natural disasters had been largely confined to property damage and loss of life. And estimations were generally limited to the immediate period of the disaster, just hours or days after the earth shook or floodwaters peaked. Now, risk-assessment models are incorporating longer time periods extending to weeks and even months, and to more diverse measures, such as disrupted commercial flows or post-traumatic stress disorders. As experts have expanded the time periods and range of losses in their models, risk assessment has become much more complex and forecasts are likely to be fraught with uncertainty. That, in turn, has added to public and leadership hesitation on how best to prepare for and react to disasters.

Risk Perception and Choice

Whereas risk assessment focuses on objective losses such as financial costs, *risk perception* is concerned with the psychological and emotional factors associated with risk. Research has demonstrated that the perception of risk has an enormous impact on behavior, regardless of the objective conditions.

In a set of path-breaking studies begun in the 1970s, decision scientists and psychologists such as University of Oregon's Paul Slovic, Carnegie Mellon University's Baruch Fischhoff, and others began studying people's concerns about various types of risks. They found that people viewed hazards with which they had little personal knowledge and experience as highly risky, and they especially dreaded their possibility. In the case of unfamiliar technologies with catastrophic potential such as nuclear power, people perceived the risks as much higher than did the experts.[2]

Research also found that people often perceive the world of low-probability and high-consequence events quite differently from experts, and that this impacts on their decision-making process and choice behavior. For years, however, this disparity was simply ignored by expert analysts, who made little effort to communicate the inventory, hazards, vulnerability, and losses from risks in ways that the public could accept and act upon. Sometimes, important underlying assumptions were not made explicit; other times, complex technical issues were not explained well; and often, little effort was made to help the public appreciate why experts could disagree with one another. Rarely were public perceptions even considered.

In recent years, however, the scientific and engineering communities have devoted increased attention to the psychological factors that impact on how individuals make decisions with respect to risks from natural and technological hazards. Rather than simply urging policy makers and organizational leaders to take actions on the basis of their traditional risk-assessment models, experts are increasingly incorporating salient human emotions such as fear and anxiety into the models.

Researchers have discovered that people are generally not well prepared to interpret low probabilities when reaching decisions about unlikely events. In fact, evidence suggests that people may not even want data on the likelihood of a disastrous event when the information is available to them. One study found, for instance, that when faced with several hypothetical managerial decisions that are risky, individuals rarely ask for data on the probabilities of the alternative outcomes. When one group was provided limited information about the choices they were facing and given an opportunity to find out more about their risks, fewer than one in four requested information on the probabilities, and none sought precise likelihood data. When another group was presented with precise probability data, fewer than one in five drew upon the concept of probability when making their choices between alternative courses of action.[3]

If people do not think probabilistically, how then do they make their choices in the face of risk? Extensive research on decision making now confirms that individuals' risk perceptions are affected by judgmental biases.[4] One of the important forms of bias in the case of extreme events such as large-scale disasters is a tendency for people to estimate the risk they face on the basis of their own experience regardless of what the experts may have communicated. If an event is particularly recent or impactful, people tend to ignore information on the likelihood of a recurrence of the event and focus their attention on the consequences should another similar disaster occur.[5] Following the terrorist attacks with hijacked aircraft on September 11, 2001, many of those living in the United States refused to fly because they believed that the chances of ending up on a hijacked aircraft were dangerously high—even though the actual likelihood was extremely low given the tightened security measures introduced in the wake of 9/11.

More generally, researchers have found that people tend to assess low-probability, high-consequence events by focusing on one end of the likelihood spectrum or the other: For some people, such events will surely happen, for others they will surely not happen, and few fall in between. For very unlikely events, however, people crowd toward the "will not happen" end of the spectrum. It is for this reason that there is a general lack of public interest in voluntarily purchasing insurance against natural disasters and in investing in loss-protection measures. People underestimate both the probability of a disaster and the accompanying losses, and they are often myopic when it comes to proper planning for disasters. If a disaster does occur, people then tend to overinvest in seeking to prevent a recurrence. Protective measures are thus undertaken when it is too late. A study of homeowners in California, for example, showed that most purchased earthquake insurance only after personally experiencing an earthquake. When asked about the likelihood of another quake occurring in their area, they correctly responded that it was lower than prior to the disaster because the stress on the fault had been reduced. And yet that is when they finally decided to acquire the insurance.[6]

Risk-Management Strategies

In developing effective risk-management strategies for reducing losses from natural and unnatural disasters, leaders of public agencies and private and nonprofit organizations will want to appreciate the findings of risk-assessment studies and the factors that influence risk perception and choice. Drawing on that research, we propose six areas for improving risk management:

1. ***Risk forecasting.*** The broadening of disaster losses to include longer-term impacts and indirect costs has made forecasting more complex. Improvement in the precision of these forecasts is critical for both averting disasters and minimizing their impacts. For example, more detailed weather forecasts of the path and severity of a tropical storm can be key to wise evacuation decisions and avoiding unnecessary flight. So, too, would be better data on the systemic risks that little regulated but highly leveraged financial products can invisibly create.
2. ***Communicating risk information.*** Because people generally dismiss low-probability events by assuming that they will not personally experience such events, expanding the time frame over which the likelihood of an extreme event is presented can garner more attention. If a company is considering flood-protection insurance for the 25-year life of a production facility, for example, managers are more likely to take the risk seriously if a 1-in-100-year flood is presented as having a greater than 1-in-5 chance of occurring during a 25-year period rather than a 1-in-100 chance during the coming year.[7]
3. ***Economic incentives.*** Both positive and negative economic incentives encourage individuals to take protective measures.

But here again, the way people process information on the costs and benefits of reducing the risk can play an important role in their decision on whether to adopt the measures.

What would be the effectiveness, of say, a policy of reducing homeowners' insurance premiums for homeowners who undertake loss-reduction measures along the Mississippi River, or a policy of incentivizing villagers in Bangladesh to avoid migrating into flood-prone areas? Given that people think only about the potential benefits of such measures over the next year or two, not the next decade or two, they may not view these measures as financially attractive if there is a significant up-front cost. Had they considered a longer time period when evaluating the protective measure, the costs may well have been viewed as worthwhile.

Fines coupled with specific regulations or building standards can also be used to encourage protective measures, but they, too, must be coupled with measures that ensure a high likelihood that negligent individuals will be penalized. If people perceive the probability of detection to be low or the cost of noncompliance as modest, they may conclude that it does not pay to take protective action.

4. ***Private-public partnerships.*** Because the public, private, and nonprofit sectors share in the costs and benefits of preparing for disasters, furthering collaboration among them ahead of time can be vital for building effective leadership and strategies for facing disasters. Public-private partnerships should thus be created before they are needed.

   Insurance premium reductions should be given to those who invest in risk-reducing measures to reflect the lower losses from a future disaster. Building codes may be desirable when property owners would otherwise not adopt cost-effective mitigation measures because they either misperceive the benefits from them or underestimate the probability of a disaster occurring. This might have been a factor in the widespread loss of life in the Pakistan earthquake, magnitude 7.6, in October 2005, which killed more than 70,000 inhabitants, many buried under poorly constructed schools and homes. So, too, with investment codes: Had there been stronger regulation on derivative products, such as insurance on subprime mortgage securities, investment bankers would have been less likely to contribute to the systemic risks that rocked the world's economy in 2008.

5. ***Reinsurance and other financial instruments.*** The shortage of reinsurance—insurance for insurance companies that allows them to offer greater protection to policyholders than the assets of the insurers would ordinarily permit—following Hurricane Andrew's damage to Florida in 1992 and the Northridge, California, earthquake in 1994, led U.S. financial institutions to market new instruments for providing protection against mega disasters. Known as catastrophe bonds, these were offered at high interest rates to overcome investors' qualms about the likelihood of losing their principal should a major disaster occur. The market for such bonds grew rapidly in the 2000s, with $2.7 billion in new and renewed catastrophe bond issues in 2008.[8]

   In anticipating exceptionally massive disasters, it may be necessary for the government to provide insurance protection to pay for losses that the private sector is not willing to cover. Florida established the Florida Hurricane Catastrophe Fund following Hurricane Andrew in 1992, for instance, when a number of insurers reported that they could no longer include windstorm damage as part of their standard homeowner coverage. After the Northridge earthquake in 1994, insurers backed off from earthquake coverage, and the state formed the California Earthquake Authority to provide homeowners with earthquake coverage.

   In providing coverage against large-scale catastrophes, it is important that premiums closely reflect risk. Equity and affordability considerations may justify some type of subsidy for those deserving special treatment, such as low-income residents. This subsidy should *not* be in the form of artificially low premiums, but should preferably take the form of a grant from the public sector. For example, if a risk-based flood insurance premium of $2,000 is considered to be unaffordable to a household in a high hazard area, the family could be provided an insurance voucher to buy a policy in much the way that food stamps are provided to those in need of household staples. If the family reduces its risks by investing in a mitigation measure such as elevating its house, it receives a premium discount.

6. ***Resiliency and sustainability.*** The resilience of a community after a disaster and its sustainability over the long run have important ramifications for estimating the extent of hazard damage and developing risk management policies. Resilience refers to the ability of a business, household, or community to cushion potential losses through inherent or explicit adaptive behavior in the aftermath of a disaster and through a learning process in anticipation of a future one. Businesses may have alternative power generators in place, households may ration their water supply, and communities may open shelters for those forced to evacuate their homes.[9]

   Resilience also includes the ability to use price signals, such as premium discounts for investing in mitigation measures, to encourage appropriate actions before and after a disaster. And it entails the ability of community, company, and other leaders to remain focused on recovery even as they may be at risk or personally suffering in the immediate aftermath of a disaster. In the wake of Hurricane Katrina, for example, the president and senior administrators of Tulane University in New Orleans were marooned on campus for four days without food, water, power, or regular contact with the outside world. Despite their severe personal circumstances, they plunged into the arduous work of staff rescue and university restoration. After "being stranded for four days," recalled the president, Scott S. Cowen, "I realized that I could either focus on the darkness, or I could try to see beyond it and focus on the light. I chose the latter." In reflecting on the experience and its personal hardships, he said, it "has taught us as an institution to stay focused on our mission and goals even in the face of financial and physical crisis. It has taught us the responsibility that comes with our role as the largest employer in our home city—a responsibility to help rebuild our city and heal its people."[10]

   Advanced economies are becoming increasingly interlinked and dependent on sophisticated, vulnerable systems—especially infrastructural services such as highways, electric supply, and the Internet—for which substitution is difficult and thus resilience more critical. When the west coast of Japan was hit by a minor earthquake in July 2007, a supplier of auto piston rings was forced to close, and because Japanese auto making was built on a just-in-time inventory system, the supplier's closing forced Toyota and Honda to suspend production.[11] Researchers have a role to play here in identifying ways to improve resilience in a more interdependent and interconnected world, such as the establishment of information clearinghouses for suppliers without customers and for customers without suppliers.

Sustainability refers to the long-run viability and self-sufficiency of the community in the face of hazard threats. The more general definition of the term emanates from economic development and stipulates that decisions taken today should not diminish productive capacity—broadly defined to include natural resources and the environment of a community—in the future. In the case of natural hazards, sustainability implies that land-use decisions made today—such as forest management or strip mining—should not place the community in greater jeopardy in the future or make it more dependent on external assistance to survive. Sustainability emphasizes the importance of integrating mitigation measures into overall economic development policy and eliminating practices that increase a community's exposure to hazards.[12]

Many developing countries are especially vulnerable to disasters because of low-quality structures, poor land use, inadequate emergency response, environmental degradation, and limited funds. Climate change may especially increase the likelihood of disasters in these areas, such as flooding in low-lying Bangladesh. Developing countries often lack the infrastructure and institutions that developed countries take for granted in formulating risk management strategies. And in areas where poverty is extreme, the indirect effects of disaster may include a surge in endemic disease, widespread starvation, and human-rights violations. In the wake of the Mozambique flooding in

2000, for instance, families irretrievably lost birth certificates, marriage documents, and land titles because few personal records had been backed up or computerized.

Guiding Principles

In characterizing and developing strategies and leadership for perceiving, assessing, and managing risks associated with extreme events, it is useful to focus on a set of guiding principles. These principles apply not only to leadership in averting and responding to natural catastrophes but also to leadership facing other extreme events, whether terrorist attacks, financial crises, or governance failures. We briefly highlight these principles here:

Principle 1: Appreciate the importance of estimating risks and characterizing uncertainties surrounding such estimates. For developing the strategies and leadership for reducing and managing a specific risk, it is essential to have reliable estimates of the likelihood of the event and its consequences.

Consider a business facing a decision on whether to invest $100,000 to make its property more fire resistant. An informed decision on whether to incur this cost depends on having accurate estimates of fire frequencies and likely losses. Its executives will be more likely to make this investment if they learn that the chances of a fire next year are 1-in-100 rather than 1-in-1,000, and if the likely property damage and business interruption would total $5 million rather than $500,000. The less uncertainty surrounding these estimates, the more confident the executives will be regarding their decision as to whether to undertake these measures.

Principle 2: Recognize the interdependencies associated with risks and the dynamic uncertainties associated with the interdependencies. Many factors contribute to extreme risk, and they are connected through ever-changing linkages. For disaster strategies and leadership, understanding the evolving interconnectedness can be very challenging because the linkages are often hidden or indistinct.

On December 21, 1988, Pan American flight 103 exploded near Lockerbie, Scotland. In Malta, terrorists had checked a bag containing a bomb onto Malta Airlines, which maintained minimal security procedures. Airport personnel transferred the bag at Frankfurt's airport to a Pan Am feeder line, and personnel at London's Heathrow airport in turn loaded the bag onto Pan Am 103. The bomb was designed to explode above 28,000 feet, a flight altitude normally attained over the Atlantic Ocean, though not over Europe. Terrorists had deliberately exploited widely varying security procedures in place across the airports and airlines. Measures to prevent an aircraft disaster were only as strong as the weakest link in the system.[13]

Relationships among these interdependencies evolve over time, and measures to thwart their catastrophic impact on others may become inadequate later on. Airport authorities around the world improved security for bag transfers in the wake of the loss of Pan Am 103, but terrorists did find other ways of working around airline security measures, as the world learned on September 11, 2001. And even though government regulators in a host of countries tightened their rules in the wake of the financial crisis of 2008, new forms of systemic risk may nonetheless insidiously reappear beyond the reach of the new regulatory provisions. Evolving uncertainties point to the need for continuous vigilance and updating of risk-projection measures.

Principle 3: Understand people's behavioral biases when developing risk management strategies. Among the well-documented biases are misperceptions of the likelihood of catastrophic events, a focus on short-term concerns and returns, and a falsely optimistic confidence that a calamity will simply not happen on my watch—the NIMTOF (not in my term of office) phenomenon. Appreciating such biases is an important step for creating remedies and building cultures that can reduce or eliminate them.

Many individuals, for instance, will not invest in protective measures for a property unless they believe they can recoup their investment in two or three years, even though the measures will be of benefit as long as the property stands. People often purchase insurance following a disaster, not before, and then tend to cancel their policies after a few years if they have not collected on their policy. Rarely do people concur with the principle that "the best return on an insurance policy is no return at all" (that is, no loss whatsoever).

Principle 4: Recognize the long-term impact of disasters on a region's or nation's politics, culture, and society. Catastrophes often create enduring change in areas far from the epicenter in ways that public and private leaders need to appreciate in taking preventive measures prior to a disaster and use to their advantage in developing strategies following a catastrophic event. The massive earthquake of 2008 in southeast China, for example, stimulated private charitable giving, attracted international support, and revised how Chinese officials view substandard schools, homes, and office buildings.

Principle 5: Recognize transboundary risks by developing strategies that are global in nature. Most disasters do not recognize political borders. The terrible Southeast Asia tsunami of 2004 killed residents of 11 countries. The Pakistan earthquake of 2008 left more than a thousand dead in neighboring areas of India. The failure of Lehman Brothers and the near collapse of other American banks in 2008 had catastrophic consequences for banks in dozens of other countries, from Britain and Iceland to China and Mongolia.

One strategy to address and minimize risks is to have countries sign a treaty to reduce certain environmental risks, such as global warming or atmospheric pollution. There are potential benefits to all societies if enough countries take action, but there is also a net cost to any single country for adopting the treaty, as the United States argued at one point in refusing to sign the Kyoto treaty. What incentive is there for any one nation to adopt a treaty if it knows that a number of other countries will not join? How can policy makers and national leaders convince countries with leverage to sign the treaty to induce others to follow suit?

Principle 6: Overcome inequalities with respect to the distribution and effects of catastrophes. Whether natural or human caused, disasters often bring disproportionate hardships to those already at risk from low income or poor health.

Public policies and private actions can help prepare a readiness plan on the part of those with more financial resources to support those in distress with fewer resources.

Consider the flow of domestic and international assistance to China's southeast Sichuan Province in the aftermath of its great earthquake in 2008, with more than 69,000 dead (including 19,000 school-children), 274,000 injured, and 4.8 million homeless. The Chinese government invested more than $100 billion in the region's restoration, dispatched more than 50,000 soldiers and police to the area, and accepted humanitarian support from abroad, including South Korea, Japan, Russia, the United States, and even Taiwan. The Red Cross Society of China and many private organizations and individuals provided rescue and restoration equipment and funds (Yao Ming, of the Houston Rockets, donated more than $300,000.) Together, they helped thousands of families of modest means recover from the disaster. The experience points to the value of having government agencies and organizations such as the Red Cross prepared to provide assistance when it is most needed.

Principle 7: Build leadership for averting and responding to disasters before it is needed. The best time to create a readiness to face and overcome a low-probability, high-consequence disaster is before the event occurs. Leadership development is a time-consuming and labor-intensive process, and investing in it now can be seen as a preemptive and cost-effective measure to ensure that the six principles above are turned into active practice.

Had American financial institutions and regulators taken greater care to understand the growth of systemic risk in the U.S. housing and derivatives market, and had they created a greater readiness among their leaders to anticipate sharp downturns in those markets, the deep recession that the systemic risk caused in 2008 might not have reached such a depth. The failures of a host of banks, insurers, and manufacturers might have been averted, and the jobs of millions in the United States and abroad might have been saved.

The risk-management strategies and guiding principles we have identified here are intended to furnish a foundation for public and private policies and practices for preventing and reducing losses from low-probability, high-consequence events. The chapters that follow expand and draw upon these strategies and principles for catastrophic risks ranging from natural disasters to financial crises, and they provide guidance to leaders in all institutions for designing and developing measures to reduce losses and create a sustainable recovery in the wake of a catastrophe.

2

Acting in Time Against Disasters: A Comprehensive Risk-Management Framework

Herman B. "Dutch" Leonard and Arnold M. Howitt[1]
John F. Kennedy School of Government
Harvard University

Overview

This chapter presents a framework for comprehensive analysis of how society can reduce the aggregate loss in social welfare resulting from disasters, identifying five leverage points in which investments in capacity can make a difference. Substantial emphasis is generally placed on two of these leverage points: emergency response at the time of a disaster and preparation for response. In addition, in the wake of a disaster, society often commits massive resources to recovery for those individuals and communities directly affected. Less attention is typically paid to prevention and mitigation efforts, which work on reducing the likelihood that a disaster will occur or on reducing the consequences of an event if it does take place. And almost entirely neglected are steps that could be taken in advance that would make recovery quicker, less expensive, or more complete. Society would benefit from developing a more balanced portfolio of investments across these leverage points. Ultimately, this is a problem of "acting in time"—of whether society can foresee hazards, figure out actions to address them, and mobilize itself to take those actions on a timely basis.

Managing Large-Scale Social Hazards

How should societies organize themselves to prepare for large-scale hazardous events—serious earthquakes, major floods, severe hurricanes, massive industrial accidents, significant terrorist events—that occur with little predictability of time and place? Obviously, such events constitute *emergencies*—urgent situations where the stakes are high, outcomes depend on the actions taken (but in a highly uncertain or significantly unknown way), and significant losses are, in the absence of effective action, highly probable. Some of the major consequences of the hazards we face can be effectively ameliorated if we act in advance; most can be responded to as they unfold; and nearly all will require significant efforts after the fact to help us recover. How, then, can we best organize our capacities—our thinking, institutions, processes, and resources—to cope with major emergencies? How can we most productively "act in time" against disasters? What actions can we take in advance—what effective, high-value investments that address the prospects and potential consequences of future emergencies can we identify and activate ahead of time—rather than simply waiting for negative events to happen and then figuring out what to do after the fact?

As they break upon us, emergencies are frightening and highly salient—images of damage and injured or imperiled people demand our consideration. Confronted by unfolding disaster, our natural instinct is to *respond*—to rescue and support the afflicted. We volunteer to help; we open our homes to the displaced; we send donations to the agencies that answered the call. Perhaps in part because of their visual and political immediacy, the most common focus of work on minimizing the overall damage and meeting the cost of disasters is by responding quickly and effectively when they occur. When a given class of disasters confronts us repeatedly—wildland fires, for example, or spring floods, or hurricanes—we generally develop enough foresight to prepare in advance; that is, we build response capabilities so as to be able to mobilize an effective response when an event occurs.[2]

The terms *crisis management* and *emergency management* are used extensively in discussions about how major social hazards are addressed.[3] These terms nearly always imply a focus on a relatively brief time window of preparation for and execution of a response to disasters. They concentrate on whether the response apparatus and procedures in place before the event are adequate to the task and on the efficiency and effectiveness of actions in the immediate aftermath of the event. Response is primarily concerned with the intense "rescue" period during which critical assets—lives, especially, and property—are directly at risk. But preparation for response—that is, making preparations so as to be able to execute response/rescue actions—is not the only way that societies can or should manage the hazards of uncertain events. More comprehensive management of large-scale risks—or to put it another way, more complete and systematic development and exploitation of cost-effective opportunities to reduce the negative consequences from major risks—requires us to expand the common but narrow focus away from mere response.

We need to extend the time frame of our examination of disasters in both directions. We need to look further into the future, after the end of the immediate response and into the longer process of recovery. And we need to look further into the past—into things that can be done to avert events (by preventing them altogether), to shape them so that their consequences are not so severe if they do occur (through efforts at mitigation), or to permit more rapid recovery from disaster consequences that still occur in spite of these efforts.

In what follows here, we build on the discussion presented by Kunreuther and Useem in the preceding chapter. They observe that social losses flow from the vulnerabilities of an inventory of valuable assets (which can be either tangible or intangible) in the face of uncertain hazards. In this chapter, we present a simple framework for systematically developing the full range of options for intervention to reduce the expected net losses from such hazards. This can include efforts to reshape the hazards themselves, and efforts to shift the vulnerabilities of the identified valuable inventory of social and individual assets, and the actions can take place either before or after the hazardous event transpires. We refer to the approach we outline here as a "comprehensive risk-management framework." In our view, this approach derives in a straightforward and logical way from a simple social optimization problem: As a society, we want to make cost-effective investments to minimize the expected net present value of damage from future hazards.[4] Societies face a series of probabilistic hazards. If we do nothing and they come to fruition unchecked, they will cause a loss of social welfare—a decline in the quality of life for some or all in the community—over some period (and perhaps indefinitely).[5] For example, a major earthquake like that recently experienced in central Italy causes losses in social welfare from loss of life and from injuries, from destruction of valuable property and assets, from lost earnings and wealth (and, therefore, a decline in consumption opportunities for a long period following the event itself), and from a lost sense of security and safety among those who remain. Losses in social welfare often continue well after the event. We can think of the total loss flowing from a disaster event as the cumulative loss of social welfare, the amount by which social welfare over time falls below what it would otherwise have been in the absence of the hazard. Figure 2.1 depicts a notional graph of the path of social welfare in the absence and in the presence of a disaster. In the example shown, in the immediate aftermath of the event, social welfare declines rapidly and precipitously, and gradually recovers over time; the area between the social welfare path that would have obtained in the absence of the event (shown by the solid black line) and the curve in the presence of the event (shown as the lower dashed black line) indicates the cumulative loss in welfare associated with the event.

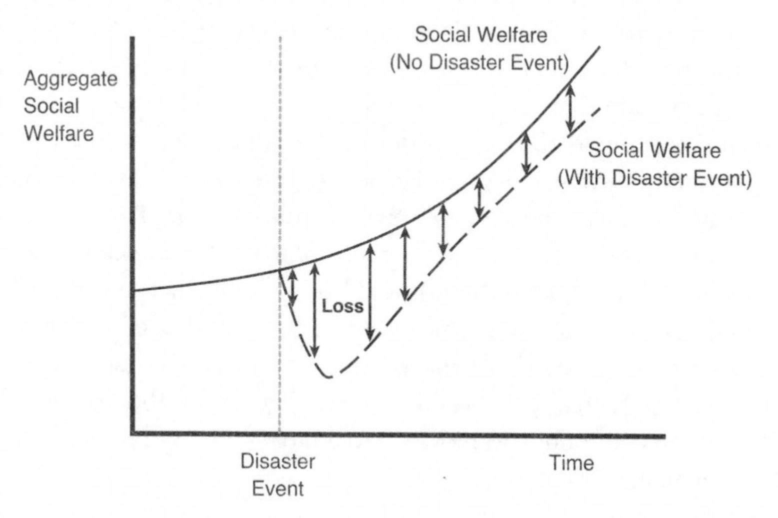

Figure 2.1 The path of social welfare with and without a disaster event

For example, imagine that the event depicted in Figure 2.1 is an earthquake in a major city. In the immediate aftermath of the event, social well-being declines rapidly as members of the community are killed or injured, property is destroyed, and economic and social activity is disrupted. With effective response and rescue, further damage from the event is minimized; and with efforts at recovery, the quality of life begins to improve. Over time, the general quality of life and economic activity returns to and then exceeds that before the event—but, in the trajectory shown in Figure 2.1, it never reaches as high a level as it would have had if the event had not taken place. For example, some businesses may fail or permanently move away and not be replaced, or the reduced sense of security may lead to a permanently lowered willingness to invest in economically productive physical assets in the affected area. In this example, the community never fully recovers from the event.

Other trajectories of social welfare in the aftermath of an event are, of course, possible. In the example shown, at every point in time after the event the level of social welfare falls below the level that it would have had if the event had not taken place. In other circumstances, the time path of welfare after the event may regain the level it would otherwise have had, or it may even exceed that level. This would be possible, for example, if a set of suboptimal capital investments—such as housing, roads, or utilities—that had been holding social welfare below its potential level were swept away in the disaster. It might not have made economic sense to destroy them before the event; but after they are destroyed *by* the event, they can be rebuilt in a more efficient social investment pattern, raising social welfare above and beyond its *ex ante* value. For example, the damage during the Loma Prieta earthquake to an elevated freeway along San Francisco's waterfront was sufficiently extensive to make the cost of repairs prohibitive, and the elevated structure was taken down. In the opinion of many, this created a renaissance in the waterfront district. It is at least possible that, at least in this limited instance, the earthquake resulted in a valuable opportunity to reconstruct an area where the productivity of social assets was far below its potential level—and the damage from the earthquake allowed the community to move on to a more valuable use of some of its remaining assets.

Indeed, not only are different post-event trajectories *possible,* but the *purpose* of our interventions in facing hazards is precisely to shift that trajectory cost-effectively in a favorable direction—to reduce the amount by which social welfare after the event falls below what it would otherwise have been. Transparently, the object of our effort should be to minimize the present value of the cumulative difference between the trajectories, taking into account the resources expended in shifting the trajectory. For example, relatively inexpensive investments in strengthening the levies in New Orleans would have resulted in vastly less destruction from Hurricane Katrina. Here, an effective intervention in advance (in the form of advance mitigation expenditures) would have resulted in a significantly less steep decline in social welfare, and a much more rapid return to a trajectory very close to or equal to what would have taken place had Katrina never come ashore. Our challenge in the face of future hazards is to find opportunities—in mitigation, in response, and in recovery—to spend resources in ways that preserve social welfare by keeping the trajectory of social welfare in the aftermath of an event, if it does occur, as close as possible to—or above!—what it would have been without the event.

Points of Intervention: When and Where Can We Invest Most Effectively?

Logically, a prospective disaster event defines three different time periods in which we can intervene against its associated future probabilistic losses: We can take actions (1) before the event occurs, (2) during or in the immediate aftermath of the event, or (3) after the event itself is over and the community is working to recover from it. And we can make these interventions in three different forms:

1. **Prevention and mitigation:** We can intervene (through prevention or mitigation measures) to shape the event itself; we can try to keep it from happening at all or can try to shift its consequences if it does occur.

2. **Crisis management and response:** We can intervene (through crisis management of the event) to execute an effective, further-damage-limiting response for those events that do take place.

3. **Recovery:** We can intervene (through recovery efforts) to push the social welfare trajectory back toward where it would otherwise have been.

Intervening by Changing the Events Themselves

The first opportunity to intervene to reduce the net present value of social losses from risk events is before the event occurs, by altering circumstances either to prevent the event entirely or to reduce the damage if it does occur. Sometimes, hazardous events may be prevented altogether, as, for example, when successful cloud seeding brings an end to what might otherwise have been a devastating drought. In other circumstances, even though the event itself may not be preventable (or may not have been effectively prevented), we may be able to take actions that will reduce the damage the event will do if and when it does take place.[6] For example, we do not currently (and may never) have the technology to prevent earthquakes, but we do have the technology to make buildings resistant to the damage that earthquakes do; with the right investments in building materials and design, we can dramatically reduce the extent of damage that a given earthquake will cause. As described earlier, Hurricane Katrina provides an object lesson in the value of advance prevention and mitigation—a comparatively small investment in strengthening the levee system would very likely have prevented the massive flooding and attendant multiyear disruption to the lives of hundreds of thousands of New Orleans residents.[7] Indeed, Hurricane Katrina probably constitutes the largest—and one of the most preventable—losses of social welfare ever to befall the United States. Katrina thus dramatically illustrates the fact that the opportunity to prevent events or mitigate their consequences provides a distinct point of intervention to reduce harms, a set of potentially cost-effective investments that might reduce the expected net present value of social loss from hazards.[8] Prevention and mitigation thus point to our first materially distinct opportunity to reduce social harm, through action in advance of an event: *Eliminate or reduce the probability of the event, or reduce its negative impacts if it does occur.*[9]

Intervening Through "Crisis Management"

Much of the public discussion of addressing prospective social hazards begins with "emergency" or "crisis" management. In terms of the trajectory in Figure 2.1, the intent here is to limit the amount of damage by intercepting the negative consequences as they unfold after the event and moving people and property out of harm's way. This reduces the amount by which the post-event trajectory of social welfare falls below its *ex ante* path and reduces the time during which it remains below the level it would otherwise have had. Actions during and immediately following the event are generally referred to as *response* or *rescue,* and, as previously noted, they tend to be the predominate focus of what is commonly referred to as crisis management. Examinations of emergency management generally focus on what can be done "in the moment," when the event is underway and the consequences of the event are still actively unfolding at a rapid pace. Studies and training in crisis management emphasize decision making and execution in stressful situations of uncertainty, with high stakes in the balance, and seek to improve performance during the event by developing the skills of crisis leaders and identifying (and, hopefully, rectifying) common errors or biases in decision making that often lead to difficulties.[10]

Of course, response and rescue will generally be much more effective if it has been planned, organized, and readied in advance, so crisis management also focuses attention on the period before the event begins. Its attention in this time period tends to be narrowly focused on supporting more effective action in response—arranging people, training, skills, equipment, procedures, systems, and organizations that will enable (and, hopefully, ensure) a rapid, reliable, and effective set of rescue actions.

Crisis management, thus, suggests two forms of intervention to reduce probabilistic harms, in two different "time zones": First, before the event, take actions to *prepare the response capability*; and, second, as the event unfolds, *respond effectively and reliably.*

Intervening Through Recovery

Finally, as the immediate response actions are accomplished, and as the active and rapid flow of consequences subsides, we move to the "recovery" period. Here, in terms of the trajectories in Figure 2.1, the intent is to shift the trajectory of social welfare *after* the event so that it more quickly returns to or near the level that it would have had if the event had not transpired. Actions taken well after the event have traditionally not been viewed as directly related to crisis management. Indeed, they are often approached as though the event itself, the source of the consequences being managed during the recovery, were no longer relevant; all that matters is what the actual consequences are or were, and the best way to manage them. In communities devastated by a hurricane or flood, we institute programs of housing and community development, often with little attention to the source of the initial damage—presumably on the theory that if houses need to be rehabilitated, it makes little difference whether it is because they sustained flood damage or were blighted by neglect or were burned out in a wildland fire. The program will simply deal with whatever damage exists and try to rectify it. Traditionally, then, the work of recovery is understood to begin (well) after the event is over and the response has ended or is imminently ending, and it is time to begin rebuilding the community and its various assets that were damaged by the event. Recovery—and actions to support recovery, like planning and community mobilization—are understood to take place after the fact. Traditional recovery discussions thus focus on one set of actions (rehabilitation and reconstruction) and on one time period (after the event).[11]

From a logical perspective, however, there is no reason that at least *some* recovery activities cannot be undertaken *before* an event takes place. Just as the response that will take place during the event can be prepared for in advance of the event (and the response can be profoundly better—faster, more reliable, more effective—as a result), there may be actions that can be taken in advance of the event that will "prepare" for a more rapid recovery. Importantly, such "advance recovery" actions are distinct from the mitigation or prevention measures described previously. Mitigation and prevention are designed to reduce or eliminate the consequences of the event—that is, to reduce the amount of recovery that is necessary. By contrast, advance recovery efforts are designed to make whatever recovery *does* need to take place more efficient, rapid, and effective.

What kinds of advance recovery actions might be helpful? To be sure, it would be foolish to make detailed plans for a recovery before a major event took place—every event is different, and most major events have a high variability in intensity, so that some areas are heavily damaged and other areas nearby are largely unscathed. Unduly detailed planning before we have knowledge of the specific damage that needs to be rectified could easily be a waste of resources.

Nonetheless, there *are* actions that we can take in advance that will shift the recovery trajectory. Generic preparation for major disasters might be effective at accelerating the pace of recovery in the aftermath of an event. For example, some more general forms of planning may be valuable as a framework for more detailed efforts after an event. Attention in advance to rules and regulations that might need to be suspended to allow rapid rebuilding (for example, public procurement regulations or building codes), or the development in advance of a planning and permitting mechanism that is designed to be nimble in the aftermath of a significant event could materially speed reconstruction. The development of financial arrangements that would facilitate access to resources after an event could enable recovery efforts that would otherwise be impossible (especially early in the recovery period) and thus may constitute an effective way to accelerate recovery. Studies of the pace of recovery after major disasters also reveal the importance of the quality of local (that is, neighborhood-based) leadership as a significant determinant of how rapidly and effectively recovery takes place—so efforts that build local leadership groups and provide them with experience in organizing their neighborhoods may significantly increase the rate of recovery.[12] For example, San Francisco currently has underway an ambitious program to identify and construct advance recovery infrastructure that will successfully accelerate recovery in the aftermath of a major seismic event and is developing planning, budgeting, regulatory, and financial tools that will yield significant dividends if a major earthquake occurs in the Bay Area.

Thus, a more robust examination of what happens during recovery suggests that seeking to reduce the net social cost of future hazards through more rapid and reliable recovery calls for consideration of actions of two kinds, in two time periods. The first category consists of actions taken after the fact to *undertake reconstruction* and thereby shift the social welfare trajectory up toward where it would have been in the absence of the event—as rapidly as possible given the event and the recovery preparations that preceded it. The second category includes actions taken in advance of the event—"advance recovery" actions—that are designed to *accelerate the planning and execution of recovery activities* should a major event occur.

Taken together, then, we have identified five different forms of action in three different time periods that, if well and efficiently undertaken, can reduce the expected net present value cost of the hazards we face. Table 2.1 lists these five alternative approaches, and Figure 2.2 shows them graphically. These alternatives for intervention collectively constitute a "comprehensive risk-management framework." Within this framework, we can identify and compare different opportunities for reducing damage from hazards. We can also search more comprehensively, seeking interventions of all possible forms instead of limiting our attention to only a subset of the five logically distinct forms of action. Ideally, we want to find the most cost-effective interventions—the actions, in any of the five categories, that most significantly reduce the expected value of future losses per unit of resources expended. In short, we want to use the comprehensive risk-management framework to help us form a balanced, efficient, cost-effective portfolio of actions across the full range of options.

TABLE 2.1 Form, Time Period, and Intended Benefits of Alternative Actions to Reduce Net Present Value of Social Damage from Hazardous Events

Investment/ Intervention/Action	Time Period	Intended Benefit
1. Prevent/mitigate	Before the event	Reduce harm created
2. Prepare a robust response	Before the event	Reduce damage in progress
3. Build recovery infrastructure	Before the event	Accelerate recovery
4. Respond	During and immediately after the event	Reduce damage in progress
5. Recover	After the event	Restore social welfare as rapidly as possible

In the context of this picture of the comprehensive risk-management framework, we can readily see the sense in which the traditional focus on crisis management is too narrow. Crisis management, as generally defined, focuses on the response itself (area 4 in Figure 2.2). To make that response effective, it also has to focus on the preparation for the response (area 2 in Figure 2.2). It does not generally concern itself, however, with the genesis of the events (or with attempts to shape those events in advance), and it also generally avoids examining either the recovery or any efforts that could be made in advance to make the recovery more efficient, reliable, and effective. Therefore, to get an appropriately balanced portfolio of investments, we need to expand the traditional focus on crisis management in both directions—further back in time, to explore opportunities for prevention, mitigation, and advance recovery, and further forward in time, to contemplate and execute the most successful possible recovery that can follow the crisis response/rescue phase of the event. A key opportunity framed by the comprehensive risk-management framework is precisely that it requires us to expand our focus in both of these directions to seek cost-effective means to reduce the net expected present value of social losses from hazards, and it is to the development of such a balanced portfolio of investments that we now turn.

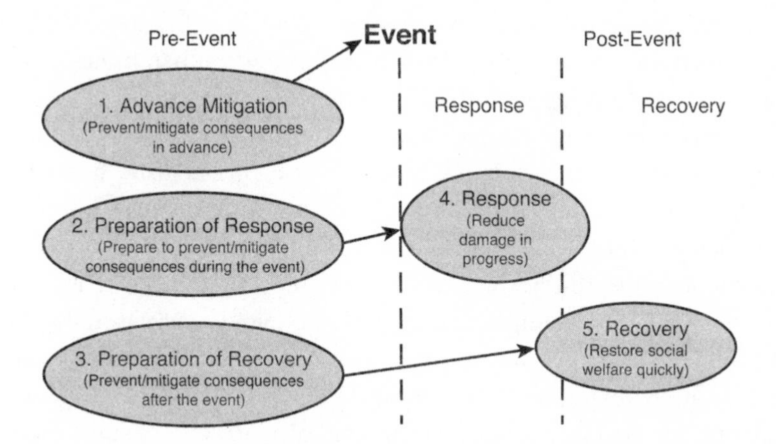

Figure 2.2 Time periods of investments to reduce social cost of disasters

The Level and Balance of the Current Portfolio of Risk-Management Efforts

Viewed through the lens of this more comprehensive framework, it is natural to inquire about the level and composition of the current portfolio of investments in hazard-loss reduction. Do we—in societies around the world —invest at roughly the right level in these strategies? And do we have reasonably coherent and efficient patterns of investments across the five possible domains?

Unfortunately, there are good reasons to believe that in most, if not all, societies, we do not. Getting an efficient level and pattern of investments across such a wide range of possibilities is intrinsically difficult, and existing institutional structures and frameworks for developing hazard reduction strategies do little to encourage integration across the spectrum we have identified. Indeed, one potential value of articulating the simple framework outlined here is simply that it may encourage more comprehensive search and analysis across the wider array of possible options.

The Overall Level of Advance Investments in Hazard-Loss Reduction

Investing now to reduce future harm is intrinsically a difficult decision to get right. The costs of such investments are, for the most part, both immediate and certain, whereas any benefits are probabilistic, uncertain, and delayed. Human beings and human organizations have always struggled with the challenge of balancing current, immediate expenditures of clearly valuable resources on things they need now against the uncertain, future, delayed, probabilistic gains they might get from diverting those resources into investments with uncertain, delayed future returns that can only be hoped for. In the preceding chapter, Kunreuther and Useem outline some of the reasons for this struggle—for example, the fact that people do not naturally think in probabilistic terms, and the widespread tendency toward myopia in making individual (and, often, group) decisions. It may be especially difficult for people to balance current expenditures against future reductions in loss when the events for which these investments would need to be made are horrible to contemplate, and most of us would thus prefer not to think about them. But political strategies have been devised to ensure funding for other investment areas that have these characteristics—national defense, for example—and we may well be making progress in dealing with some other areas like this, including preventive health and climate change. Kunreuther and Useem outline a series of principles of social risk management designed to help construct social decision mechanisms that can help counterbalance biases toward myopia in the face of probabilistic events. And a central theme of a number of the chapters in this book that look at specific hazards is that there are politically feasible ways in which a better balance might be struck between current resource demands and future hazard reductions. The fact that this remains a significant focus of research and political effort, however, suggests that in general the overall level of investments to reduce losses from future hazards probably falls short of the socially optimal level. For example, although it might not be possible with current knowledge and technology to assess the optimal level of investment that we should be making to avoid climate change (or the consequential damages of climate change), most knowledgeable observers believe that we are currently well below the optimal level of mitigation and adaptation efforts (to use the phraseology common in climate change discussions). One virtue of outlining the comprehensive risk-management framework should be that it helps us to search more effectively for a broader range of possibilities, and allows us more systematically to compare investments of different types by treating them all as variations on the same general theme of reducing the expected net present value of future social losses, and thus putting them on a more commensurable basis.

The Balance Among Different Forms of Loss-Reducing Investments

It also seems likely that some areas of investment in loss reduction attract relatively more resources than others—that is, that the portfolio of investments, in addition to being on average smaller than it should be, is also imperfectly balanced. What keeps us from having a balanced pattern of investments? One important factor is that some forms of investment are dramatically more salient than others (both visually and emotionally) and thus are more likely to attract resources. For example, the rescue or response period in major disasters is highly visual and emotionally galvanizing and therefore tends to generate a sense that we must do everything possible—so "all available" resources are often mobilized after a major event has begun. Similarly, after an event has taken place, there is little choice but to expend resources, subject to the limits of availability, to recover from the consequences. When a community lies in ruins, we generally rush to provide resources for the rebuilding. After an event, the losses are no longer uncertain, probabilistic, or in the future—they are here, now, visible all around us, and they cry out for help and resources. No matter how much less it might have cost if we had made investments in advance to avoid the tragedy, when it has befallen us, we have little choice but to front the resources to make the community at least partially whole again, whatever that may now cost.[13] Therefore, the response itself and the recovery (investment areas 4 and 5 in Figure 2.2) tend differentially to be able to attract and command (and consume) resources and are thus probably at least relatively overrepresented in the array of disaster-related investments.

There is reason to believe that preparation for response (investment area 2 in Figure 2.2) also differentially attracts resources, particularly after a major event has passed (in preparation for the next event). This is because, during the highly salient rescue period of the last event, it never seems that we have enough preparation, resources, and readiness to deploy quickly enough; there never seem to be enough fire trucks, and they never arrive as soon as we would like. In critical discussions after the fact, highly animated victims of the last event (naturally enough) often demand explanations for why the response was not faster, bigger, better. A common response is to increase the preparation budget so as to have a larger fleet of fire trucks available when the next event takes place.[14] During periods with few events, however, declining salience and memory sharpness lead to lessened political demand for disaster protections. Often, political interest in sustaining these investments wanes, leading to cuts, and thus sets up the next cycle of disaster followed by reinvestment. Whether investment area 2 is over- or underinvested in may thus depend in part on where we are in the cycle of disasters. Nonetheless, the salience of response and the prospect of future needs probably generally inclines investment area 2 toward differential ability to attract resources, particularly in the immediate aftermath of a major event.

By contrast, two other investment areas seem to get comparatively little attention. Prevention and mitigation efforts (investment area 1 in Figure 2.2) and advance recovery activities (investment area 3) are both disadvantaged (in the same way as are all hazard-reduction investments) by the fact that their costs are immediate and certain, whereas their benefits are probabilistic, uncertain, and delayed. That is, they are subject to the same myopia that generally plagues individual risk perception and assessment. But they are *further* disadvantaged by the fact that their potential benefits are less visible (at least, until the event takes place). Prevention and mitigation famously create invisible benefits; we rarely are in a position to observe what was prevented. The need to prevent or to be ready to recover is intrinsically an abstraction, an idea. By contrast, the need to be ready to respond is vivid, and the need to recover after an event has occurred is visible all around us. This is the flip side that response and recovery after the fact get so much more attention than prevention, mitigation, and advance recovery before the fact. The event and the recovery from the event that was uncertain and off in the future (and therefore attracted relatively little prevention, mitigation, and advance recovery planning attention in advance) has become immediate, inescapable, certain, and *now*. It is therefore able to get many times the resources that might have been necessary to prevent it, reduce its consequences, or prepare a more rapid recovery from its after-effects.[15]

Institutional Challenges

An additional problem further enhances the difficulty of forming a fully efficient social portfolio of investments across the range of opportunities to intervene to reduce social losses: The institutional structure of governments in most countries gives responsibility for various components of these investments to different agencies and, frequently, to different levels of government, which makes it difficult to compare them (or even to assemble a comprehensive picture of them).

Consider, for example, floods as a social hazard in the United States. Responsibility for flood control—what we have referred to here as prevention and mitigation of the consequences of floods—lies with the Army Corps of Engineers (in the U.S. Department of Defense) and with some state and local agencies. This, by itself, is a complicated start, forced by the multilevel U.S. governmental structure, driven by the fact that floods are often large-area events that will involve many different jurisdictions, and reflecting the fact that the best place to control a flood may be many hundreds of miles (and multiple jurisdictional boundaries) upstream from where the flood may take place.[16] Preparation for response is the domain of planning and organizing and first-responder agencies—at the federal level, the Federal Emergency Management Agency (FEMA), which will mobilize many other organizations, including contractors and state and local government agencies outside the affected region, and the Coast

Guard; at the state level, the National Guard and other state agencies; at the local level, police and fire departments. There is little attention to advance recovery, and no agency appears to have an extensive mandate for this area of investment. And recovery will be in the province of FEMA, the Department of Housing and Urban Development, and a variety of state and local agencies.[17]

From an institutional perspective, different possible interventions suggested by the comprehensive risk-management framework lie in multiple agencies in multiple jurisdictions at multiple levels of government. Developing a comprehensive picture of the different responsibilities of and investments being made by these different players would be a daunting undertaking—and this is only one of many major hazards for which the society should want to have a comprehensive, balanced portfolio of investments before, during, and after an event. The complex structure of institutions involved in these matters is thus an additional barrier to examining the existing investments, forming a more comprehensive picture, and developing a more efficient portfolio of social hazard reduction strategies and investments.

The net result of these systematic forces acting upon our (largely disconnected and independent) decision-making processes for investments in social risk loss reduction appears to be (1) that we wind up spending too much on response to and recovery from events that we should have instead figured out how to prevent or mitigate, and (2) that our recoveries are generally slower than they should be, exacerbating social losses, because we have not built the necessary or useful infrastructure for rapid recovery in advance.

The fact that these forces probably result in an inefficient distribution of investments across hazard-loss reduction investment areas is precisely why we need a comprehensive risk-management framework in the first place. In its absence, we have to try to identify and carry out investments of different kinds in an independent and disconnected form, with little comparative attention to where the greatest opportunities and most efficient investments lie. By contrast, if we use a comprehensive risk-management approach, we should be able to build a more balanced portfolio with higher average returns on our investments.

Consider, for example, the problem of the management of wildland fires in the southwestern United States. Over the past century, recurrent fires in fire-adapted ecosystems have become more intense and more damaging as a constellation of forces has systematically increased the hazard and built up the inventory of valuable assets in high-hazard zones. Traditionally, risks to life and property from wildland fires were managed through a standard crisis management response approach, with growing investments in fire-suppression technology and efforts. Recurring dramatic (and highly photogenic) events—including 200-foot-high flame walls driven by high winds at great speed toward vulnerable communities, and the charred remains of homes and their treasured contents, and, far too often, the bodies of fire victims—galvanized massive efforts to increase resources for traditional responses designed to suppress fires after they had started. Paradoxically, these (often partially successful) efforts to suppress fires led to a systematic buildup of volatile fuels in wildland areas, which actually increased the hazard by making fires both more likely and more intense. Meanwhile, politically popular (but myopic) land-use policies (encouraged by false confidence in our presumed ability to continue to suppress fires) permitted fire-prone areas to be colonized by suburban real estate development and extensive building of second homes deeply embedded in fire-adapted ecosystems. The results have been utterly catastrophic: Costs of fire suppression and of property losses have spiraled upward, and both civilian and firefighter deaths and injuries have increased. Far from investments that have reduced the present value of loss from future hazards, policies and investments in this domain have systematically *increased* losses, lowering the expected path of future social welfare.

How might the application of the comprehensive risk-management framework developed here help us organize our investments more judiciously in the face of this challenge? It would focus attention on the full range of possible investments, including prevention and mitigation, response and recovery. Doing so should help us notice that we have made enormous investments in response and in preparation for response and have been forced to make enormous expenditures for recoveries—but have made only small investments in (1) prevention (through land-use policies that would discourage embedding vulnerable high-value properties in fire-prone areas); (2) mitigation (through treatment of areas to reduce the buildup of natural fuels in areas with concentrations of valuable property and through taking defensive measures like clearing brush in the immediate vicinity of structures in wildland areas); and in (3) preparation for rapid and less-expensive recovery. A more balanced analysis, structured by the comprehensive risk-management framework, will allow us to formulate a more judiciously balanced array of investments—and, thus, to reduce expected future social losses substantially.

It is reasonable to ask what institutions might conduct this cross-agency, cross-jurisdictional, cross-level-of-government analysis and how the decision-making process might be structured. In many ways, this problem recalls the efforts since the early 1960s to develop comprehensive, analytic budgeting systems (for example, the Kennedy-Johnson administrations' promotion of the Planning-Programming-Budgeting System [PPBS], first in the Pentagon and then across the federal government).[18] PPBS was much less successful than desired, in part because even when analysis of major "programs" in the Defense Department alone were conducted, it was exceedingly difficult to make and enforce executive decisions based on this analysis. The "best" course indicated analytically was often lost in the intensely political budgetary bargaining within the Pentagon, between the Department of Defense and the White House and between the executive branch and Congress in a fragmented authorization and appropriations process. Similar, perhaps even more complex, forces operate in the current Homeland Security arena in the United States.

Nonetheless, the likelihood that a more comprehensive analytic process might not be perfectly effectuated in decision making should not preclude making the effort to think more systematically and comprehensively about the full portfolio of investments that societies make to reduce the net losses from disasters of all types. One approach that might prove beneficial would be to develop "balanced scorecards" for a "virtual" homeland security sector either in an individual jurisdiction or for a system that cuts across agencies, jurisdictions, and levels of government.[19] Good analysis, effectively articulated and publicized, can shape public discussion and constrain policy politics even if it does not wholly "win out" in the final political decision-making process. The difficulties of institutional setting will remain, but the public debate—and the direction of the outcomes—can nonetheless be altered over time.

The More General Problem of Acting in Time

Identifying a more robust set of possible cost-effective social hazard-loss reduction opportunities—which the comprehensive risk-management framework should help us to undertake—is, in the end, only one part of the problem of actually addressing the hazards and reducing the prospective losses. Before they can find strategies for expected loss reduction, societies need to identify areas of hazard that are worth investigating. And, in addition to finding strategies for addressing the hazards they focus on, societies need to carry those strategies into action.[20] Thus, the risk-management framework needs to be seen as part of the larger challenge of organizing and mobilizing public action. The losses from hazards (and the benefits from hazard-loss reductions) are intrinsically in the future, so we can view this wider challenge as a problem of "acting in time"—that is, of taking action against future harms (or in favor of future opportunities) while there is still time to do so.[21]

What does it take to act in time against a future hazard? First, the hazard itself must be identified with sufficient clarity to permit us to develop possible actions that could reduce its expected future damage. If it cannot be (or is not) foreseen, we cannot take specific action against it. Second, if it is observed, then we next have to identify actions that could cost-effectively reduce its future impacts. (This, of course, is the challenge to which the comprehensive risk-management framework previously described is directed; it is designed to help in the effective search and comparative evaluation of alternative strategies for reducing future damage from probabilistic events.) Third, once we have identified or developed potentially valuable actions that can be taken to reduce expected future harms, we have to figure out how to mobilize the resources and actions implied. Figure 2.3 illustrates these phases of being able to act in time. We refer to the first phase as *visibility*: Can the hazard be perceived clearly enough to be acted upon? The second can be described as *actionability*: Can we identify cost-effective actions that would reduce its expected harms? The third can be referred to as *mobilizability*: Is this hazard, and the associated set of actions for addressing it, something around which we can mobilize people and institutions to take action (and expend resources)? Only if we can work our way successfully through each of these steps will we be acting in time. Otherwise, we may have general preparations for dealing with the consequences of this particular risk, but we will not have acted in time in the face of this risk as effectively as we might have.

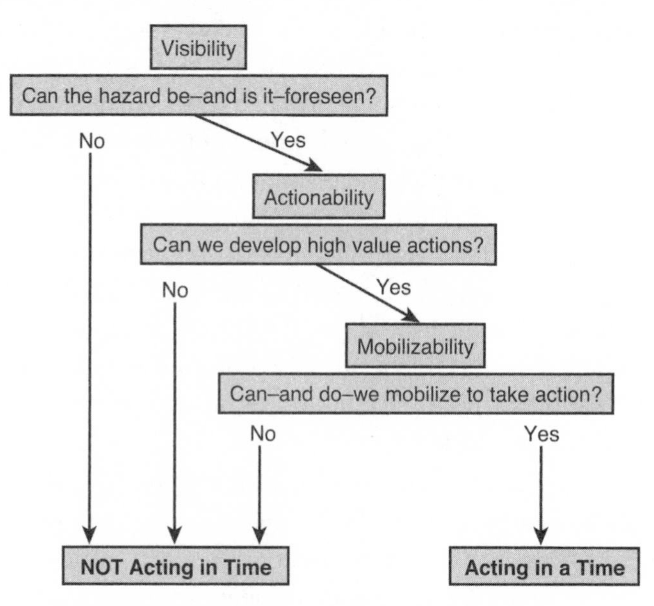

Figure 2.3 The simple analytics of acting in time

As an example of the "acting in time" challenge, we can return to the wildland fire management problem discussed earlier. In this case, the hazard is certainly visible. Through application of the comprehensive risk-management framework, we can develop a more judicious and balanced set of investments across the full scope of opportunities to address the hazard. These range from prevention and mitigation (through better land use and wildland fuel reduction) to right-sizing the response capabilities that will be required in the lower-hazard environment thus created to developing rapid recovery mechanisms for circumstances where damage still occurs. Thus, the comprehensive risk-management approach helps us to explore and develop opportunities for investment and thus helps generate actionability. The remaining problem for acting in time against this hazard, then, is mobilizing communities to actually undertake the resulting, more balanced set of investments. This is a problem of political visioning and of developing the will to act, and it has proven immensely difficult to solve. There are, however, communities where significant rebalancing of efforts has been undertaken. In Ventura County, California, for example, extensive efforts at brush clearing on public lands and the development and enforcement of ordinances requiring brush cutting around homes to create "defensible space" have dramatically reduced the number of homes lost to wildland fire (in comparison with other nearby areas). "Positive deviants" like Ventura County may help us spot conditions in which individuals and communities are more likely to address these challenges successfully.[22] The challenge of mobilizing is partly a problem of risk perception and assessment (as described in the preceding chapter), partly a challenge of finding mechanisms to collectively overcome the systematic forces of myopia, and partly a challenge of generating the will to carry through on a decision to act. Throughout the remaining chapters of this book, the issue of how the acting in time problem of creating visibility, actionability, and mobilizability can be successfully addressed for different social hazards will be a recurrent theme.

Conclusion

The comprehensive risk-management framework focuses attention on five different kinds of actions that can be taken at different times (three before the event, one during and in the immediate aftermath of the event, and one that continues long after the event) to reduce the expected present value of the losses associated with a future hazard. Examining risks to social welfare in this framework will permit the development of a portfolio of interventions that is balanced across the different points of entry, encouraging us to seek cost-effective investments in all five of these areas and allowing us to compare investments in different areas to see which will provide the greatest anticipated net reduction in losses associated with the hazard—that is, the greatest return on our investments in expected hazard-loss reduction.

The useful risk-management work outlined by the comprehensive risk-management framework, however, cannot be undertaken without prior work to identify hazards that can be acted upon—and it will not be useful unless the high-value investments it identifies are actually undertaken.

Identifying the opportunities to intervene, designing interventions, and actually making these investments in time to matter thus requires that we "act in time"—and this implies that the comprehensive risk-management framework needs to be embedded in the larger framework of acting in time: (1) identifying or perceiving hazards clearly enough to permit investments to be made to reduce their expected future costs; (2) using the comprehensive risk-management framework to design alternative interventions and determine which of them provide the greatest reduction in expected future losses per unit of resources expended; and (3) mobilizing the political and social will to expend current and future resources against the probabilistic prospect of reduced social losses if a possible hazard turns into an actual event. Only if we can manage each of these challenges will societies construct a fully systematic, efficient, and effective approach to social risk management.

3

Forecasting and Communicating the Risk of Extreme Weather Events

Geoff Love and Michel Jarraud
World Meteorological Organization[1]

Overview

This chapter analyzes the approaches being taken by those who provide public forecasts and warnings for extreme hydro-meteorological events. It notes that all forecasts have a degree of uncertainty about them and that meteorologists have developed a variety of methods for expressing this uncertainty. Weather forecasters have traditionally used qualifiers in their forecasts to express uncertainty consistent with guidelines developed by the World Meteorological Organization. In the domain of climate analysis and prediction, the Intergovernmental Panel on Climate Change has provided a framework for expressing uncertainty, both as reflected by general qualitative assessments and by quantitative assessments aimed specifically at decision makers. Often missing in the weather warning or climate information is the assessment of the vulnerability of threatened communities. This chapter outlines methods of filling this gap and integrating the resulting estimation of risk and uncertainty so that decision makers of all types can make better use of hydro-meteorological information in their efforts to reduce disaster risk.

Introduction

Traditionally, risk assessment considers two dimensions: the likelihood of a disastrous event and the expected impact of the event. For a range of hydro-meteorological extreme events (droughts, floods, tropical cyclones, forest fires, tornadoes, heat waves, and so on), this chapter examines the ways in which the uncertainty in the assessment of both the likelihood and impact of the event can be characterized. Various techniques allow for an objective assessment of the uncertainty associated with the event's likelihood, but the uncertainty associated with its impact is more difficult to quantify, and, as the risk of an event is the product of these two factors, the assessment of risk has a degree of unresolvable uncertainty attached to it. The challenge faced by National Meteorological and Hydrological Services (NMHSs) is characterizing these uncertainties in such a way that the public generally, and their community leaders, can integrate the information into their risk assessments, thereby facilitating timely and cost-effective decisions that enable them to manage properly the risk associated with extreme weather, climate, and hydrological events.

The Concept of Risk

The generally accepted concept of risk[2] has two key elements, both of which involve uncertainty. First, the concept relates to an event that has not happened but for which there is a belief that there is a nonzero likelihood (or probability) that it will occur in some specified future time period; because all future events are to some degree uncertain, this element of the concept introduces an element of uncertainty. Second, the concept relates to the expected impact the event: Because the state of the systems that will be affected by the event cannot be precisely specified (if for no other reason than it is not clear when the event will occur), nor can the event's interaction with them, then there is an element of uncertainty in the event's impact.

The risk associated with a particular event is then the product of the likelihood (or probability[3]) of occurrence and the impact:

Risk = (Probability of an event occurring) × (Impact of the event should it occur)

Graphically, the risk arising from three types of extreme meteorological events might be represented in "risk space," as depicted in Figure 3.1. Each shaded area (event) in this space is a schematic "estimate" of the risk. The boundaries of the shaded areas correspond to some confidence limit (say, for example, 95 percent of events would be expected to fall within this area), thereby characterizing the uncertainty associated with the best estimates of probability of event's occurrence and its impact.

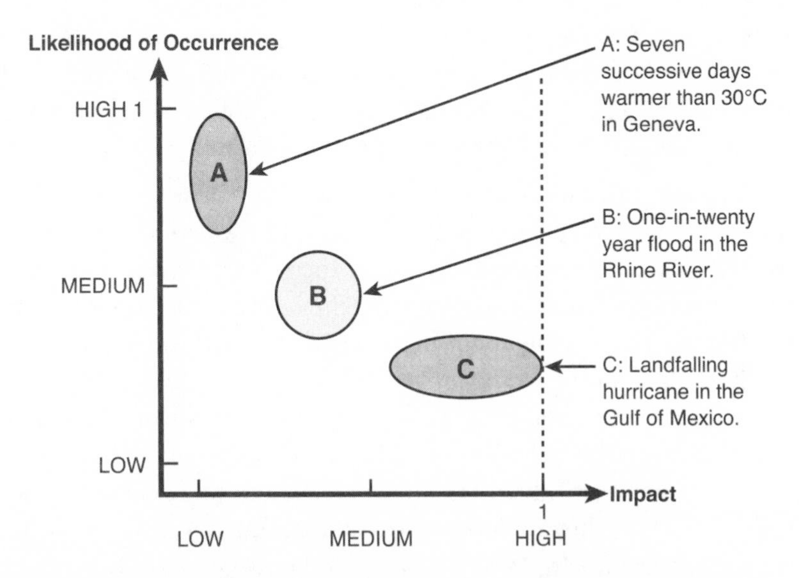

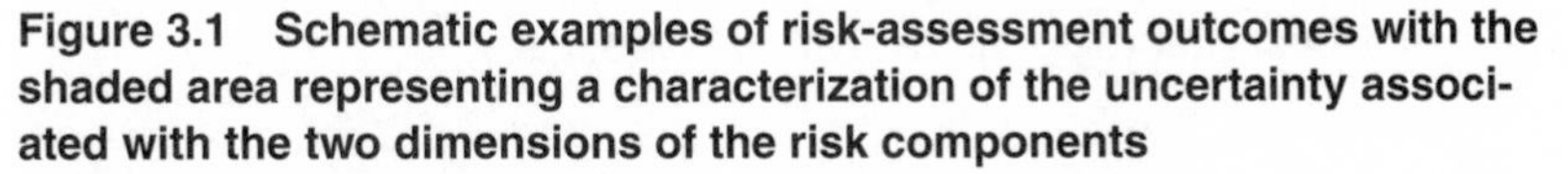
Figure 3.1 Schematic examples of risk-assessment outcomes with the shaded area representing a characterization of the uncertainty associated with the two dimensions of the risk components

Area A on Figure 3.1 is a schematic depiction of the risk of a longer-than-usual sequence of hot days in Geneva occurring in a particular year. Such an event will occur from time to time, possibly disrupting public transport and placing unusual demands on energy supplies. The impact is relatively low, and were it not for climate change, the probability of occurrence could easily be calculated from a statistical analysis of the last 150 years of climate data for Switzerland.

Area B on Figure 3.1 is a schematic depiction of the risk of the 1-in-20-year flood occurring in a particular year. The analysis of past floods would establish a flood level for the 1-in-20 year flood and also provide a good estimate of the likelihood of occurrence and the impact; however, changing levels of development in the catchment and changing types of land use would affect flood likelihood and flood impact in ways that cause uncertainty.

Area C on Figure 3.1 is a schematic depiction of the risk associated with a hurricane land-falling on a particular 60 mile (100 km) stretch of the coast of the Gulf of Mexico in a particular year. Depending on the time of day and how effective early-warning procedures have been, there can be a great deal of difference in impact. In addition, the year-to-year variability of hurricane occurrence and the effects of climate change make future predictions of probability, based on the climatology of past events, somewhat problematic.

The second important concept related to risk assessment is risk management. Every community is exposed to weather, climate, and hydrological extreme events. Whether these become major disasters, minor inconveniences, or something in between depends in large part on the risk-management decisions taken by those in leadership positions. One of the challenges faced by professionals in NMHSs[4] is to provide information to all those decision makers who require the information on the full range of hydro-meteorological extreme events in a manner that identifies their likelihood of occurrence, and impacts, as best they understand them. NMHSs must also characterize the uncertainty in the information and present the information in ways that best meet the decision-maker needs.

The Role of Atmospheric and Hydrological Scientists

Atmospheric and hydrological scientists use data from past events to provide statistically based predictions of the likelihood of future occurrences. They also use numeric models, built through a combination of the basic laws of physics, particularly those that govern fluid flow, and process understanding acquired through 150 years of systematic research into the behavior of natural systems, to provide model-based predictions of the likelihood and possible impact of extreme weather, climate, and hydrological events occurring at some future time. These statistical systems and models are almost invariably accompanied by tools that can provide an estimate of the uncertainty associated with the likelihood assessment, thus providing data for the vertical dimension of the risk-assessment chart (Likelihood of Occurrence, Figure 3.1). Assessing this vertical dimension of the risk "space" is the expertise of atmospheric and hydrological scientists.

The horizontal axis of the risk space (Impact, Figure 3.1) provides a different range of challenges. The impact of an extreme weather, climate, or hydrological event comes about, to a significant extent, because of the interaction between the natural world and systems and infrastructure put in place by humans. Whether a levee will break under the weight of a particular storm surge, whether railway lines will buckle in a heat wave, whether the authorities can clear snow from key roads during and after a blizzard, whether a bridge will be washed away in a 1-in-20-year flood are all questions beyond the atmospheric scientists or hydrologists alone to answer. In a similar fashion, the associated questions of what might be the range of community impacts, such as school closures, job losses, industry failure, and so on, should these extreme weather, climate, and hydrological events occur have also traditionally been beyond the scope of the work of the physical science community. Nevertheless, it is becoming increasingly clear that physical scientists need to work closely with the engineers, land-use planners, social scientists, and other professionals with an understanding of the impacts of natural disasters so as to ensure that risk assessments and uncertainty characterizations from the science community are compatible with the decision-making processes of those using them.

Assessing Risk and Characterizing Uncertainty on Climate Timescales

Assessing the risk of long periods of hot weather (heat waves) is an important task of NMHSs and community leaders in countries subject to subtropical and mid-latitude climates. The heat wave in Western Europe in 2003 lasted for different periods in different locations. In Paris, France, for example, there was a sharp upward spike in deaths of the elderly, who are least capable of dealing with extreme heat, throughout the period a day or so after the maximum temperatures exceeded around 27°C (Figure 3.2), which was from around August 4 to 14.[5] Associated with the heat waves were also an increased incidence of fires in Mediterranean countries and the loss of agricultural production throughout the region,[6] all demonstrating the vulnerability of communities adapted to a cooler climate to long periods of high temperatures.

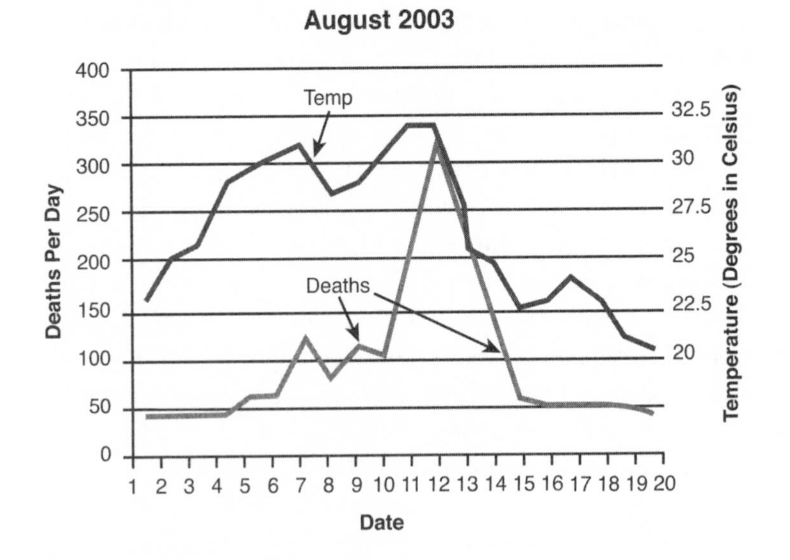

Figure 3.2 Deaths per day and maximum temperature in Paris, France, for the first 20 days of August 2003[7]

In Australia, in March 2008, Adelaide, the capital city of South Australia, experienced 15 days of temperature above 35°C (Figure 3.3). Prior to this event, the previous longest run of consecutive days above 35°C in the modern instrumental record was 8. This event was well forecast, in large part due to the excellent weather model forecasts available from centers operating and publicly exchanging the output from global and regional numeric weather prediction models. The risk of this expected extreme event was then well accepted by the community as it developed, because its unusual nature was characterized in media releases as an exceptional event. Staff of the Australian NMHS (the Bureau of Meteorology) were aware, from historical data, that on average, a run of 8 hot days (temperature above 35°C) in Adelaide occurs around once a decade and that hot periods had not extended beyond 8 days. Placing the predicted 15-day sequence of hot days on the chart suggested that Adelaide was to experience a once-in-3,000-year event. This message was conveyed widely through the media and became the talking point of the city. As the heat wave developed, local energy companies made provision for additional energy to meet the expected air-conditioning demand, outside sports events were canceled, water restrictions were put in place, and the community took a wide range of local actions to mitigate its effects.

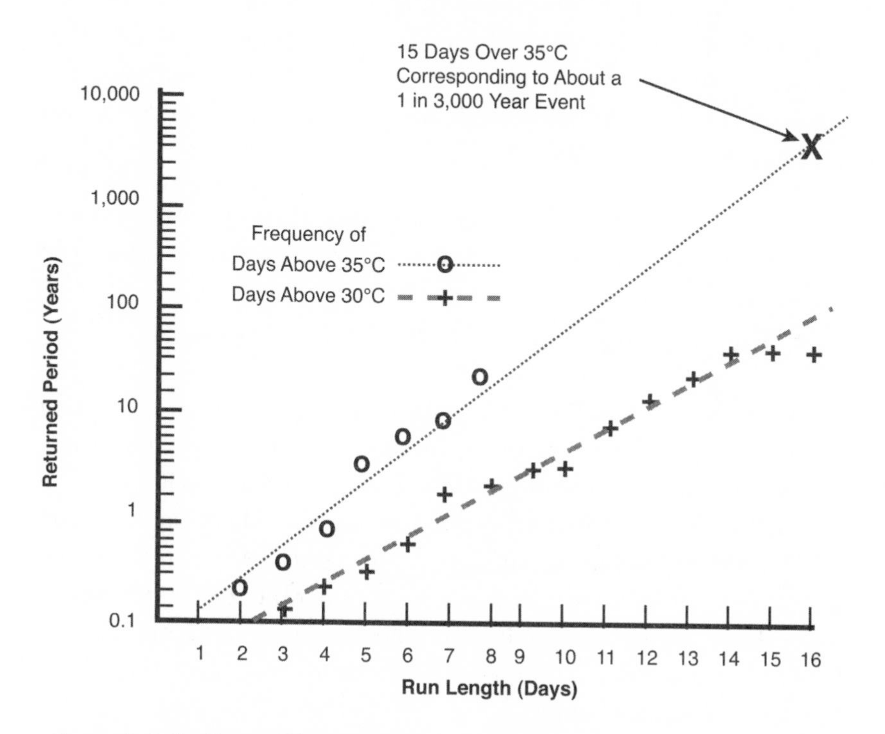

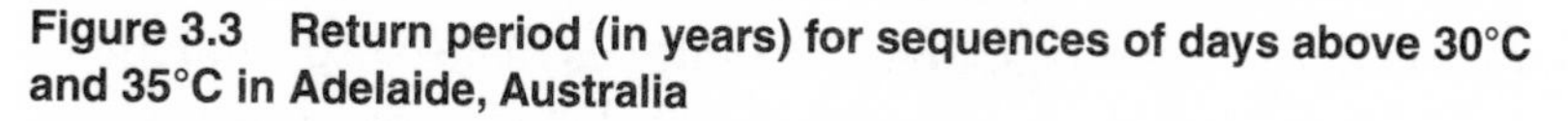
Figure 3.3 Return period (in years) for sequences of days above 30°C and 35°C in Adelaide, Australia

Not unlike the Adelaide heat wave, the hot summer in Western Europe in 2003 also appears to be an extreme outlier when compared with the long-run data from the available instrumental record. Summer temperatures for Switzerland (average for Basel, Bern, Geneva, and Zurich) for the 136 summers to 2000 fell between 15°C and 20°C, with an average around 17°C. The 2003 summer average temperature was in excess of 22°C, an average temperature falling 5.4 standard deviations from the 137-year sample mean.[8]

In some fields of science (for example, hydrology), data points that fall well away from other data in the sample (outliers) are sometimes removed. An explanation for removing outliers is sometimes given in terms of an experiment to determine the value of a known constant (for example, the speed of light) where all the data points with one or two exceptions cluster around a single value, and that averaging the defective points with the good ones would lower the accuracy of the estimate. Such a justification is based on two assumptions:

1. In such experiments the techniques and processes have been appropriate and that for the outliers gross errors of some type have been made.
2. The parameter being investigated is indeed not variable.

In the summer of 2003, there were no gross errors in measuring the temperature in Switzerland, or elsewhere in Western Europe, and second, the mean summer temperature in Switzerland is not a constant over time. Clearly, the 2003 outlier should not be discarded in any estimates of future summer temperatures for Switzerland. The distant past and its statistical characteristics may not be a good indicator of the future in this case because the sample of data from the past is very likely to have different characteristics to that of the future because of climate change.

The occurrence of these heat waves, more severe than any found in the modern instrumental record, indicates that statistical methods to assess the risk of these extremes are likely to give incorrect probability estimates. The alternative to the use of statistical methods is to employ models of the earth-atmosphere system that take into account changing climate and then to deduce, to the extent possible, the effects of changing climate on the climatology of extreme weather events through a detailed study of the model's climatology of such events.

The Intergovernmental Panel on Climate Change (IPCC) developed an agreed language to characterize uncertainty and provides a

IPCC Terminology

The IPCC[9] used the following terms to indicate the assessed likelihood of an outcome or a result:

- *Virtually certain* > 99% probability of occurrence
- *Very likely, 99% to* 90%
- *Likely,* 90% to 66%
- *About as likely as not, 66% to 33%*
- *Unlikely,* 33% to10%
- *Very unlikely,* 1% to 10%
- *Exceptionally unlikely,* less than 1%

The following terms were used to express confidence in a statement:

- *Very high confidence,* at least a 9 out of 10 chance of being correct
- *High confidence,* about an 8 out of 10 chance
- *Medium confidence,* about a 5 out of 10 chance
- *Low confidence,* about a 2 out of 10 chance
- *Very low confidence,* less than a 1 out of 10 chance

comprehensive account of all aspects of assessment of the risks associated with climate change.

The IPCC's Working Group I Fourth Assessment Report[10] examined the likelihood of all aspects of climate change from a global and regional perspective (that is, the vertical axis of Figure 3.1) and used many ways to assess the risk of future global warming and the likely change in the climatology of extreme and other weather events. Table 3.1, drawn from the Working Group I Report, summarizes these. The use of everyday expressions such as *very likely* with associated probability ranges is intended to bridge the understanding of the quantitative scientists and decision makers with experience in weighing options expressed qualitatively.

TABLE 3.1 Recent Trends, Assessment of Human Influence on the Trend, and Projections for Extreme Weather Events for Which There Is an Observed Late-Twentieth-Century Trend

Phenomenon and Direction of Trend	Likelihood That Trend Occurred in Late Twentieth Century (Typically Post-1960)	Likelihood of a Human Contribution to Observed Trend	Likelihood of Future Trends Based on Projections for Twenty-First Century Using SRES[11] Scenarios
Warmer and more frequent hot days and nights over most land areas	Very likely	Likely (nights)	Virtually certain
Warm spells/heat waves. Frequency increases over most land areas	Likely	More likely than not	Very likely
Area affected by droughts increases	Likely in many regions since 1970s	More likely than not	Likely
Intense tropical cyclone activity increases	Likely in some regions since 1970	More likely than not	Likely

Source: IPCC[12]

The IPCC's Working Group II[13] considers, *inter alia,* the impacts of climate change (the horizontal axis of Figure 3.1). Taking the example of heat waves, from Table 3.1, it can be seen that the likelihood of an increase in the number of heat waves occurring is in the 90 percent to 99 percent probability range and will have associated significant and costly impacts on the affected communities if they occur. The IPCC's Working Group II[14] essentially considers vulnerability to climate change (the vertical axis of Figure 3.1). The Working Group II Report considers a range of harmful impacts arising from an increase in the frequency of heat waves and assigns a "moderate" confidence level to their occurrence (that is, the associated impacts are expected with a confidence attached to their occurrence of between three and seven chances in ten). These two assessments can be combined in a two-dimensional risk space giving a decision maker more available information in a graphical form (see Figure 3.4).

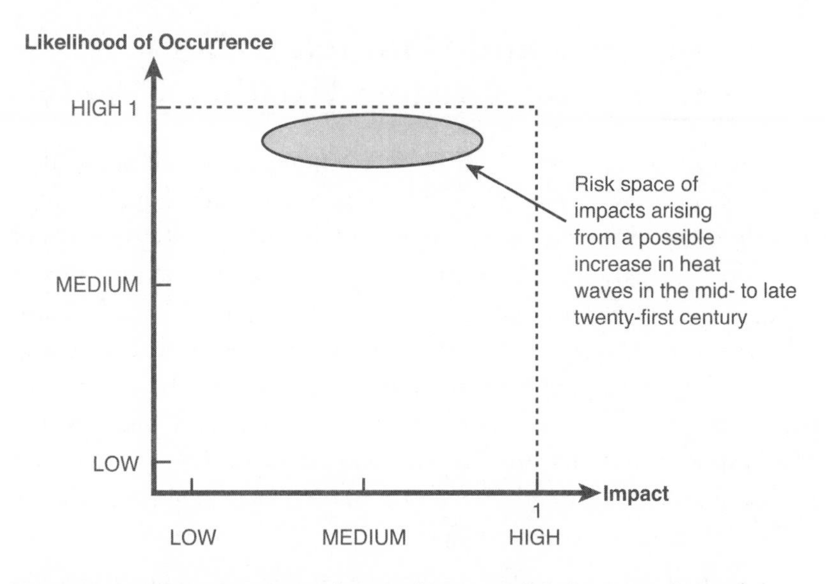

Figure 3.4 Risk space associated with a possible increase in heat waves in the mid to late twenty-first century

It is argued here that a true synthesis of the many global, regional, and local changes to climate as a result of global warming is possible through generating a series of risk space diagrams. As previously noted, the IPCC Working Group I uses language that facilitates quantification of the uncertainty for a range of possible climate-change-related events and in so doing provides information for the vertical axis of risk space diagrams. The IPCC Working Group II has identified the impacts on communities and biological systems and processes from these same events, again in terms that enable quantification of uncertainty, thereby specifying the horizontal axis of a series of risk space diagrams. What the IPCC did not do was to visually depict the risk space from these events. Figure 3.4 provides an example of the risk space for heat waves, as specified by the IPCC Working Group I and II reports. Were such risk space diagrams generated for a range of possible impacts for a country or region that is reasonably homogeneous in terms of exposure to disaster risk, then what would quickly emerge would be a relative ranking of possible events (as schematically shown in Figure 3.1), thereby assisting decision makers when determining the relative level of resources to be applied nationally to deal with a range of possible impacts.

Assessing Risk and Characterizing Uncertainty for Extreme Weather Events

The role of an NMHS is to assess continuously, on all timescales, the likelihood of extreme weather, climate, and hydrological events that threaten the nation they service. Outputs from statistical- and model-based analyses and forecasts are used to assess the threat from wind, flood, and fire from a range of weather events. Because NMHSs maintain 24x7 monitoring for all weather events, including those that have the potential to cause disasters, they have a role to play as an integral part of the national disaster risk-reduction system. The NMHS role then is to advise decision makers of the background risk from a range of weather events and then issue real-time advices and warnings as the risk increases.

The warning time differs by hazard, and by the stage in the life cycle of the hazard. For a tornado, the general conditions may be diagnosed several days ahead, but specific locality warnings can be issued only minutes to an hour ahead of impact after the tornado has formed and its track is apparent. For a forest fire affecting a rural or semi-urban community, hours to days of warning may be available. A community threatened by a tropical cyclone may receive many days' notification of the threat but only 24 hours or so of warning that their community will be struck.

A factor that amplifies uncertainty is the spatial scale of the forecast. To say that a tropical cyclone will strike the Florida west coast in 24 hours time is qualitatively a less uncertain forecast than to say the cyclone will strike within a 100-mile (160 Km) segment of the coast centered on Tampa. Global uncertainty (for example, the expected number of tropical cyclones in a year, usually about 80) is less than regional uncertainty (for example, the number of tropical cyclones that will affect the Gulf of Mexico in a particular year), which is, in turn, less than local uncertainty (for example, the number of tropical cyclones that will affect Tampa in a particular year). But the emergency manager in Tampa is not so much concerned with the annual number of tropical cyclones but the likelihood that the 100 miles of coastline centered on Tampa will receive a direct hit, and so he or she is always working in the domain of greatest uncertainty. To do the job most effectively, the manager will need to rely heavily on warnings and advice from the NMHS.

Advice and warnings of extreme weather events are communicated by multiple pathways. These pathways include the traditional media (newspapers, radio, and television) and also the Internet and pager alerts. The messages are tailored to the medium carrying them; television requires moving imagery, the Internet a blend of static graphics and statistical and other detail, and radio requires a minimum of technical detail but adequate qualitative information for the recipient to assess the hazard. Alerts sent on pagers and via telephone SMS messages convey the bare essentials to enable the recipient to decide whether to act immediately to obtain further information or whether the message can be disregarded. The characterization of uncertainty is then dependent on the transmission medium being used.

Modern weather forecasting blends the increasingly accurate numeric weather prediction models that depict the evolution of weather patterns on a global scale with a spatial (horizontal) resolution of tens of miles and on a regional- or meso-scale to a resolution of around 1 mile or less, and of human forecasters who add a knowledge of local weather and hydrological vulnerabilities and other effects. These forecasters then link with media commentators, emergency service professionals, and other community decision makers to help interpret warnings and highlight unique aspects of each developing extreme event, and it should be emphasized that each such event is unique and that yesterday's plans and responses may not be appropriate in today's circumstances.

As the NMHS is often one of the few national institutions to operate 24x7, with continuous contact with the media and emergency services, its hazard threat advisory and warning messages often carry information on behalf of other government agencies, including the state or national agencies responsible for managing roads, forest fires, floods, and the like. In those countries where the NMHS is inadequately resourced, or has failed to build an effective level of multihazard warning capability, the risk of an extreme weather event becoming a disaster is much higher than it need be (as discussed in the next section). The World Meteorological Organization is working closely with all NMHSs to increase its capacity to provide early warnings of extreme weather and hydrological phenomena such as tropical cyclones, forest fires, and floods.

Tropical Cyclones: Risks and Uncertainties

Perhaps the most mature early warning service of the NMHSs is the tropical cyclone warning service. In general, the weather in the tropical regions of the world is relatively benign, with warm, dry trade winds in the winter season and moist monsoon winds in summer, with the occasional squally rain shower or thunderstorm embedded within the monsoon. However, this benign picture is interrupted from time to time by devastating tropical cyclones that bring with them deadly winds and abnormally high tides, potentially causing loss of life and the destruction of property in exposed coastal communities.

In countries with well-developed disaster risk-reduction strategies, various measures are in place to reduce the risk of disasters related to tropical cyclones.

First, the NMHS has a long history of working with the general population, emergency services, and community leaders to inform them of the climatological risk profile of their community, based on the historical record of extreme weather events.

Second, NMHSs have access to the full range of meteorological observations (conventional *in situ* observations at the surface, and radar and satellite imagery necessary to detect and monitor the tropical oceans adjacent to their country). To make effective use of this data, NMHS staff receive basic training in meteorology, specific training in the use of the output from the advanced centers that supply forecasts from numeric model systems, and training in the use of modern data assimilation and forecaster support systems. In addition, the staff needs access to the data processing and communications equipment necessary to evaluate the incoming data streams, generate advice warnings, and disseminate these in a timely fashion to all those who require them. Finally, the NMHS would be an active participant in the regional tropical cyclone committee, which is coordinated by the World Meteorological Organization. Meeting these criteria supports the provision of data and information to the public similar to those in Figure 3.5(A), which graphically shows the areas expected to be affected by the tropical cyclone, along with real data (Figure 3.5[B]), which enables the public to "confirm" the forecasts and warnings they are receiving.

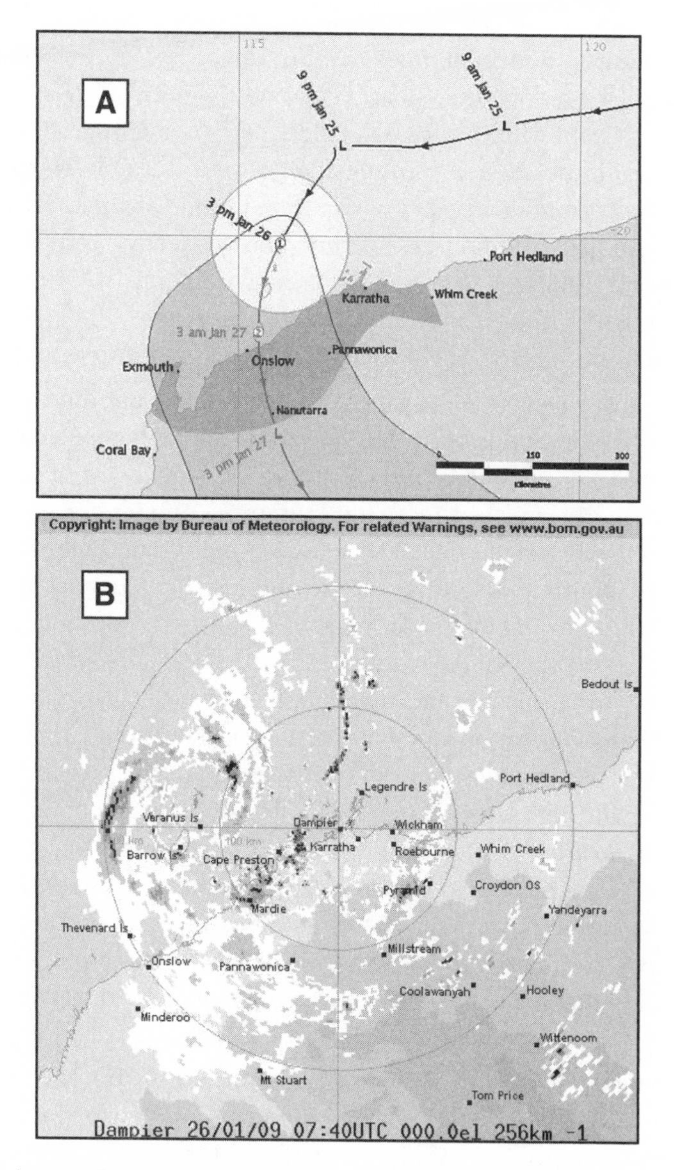

Source: Australian Bureau of Meteorology

Figure 3.5 (A) Graphical track map for tropical cyclone Dominic depicting the radius of gale force winds, and (B) a radar image from a nearby coastal radar station at about the same time

Upon detection of a tropical cyclone, advice will be issued. Then, as the risk rises, warnings will be issued to the threatened communities. The advice and warnings may be graphical (highlighting the extent of threatened areas), textual (describing the technical aspects of the hazard), and sometimes aural (perhaps a siren preceding the warning) (see following sidebar). These messages would be expected to be consistent with the WMO's guidelines[15] on incorporating uncertainty into forecasts and warnings. Very often, these warnings carry information from emergency services and other organizations advising threatened communities of their most effective response. The information flow from the NMHS to the community will be continuous throughout the event, and as the threat recedes, the information flow from the NMHS would revert back to the pre-threat level.

The effectiveness of warning systems is a key question for those responsible for public safety. However, there have been no consistent multicountry assessments of the economic effectiveness of multihazard warning systems. Instead, the literature contains assessments of the effectiveness of particular systems in single communities.[16] At the risk of generalizing the results of such studies, the outcomes appear to show that when members of the community are questioned about their understanding of the warning system, a high percentage indicate that they are aware of, and understand it, yet detailed questioning shows that significantly less than 50 percent have a full appreciation of the types of warnings that will be issued and in what circumstances. This said, the high levels of national and international media coverage of recent weather-related disasters such as Hurricane Katrina in the United States, tropical cyclone Nargis in Myanmar, the bushfires in Australia (among many) raises community awareness of warning systems, but more needs to be done with respect to both public education and evaluation of effectiveness using standardized metrics.

There is good evidence that the meteorological community has been steadily improving its capability to forecast the tracks of tropical cyclones as measured by, for example, the ability to forecast the location of a tropical cyclone at some future time (for example, Figure 3.6, with similar figures available from most countries preparing tropical cyclone warnings). The impact of this improved accuracy can be quantified with a simplified warning strategy analysis. Let us assume that a land-falling tropical cyclone brings with it an area of destructive winds around 100 miles (160km) in extent. Furthermore, from Figure 3.6, we can see that in 1990 the typical error in forecasting (following the least squares line of best fit) the location of the cyclone by the U.S. National Weather Service 48 hours ahead of land fall was about 200 miles (320km). Therefore, a warning message to communities likely to be affected by the land-falling cyclone might reasonably cover 300 miles (480km) of coastline—that is, the area of destructive winds plus the known uncertainty in forecasting the position of landfall. In 2007, after 17 years of improved science and technology, the 48-hour track forecast error has been reduced to about 80 miles (105km), and so a warning alerting communities of destructive winds, using the same approach as previously, would only need to address communities within 80 miles plus 100 for the extent of destructive winds (that is, 180 miles or 265km). Remember that real-world warning strategies are significantly more complex than this very simplified example because they must factor in the uncertainty associated with each forecast, the communities likely to be affected, the topography of the threatened communities, the amount of flooding due to prior rainfall, and many other elements.

Australian Government Bureau of Meteorology Western Australia

Media: Transmitters serving Onslow and adjacent areas are requested to use the Standard Emergency Warning Signal before broadcasting the following warning.

TOP PRIORITY FOR IMMEDIATE BROADCAST

TROPICAL CYCLONE ADVICE NUMBER 11

Issued at 3:50 pm WDT on Monday, 26 January 2009

BY THE BUREAU OF METEOROLOGY

TROPICAL CYCLONE WARNING CENTRE PERTH

A Cyclone WARNING is current for coastal areas from Whim Creek to Exmouth including adjacent inland parts of the west Pilbara.

At 3:00 pm WDT Tropical Cyclone Dominic, Category 1 was estimated to be 110 miles (175 kilometres) north northeast of Onslow and 95 miles (150 kilometres) west northwest of Karratha and moving south southwest at 10 miles per hour (15 kilometres per hour).

Tropical Cyclone Dominic is moving toward the west Pilbara coast. Gales with gusts to 75 miles per hour (120 kilometres per hour) are likely to develop in coastal areas this afternoon or overnight. The system is likely to cross the west Pilbara coast between Exmouth and Karratha, most likely in the vicinity of Onslow, overnight.

Destructive gusts to 75 miles per hour (120 kilometres per hour) may be experienced for a period close to the cyclone's path; however, periods of gales are possible in all parts of the warning area.

Tides between Exmouth and Whim Creek may rise above the normal high tide mark as the cyclone approaches the coast, with very rough seas and flooding of low lying coastal areas. Heavy rain is likely to be confined to coastal and adjacent parts.

- Details of Tropical Cyclone Dominic at 3:00 pm WDT:
- Centre located near......20.1 degrees South 115.6 degrees East
- Location accuracy......within 30 miles (46 kilometres)
- Recent movement......toward the south southwest at 10 miles per hour (15 kilometres per hour)
- Wind gusts near centre......75 miles per hour (120 kilometres per hour)
- Severity category......1
- Central pressure......987 hectoPascals

FESA-State Emergency Service advises of the following community alerts:

YELLOW ALERT: People in or near Onslow and adjacent inland communities should be taking action in preparation for the cyclone's arrival.

BLUE ALERT: People in or near the communities of Roebourne, Wickham, Point Samson, Karratha, Dampier, Panawonica, Nanutarra and adjacent inland communities should be taking precautions.

The next advice will be issued by 7:00 pm WDT Monday, 26 January.

Cyclone advices and State Emergency Service Community Alerts are available by dialling 1300 659 210.

A map showing the track of the cyclone is available at www.bom.gov.au/weather/cyclone.

Let's briefly return to the simplified warning scenario. If the 48-hour warning were one that required evacuations, then the number of persons to be evacuated would have been reduced by around 58 percent (assuming that the population is evenly distributed along our hypothetical coastline) over 17 years if the warning were issued in 2007 as opposed to 1990. Of course, in most coastal zones, the population exposed to the threat of tropical cyclones is increasing, and so the actual number of persons that would be able to avoid evacuation would have increased by more that 58 percent over the 17 years.

To understand the cost-benefit of improving warnings, it is necessary to compare the cost of research over the 17-year period against the cost of avoided evacuations. Such an analysis is beyond the scope of this chapter, but useful indicators point to the scale of some of the costs. The cost of evacuations is highly variable depending on the population density in the area to be evacuated and the infrastructure available for the evacuation (roads, railways, and so forth). An often quoted typical figure applicable to the United States is $1 million per mile of warned coastline. However, it has been noted that "hurricane evacuation costs for ocean counties in North Carolina range from about $1 million to $50 million depending on storm intensity and emergency management policy. These costs are much less than one million dollars per mile of evacuated coastline."[17] For families, there are substantial evacuation costs to be met that do not appear in the official statistics (lost hours at work, fuel to drive to and from their refuge, hotel bills and meals).[18] It is difficult to weigh the costs and benefits of reducing warning areas through improved investment in science and technology against the cost of ineffective warning, but it is clear that the current political judgment in many countries is that it is a wise community investment to improve early warning systems to the extent reasonably possible.

The reasons for improvement in the skill of tropical cyclone track forecasting are essentially twofold:

- With the improvement in coastal radar networks and availability of real-time satellite imagery, the errors in locating tropical cyclones have decreased steadily, and a better initial location of a tropical cyclone leads to a better forecast of its future track.
- The numeric weather prediction systems of the world's most advanced meteorological centers have steadily improved in

their capability to resolve and predict tropical cyclones as both the computing power available and the scientific understanding of these systems have increased.

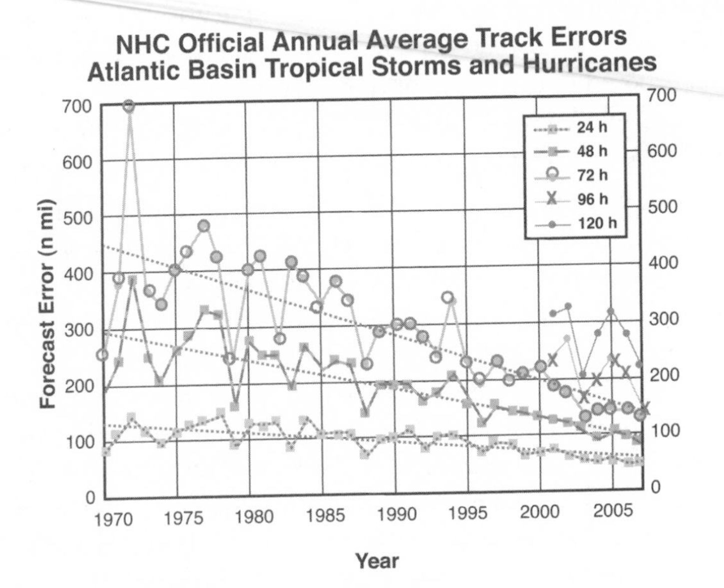

Source: NOAA[19]

Figure 3.6 The U.S. National Hurricane Center annual average track errors for the Atlantic tropical cyclone basin, 1970 to 2007, with least squares fit lines superimposed

As a result of the coordination and cooperation facilitated by the World Meteorological Organization, every NMHS worldwide has free and open access to the global database of meteorological observations and to output from forecast models run by the advanced centers. A task of the World Meteorological Organization is to assist all countries to make the best use possible of these tools to provide early warnings for extreme weather events. A highly significant benefit from this widespread access to the steadily improving products from the major centers has been the greater willingness of the community and community leaders to act promptly upon the advice and warnings of NMHSs.

Forest Fires: Risks and Uncertainties

Many regions in subtropical areas around the globe[20] experience devastating forest fires.[21] In essence, after a prolonged period of dry weather and high temperatures, grasslands and forests are susceptible to uncontrolled fires when wind speeds are high, temperatures are high, and the relative humidity (air moisture content) is low. These conditions are often present ahead of the passage of the cold front that heralds relief from a heat wave. Often associated with the air mass ahead of the cold front are high-based thunderstorms that deliver little or no rain but many lightning strikes capable of igniting the dry vegetation and giving rise to forest fires.

The provision of fire weather forecasts is a key role for NMHSs in countries susceptible to the conditions just described. The communities under threat are often those in rural areas, or those living on the fringes of major cities seeking a wilderness-style living environment while having access to the amenities of a major city. For example, significant communities throughout Australia, on the west coast of the United States, and on the Mediterranean coast certainly fall into this second category. Uncontrolled forest fires can also devastate national parks and plantations.

The NMHSs that provide fire forecasts often do this in close cooperation with one or more agencies that have direct responsibility for either forest management or for fire services. Regardless of the governance arrangements, the NMHS will advise the community and relevant decision makers on the buildup toward dangerous conditions and advise all relevant agencies when critical thresholds are likely to be reached that will require the issuance of public warnings. Because the NMHS has strong links with the media and emergency services, they often undertake the warning dissemination, the warning being a composite of meteorological data and other information such as fuel loadings, threatened communities, evacuation instructions, and the like (see the following sidebar).

Australian Government Bureau of Meteorology Western Australia

FIRE WEATHER WARNING

Issued at 3:45 pm WDT on Sunday, 25 January 2009

For the Central West inland sub district, Central Wheat Belt, eastern districts of the Great Southern and Southeast Coastal districts for Monday.

Fresh winds and high temperatures are expected to result in an EXTREME fire danger in the Central West inland sub district, Central Wheat Belt, eastern districts of the Great Southern and Southeast Coastal districts for Monday.

FESA advises

All residents should take necessary precautions to ensure the safety of life and property. No fires including solid fuel barbecues may be lit in the open during the warning period.

Local authorities should consider harvest and vehicle movement bans for the period of the warning.

To report fires, dial triple zero.

Conclusion

The assessment of risk is a traditional task of those who provide public forecasts of extreme hydro-meteorological events. In the past, this assessment was largely a matter of professional judgments developed over years of undertaking the task. As the science of risk assessment has grown, and as demands for transparency and accountability in public decision making has risen, the need for more formal, documented processes consistent with the science of risk assessment has increased. The key aspect of identifying the impact of an extreme event on a system or community provides a challenge to physical scientists that requires that they reach out, through cooperative arrangements, to professionals in a range of disciplines that are better placed to assess economic and social impacts of extreme events.

Noting that all forecasts have a degree of uncertainty about them, meteorologists have developed a variety of methods for expressing this uncertainty. Weather forecasters have traditionally used qualifiers in their forecasters to express uncertainty. In the domain of climate analysis and prediction, the IPCC has provided a framework for expressing uncertainty, both as reflected by general qualitative assessments and by quantitative assessments aimed specifically at decision makers. The World Meteorological Organization has provided extensive guidance to the field of weather forecasting on the ways uncertainty in forecasts can be communicated.

A key challenge is to ensure that those charged with forecasting extreme hydro-meteorological events—and those who use their warnings—fully appreciate the risks along with the uncertainty. Very often, the missing element in the flood, weather, or climate warning is the assessment of the vulnerability of the threatened community. To fill this gap, there is a great need to integrate further the estimation of risk and uncertainty so that decision makers of all types can make better use of warning services in their efforts to reduce the risk of local disaster.

4

Cognitive Constraints and Behavioral Biases

Seán Cleary
Parmenides Center for the Study of Thinking

Overview

This chapter discusses cognitive constraints and behavioral biases that influence our appreciation of the complex systems that characterize many natural disasters. Both personal behavior and public policy often lead to perverse results. Although traditional economic theory suggests that people make rational decisions based on information about costs and benefits, we cannot do this when addressing the complex systemic interactions that give rise to many natural disasters. We have too little information to make rational choices. We also assess risk subjectively, based on our beliefs, feelings, and prior intellectual constructs. Public policy makers must provide the common goods necessary for social well-being and incentivize individual and private behavior to assist in mitigating risks, but face the same constraints. As we address these challenges, we must be aware of the limitations of our minds and our models, and shape our, and society's, expectations accordingly.

Introduction

Most citizens in "developed" societies display a low tolerance for risk, and many expect that they should be protected from the risk of disaster. Although this is impossible, the expectation influences policy, sometimes for the better, oftentimes with perverse results.

Neither individuals, nor policy makers, have responded successfully to the challenges posed by natural disasters. Much individual behavior[1]—efforts to secure a *free ride*—and public policy[2]—statutory reduction of insurance premiums to levels lower than the risks justify, to extend coverage—have perverse effects. Insurers, for example, have been rendered unable to offer policies on economic terms and have had to withdraw from certain markets, leaving property owners without adequate cover.

This is not limited to natural disasters. A recent study[3] confirms that "policies to promote public health and welfare often fail or worsen the problems they are intended to solve. Evidence-based learning should prevent such policy resistance, but learning in complex systems is often weak and slow." What accounts for this?

Traditional economic theory suggests that people make *rational* decisions based on relevant information. When confronted with uncertain outcomes, economic actors are said to assess the probability of each alternative and to select the one likely to maximize the expected return. This theory rests on assumptions that there is symmetry between risk and return, that investors are risk averse, and that they possess full information when deciding.

We do not have full information when we confront the complex systemic interactions that give rise to some natural disasters. Each person's assessment of risk is subjective, moreover: Personal beliefs, feelings, and concepts affect the way each of us perceives the world and calculates risk and return.

Governments are charged to protect their citizens and to provide the common goods that society needs. They seek to incentivize individuals and companies to assist in mitigating risk. Many researchers, several of whom are represented in this book,[4] have provided analysis and advice on how to facilitate this.

Much of the literature assumes economic rationality and draws on experiments based on game theory. Game theoretical models are valuable when considering the behavior of individuals who reside in floodplains, earthquake zones, or coastal areas prone to hurricane or typhoon activity but do not help us grapple with the policy failures that arise from poor understanding of the interactions within complex systems. Simple models cannot approximate the dynamic complexity of climate systems or the ecosystemic interactions that exacerbate extreme weather events. It is also unclear how far we can generalize conclusions drawn from the behavior of actors in laboratory games to predict how people from different cultures will act when confronting varied choices in conditions of uncertainty.

The difficulty of making sound policy at the national level is greatly compounded by the additional complexity inherent in taking analysis, advice, and implementation to a global scale.

If we are to provide better advice, we must understand the cognitive limitations and behavioral biases that influence our ability to grasp the workings of complex systems and to act rationally in response to our appreciation of the challenges they pose.

Thinking About Complex Systems

Thought Patterns

It might be useful to start by reflecting on the *thought patterns* that underpin human thought and behavior.

A *thought pattern*—which may be *idiosyncratic* (personal), *cultural*, or *disciplinary* (for example, mathematical reasoning[5])—has three elements: a *paradigm* (a theoretical framework), a *reasoning method* (a means of approaching the challenges the paradigm poses), and one or more *heuristics* (indicative solutions that may help efficient searches).

The history of science is full of *paradigms*, with the transition in physics from the Newtonian to the relativistic and quantum theoretical paradigms in the early twentieth century being the most familiar. The rational secular-humanist worldview, which has underpinned Western polities since the nineteenth century, is a *thought pattern*, as is *rational choice theory:* Each is defined by a *paradigm,* includes indicative *reasoning methods,* and is replete with *heuristics.*

Insights from Experimental Psychology and Behavioral Economics

Not all *thought patterns* are rational; indeed, many are not! Kahneman and Tversky's experiments[6] in *behavioral economics* tested how people behaved when assessing situations and making choices. They found that we act largely intuitively, on the basis of limited information, inadequately selected, and poorly employed. Why does this occur?

The complex systemic interactions of the cosmos and our ecosystem and the psychological-social complexity of human systems vastly exceed the limits of our comprehension. In 1957, Herbert Simon described the principle of "bounded rationality" for which he won the Nobel Prize in 1978:

> The capacity of the human mind for formulating and solving complex problems is very small compared with the size of the problem whose solution is required for objectively rational behavior in the real world, or even for a reasonable approximation to such objective rationality.[7]

What Are Our Limits?

In evolutionary terms, human brains have specialized in rapid decision making under threat, at the expense of an ability to process complex interactions. Survival under threat requires rapid appreciation of new or uncertain events and effective responses to them. The adrenal reaction, equipping us to fight, flee, or play dead, depending on our sense of a threat, is a simple example.

Our "working memory"—the ability to remember and manipulate information over brief periods—is small. The "seven, plus or minus two" limit on the "chunks" of information we can process and recall without training is well documented.[8] We also cannot manipulate more than four variables *in relation to one another* at the same time.[9]

The syntax of language, moreover, is sequential; words must follow one another in predetermined ways to make our thoughts intelligible to others. This forces us to describe complex systemic relationships in inappropriate linear terms.

These limitations constrain our ability to appreciate, interpret, and assess complex issues and systems and therefore lead to distortions, three of which are common:

- **Monocausal assumptions:** We often assume that an event has one cause: A→B; B←A. This is rarely (if ever) true in complex systems, but it is a pervasive assumption that misdirects behavior and produces unintended outcomes. The assumption that removing the Taliban from power in Afghanistan and displacing Saddam Hussein in Iraq would bring security and stability was clearly wrong. Creating stable societies requires much more than "regime change," and the military interventions in both countries were exploited by radicals to justify a "defensive jihad" against the "West."
- **Egocentric interpretation:** Every person who is charged to develop policy, or to act on behalf of others, brings to the task many subjective perspectives that derive from individual experience and insight. Two results are worth noting:

  Unconscious framing: The way one defines an issue—the conceptual *frame* one uses—determines which information one seeks and employs (and ignores or discards) in filling the frame. It also shapes the interpretation of the material we select. Two commonplace examples from the political world illustrate this:

  Government leaders use *domestic political relevance* as a frame when they decide what should enjoy priority, given scarce resources and limited time. As national leaders are accountable to their domestic constituencies, few have been prepared to prioritize threats to the *global commons* like the impact of carbon emissions on climate change, above more politically salient considerations such as holding down the price of fuel.

  Defining a state as a "state sponsor of terrorism" creates a frame that dictates certain security responses, discourages diplomacy, encourages intelligence agents to search for evidence that suggests sponsorship of terrorism, and leads analysts to look for patterns to confirm it. The frame can also be used to justify other actions. The U.S. engagement with Iraq, one of the four countries[10] defined as a state sponsor of terrorism in

1979, illustrates this: Iraq was said to be providing bases to four terror groups[11] and was sanctioned. It was removed from the state terrorist list in 1982 to allow Washington to provide its government with weapons during Iraq's war with Iran and put back on in 1990 after it invaded Kuwait. It was removed again on September 25, 2004.[12]

Pervasive incorporation of prejudice: Each of us has a unique pattern of attitudes, beliefs, preferences, and prejudices (conscious and unconscious) that derives from our experiences since birth. These beliefs and assumptions inform our view of every event and of the context in which it occurs. We thus transfer emotional and attitudinal prejudice to each circumstance. Take the word *environmentalist:* Depending on one's background and experience, the word might elicit the image of "a responsible person concerned about the future of the earth" or the image of "a tree-hugger." Likewise, hearing that someone is a banker, a politician, an Arab, an Israeli, a hippie, or a rock musician creates an impression that colors any further information provided.

- **Weighting or calculus distortions:** Our ability to apply, consistently, arithmetical calculations of probability to events that evoke emotional responses—like *gain* and *loss*—is remarkably limited.[13] We often act without calculating the odds. Most people instinctively seek to avoid loss, even when this means forfeiting a larger gain. Much bureaucratic inertia is due to this, as are some elements of investment theory.[14] Prior to a disaster, many people assume that "it can't happen to me," and do not take precautions against severe risk, even when the cost of insurance is quite affordable. After disaster strikes nearby, many overreact in the opposite direction. The fact that the complex workings of nonlinear systems exceed our mental grasp compounds the problem.

How Do We Cope?

Operational Heuristics

We can make rapid, and often effective, decisions in simple situations by relying on *learned behaviors*—rules of thumb—or *heuristics.* This works well when we face familiar challenges. Indeed, we could not cope with daily life without these shortcuts.

However, many *heuristics* that we use to address the risks flowing from complex systems are oversimplified *cognitive biases* that we use to make "sense" of complex interactions that we cannot understand. This is dangerous because simple models cannot explain or predict the outcomes of complex interactions.

These heuristics also lead one astray when one is confronted with a new situation. One tends to frame it in the light of what seem to be similar prior experiences, thus misdirecting one's response.

Many cognitive biases, moreover, combine and exacerbate their perverse effects. Five of the most familiar[15] are worth listing.

- **Availability:** We tend to interpret any story through the lens of a superficially similar account. We recall unusual, emotionally charged events more easily and unconsciously adjust the specifics of the new case, and of our recollections, to make the two fit. This distortion often leads to our misjudging the probability of an event, as things that we can recall easily seem more likely.
- **Representativeness:** We judge the substantial similarity of events based on superficial, perhaps insignificant, resemblances. We also tend to see *patterns* in circumstances where none exist.
- **Confirmation bias:** We underpin an assumption by focusing on instances that confirm it, while ignoring those that don't.
- **Anchoring:** We cling mentally to a number or "fact" that we have absorbed in a particular context, and employ it more generally across a presumed field, even when it is irrelevant or misleading in another context.
- **Overconfidence:** We tend to overestimate the probability of our success in actions that we plan. This is associated with the illusion of superiority. Many successful people see themselves as always right, or at least right more often than others. Exceptionally high percentages of men believe that they are "better than average" drivers! We also claim more responsibility for our successes than we accept for our failures.

Many factors combine to distort our perceptions of risk. Figure 4.1 illustrates the potential relationships between the *heuristics* we employ in assessing what we experience, the *prejudices* that shape our responses, and the *cognitive errors* that result from these interactions. Our prior experiences, prejudices, and emotive-cognitive interactions[16] lead to three categories of common errors—those involved in *framing*[17] (or *contextualizing)* the risk, in defining its *content,* and in *calculating* its probability and impact.

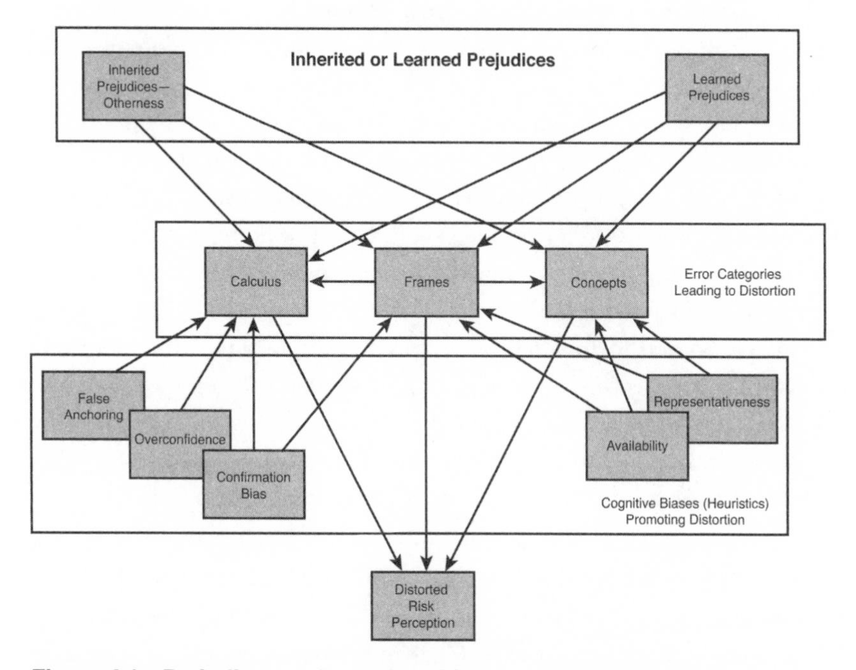

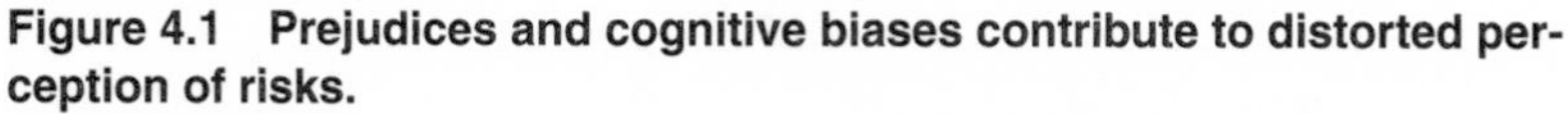

Figure 4.1 Prejudices and cognitive biases contribute to distorted perception of risks.

Group Behavior

Understanding our cognitive limitations and idiosyncratic biases is necessary if we are to address our institutional weakness in identifying, analyzing, and mitigating risk in complex systemic conditions. Because large numbers of people are often involved in assessing and mitigating risk in natural disasters, however, we also need to take account of the effects of *group behavior.*

Most group behaviors are caused by the natural desire of individuals to be accepted by their peers. They are reinforced by pressure to achieve consensus, and by a tendency to adjust to an emerging herd view when dominant figures lead the way.[18] Self-censorship by potential dissidents, mutual delusional reinforcement about capacity, group resonance reinforcing established behaviors, and distorted perceptions of the external environment, all reinforced by managers acting as group vigilantes, often weaken the performance of groups in assessing risks.

Although diversity can be an effective counter to "group think," and some successful leaders do encourage cabinet members, senior executives, or other employees to challenge the established wisdom, political memoirs are filled with examples of leaders reinforcing a propensity to "loyal" behavior by those in their circles who are party to important decisions.[19] The sustained, increasingly delusional behavior of finance professionals in some of the world's leading banks, which led to institutional collapse and required unprecedented public rescue packages to avert implosion, illustrates another pernicious form of group behavior. In a notorious statement, Citigroup's Chairman and CEO "Chuck" Prince observed in July 2007, less than a month before the subprime crash, "As long as the music is playing, you've got to get up and dance. We're still dancing."[20] The collective decision by the executives of the leading finance institutions to continue their bacchanal whirl took the global economy into its deepest recession since World War II.

Other agents, including regulators, activists, and powerful media, can also influence herd behavior. Compliance with what is seen to be politically correct or dogmatically sound at a certain time is common. The former Federal Reserve Chairman Alan Greenspan has been criticized for rejecting fears that the housing boom was turning into a speculative bubble. His views, given his status, undoubtedly influenced others.[21]

Risk Culture and Risk Tolerance

Personal experience affects one's perception of risk in several ways. The tolerance that individuals and groups have developed over time for specific risks influences the way they assess and respond to them. Living with a risk leads individuals and communities to take it for granted and *discount* it, whereas unfamiliar risks are viewed with far greater concern. The risk of *terrorism* is seen quite differently by residents of Gaza and Zurich.

Risk tolerance appears to be a function both of familiarity with a risk and one's sense of one's [in]ability to mitigate it. People living in

Tokyo, where the Kanto earthquake claimed 142,800 people in September 1923; in San Francisco on the San Andreas Fault, where the last major earthquake to take thousands of lives occurred in 1906[22] and resulted in 3,000 deaths; in Gujurat state in northwestern India, where an earthquake killed nearly 20,000 people and made more than a million homeless in January 2001;[23] and in Bam in southeastern Iran, where an earthquake killed at least 15,000 people in 2003[24]—all display high levels of tolerance for the risk of death or injury and the destruction of property by earthquake. The reasons may be different.

One might hypothesize that, in the aggregate,[25] temporal distance from the last major earthquakes, better building standards, and insurance coverage facilitate tolerance in San Francisco and Tokyo, whereas cultural-religious fatalism and the absence of material choice invoke it in Iran and India. It is also likely that group resonance discourages individuals from deviating from the group norm in such cases.

Implications for Efforts to Mitigate Risk

Efforts to reduce risk from natural disaster must be carefully designed. People in all communities may "compensate" for the lowering of risk through protection, by a form of *risk homeostasis.*[26] This is a controversial theory that suggests, first, that each individual has an inbuilt sense of what constitutes an *acceptable level of risk,* which is resistant to change, and that, as a result, traditional safety campaigns tend to *displace* risk-taking behavior rather than *reduce* it. The theory also suggests that some policies may have perverse effects, in that many people may be less cautious when they feel better protected.

A representative sample of Munich taxi drivers, half of whose taxis were equipped with antilock braking systems (ABS) whereas the other half had standard systems, saw similar accident rates in both groups. ABS drivers apparently drove faster, followed closer, and braked later. Similar tests involving drivers and seatbelts, children and cycle helmets, and scuba divers with differing levels of safety equipment show similar results. Some studies suggest that traditional means of influencing behavior—education, engineering, and enforcement in the case of traffic safety, for example—do not reduce accidents per hour in traffic.[27]

Most research in this area is related to risk taking in the context of road safety, however, and the principle of risk homeostasis is still contested and may not apply equally in all fields of activity.[28] We need to study more carefully how it may apply to mitigation of risk behavior in the context of natural disasters.

Although there are limits to policy makers' ability to promote risk aversion, there are possible avenues: First, those who place a higher value on the future indulge in less risk-taking behavior than those who discount it. Second, there is evidence that a reduction in risk-taking behavior may be achieved by interventions that reduce the level of risk that people accept. One study in Japan also suggests that improved access to information on the risks associated with environmental issues may increase the public's *participation in policy decisions* and that better access to information will improve interactions between the public and environmental policy makers.[29]

The "Neuroeconomics" of Risk

Building on the insights from psychology that inform behavioral economics, *neuroeconomics*[30] has emerged from neuroscience, drawing on brain imaging[31] and the study of the behavior of patients with brain damage, disease, or disorder.[32] Three pioneers—Colin Camerer, George Loewenstein, and Drazen Prelec—observe from the studies that "the Platonic metaphor of the mind as a *charioteer driving twin horses of reason and emotion* is on the right track, except that *cognition* is a smart pony, and *emotion* a big elephant."[33]

The metaphor, which suggests that emotion often displaces rational calculation, leads to the distinction between *cognitive (or rational) processes* (which address logical questions) and *affective processes* (which relate to emotions and emotional responses). Examples of the latter include *fear*, which prompts flight, attack, or freezing; *anger*, which prompts aggression; and *pain*, which encourages action to relieve it. These experiences leave memories, induce preferences, and influence future perceptions.

Human activity is shaped by interactions between *controlled* and *automatic* processes in our *cognitive (analytic)* and *affective (limbic)* systems. Automatic processes, which evolved to address evolutionary challenges, are faster than conscious thought and occur effortlessly. They are the product of our limbic systems, which are common to humans and animals. Human decision making is thus shaped by interactions between the limbic system (which governs intuitive responses) and the analytic system (which enables structured thought).

Brain-imaging experiments indicate that when we make decisions in conditions of uncertainty—as we inevitably do with complex systems—instincts and emotions conflict with rational choice. As *automatic* processes occur continuously,[34] the *controlled* (cognitive) processes necessary[35] for rational decisions have to override the automatic processes. Sustained rational behavior is therefore difficult.

Neuroscience offers insights into three phenomena that affect the appreciation of risk in the context of uncertainty and are central to efforts to plan for the effective mitigation of natural disasters: fear, trust, and the discounting of future rewards.

Fear

There is a neural basis for fear that influences decisions under uncertainty. When confronted with an unfamiliar figure or event, one is often able consciously to assess the risk and decide on the balance of risk and reward that one finds acceptable. In some cases, however, an immediate threat or great uncertainty may induce fear, which leads to an automatic, rather than controlled, response.

Fear is triggered by the amygdalae, almond-shaped groups of neurons in the medial temporal lobes of the brain, which register and form sensations of fear when unfamiliar stimuli appear. This leads to immobility, rapid heartbeat and breathing, and the release of stress hormones. The amygdalae also store associations between stimuli and the fear-inducing events they predict, allowing us to learn and unlearn what to fear.

Damage to the amygdalae inhibits fear. Impaired ability to register fear leads to greater risk-seeking behavior, whereas intense fear inhibits the rational assessment of risks and may cause freezing.

Interpersonal Trust

Trust underpins joint action, social cooperation, and economic exchange. The success of nations is correlated with the institutionalization of trust, whether through contract law or through social institutions like *guanxi.*[36] Transaction costs are lower if trust is widespread.

Subjects who experience mistrust[37] at others' behavior display increased activity in the insula cortex, which encodes pain, the anterior cingulate cortex (ACC), which processes abstract thinking and emotions, and the dorsolateral prefrontal cortex (DPC), which is associated with planning. The ACC seems to "balance" the discomfort at the "unfair" offer[38] with the prospect of financial reward.[39] The same areas of the brain are involved in calculations about risk. As trust involves accepting personal vulnerability when one has positive expectations about the behavior of others, this is not surprising.[40]

The hormone oxytocin, whose levels rise in social bonding, also plays a role. Higher oxytocin levels reflect greater trust. We may also "neurally encode" trust: When subjects are shown the faces of people who have cooperated with them in negotiations, activity in the ventral striatum, a reward area of the brain, is triggered.

Men and women may assess risk differently. In a game developed to measure trust, the medial cingulate sulcus (MCS) was active when men calculated how much to trust and was deactivated after the decision was made. Women behaved differently: After the decision, the caudate nucleus, which specializes in error detection, became active. Unlike the men, the women apparently questioned whether they had acted correctly, after deciding.[41]

Dealing with natural disasters requires populations to trust the explanations the scientists provide and the policies that governments propose. Take climate change: Sharply reducing carbon emissions demands changes in the behavior of citizens in developed countries. Growth must be delinked from carbon for much energy generation, and people must separate their sense of well-being from excessive consumption.[42] Achieving change will require a mix of education, regulation, and incentives, and will succeed only if citizens and policy makers trust the science and citizens trust their governments.

There are challenges in both areas: Surveys indicate that most U.S. citizens believe that climate change poses serious risks, but even educated citizens believed until recently that one could wait to reduce emissions until there was more evidence that climate change was seriously harmful.[43] Many policy makers are hesitant to introduce a carbon tax that will incentivize investment in research and development into alternative technologies, but increase the price of fuel; or to force the introduction of carbon capture and storage, which will raise energy costs for domestic users. They use the uncertainty of future events as an excuse to defer action.

This dilatory behavior ignores the impact of atmospheric accumulation of greenhouse gases, the very long delays in the climate's response to a subsequent reduction, and the risk of the inflection points in complex nonlinear systems causing immense ecosystemic disruption.

Policy makers wanting to effect change are challenged. Citizens in societies that reward individualism are suspicious of "expert" evidence that would inconvenience them if acted upon. Many believe that those in power manipulate information for political purposes. With no independent access to the science underpinning recommendations on a complex issue, and unable to evaluate alternative policies, their skepticism and resistance to inconvenient proposals is understandable.[44]

Future Rewards and Time Inconsistency

Although neoclassical economic theory suggests that we apply a rational, declining *discount factor* in measuring present rewards against future ones, we actually behave inconsistently when the rewards are uncertain.

The role of the analytic system is constant, but the limbic system overrides it when immediate rewards are offered. The possibility of immediate gratification displaces accurate calculation. We are more rational in calculating costs and benefits when the prospect of reward is moved further into the future.

The interaction between automatic and controlled behaviors produces inconsistent discounting. Decisions involving different time horizons require us to identify a pattern, categorize it, and match it against already familiar conditions. Self-control—essential for delayed gratification—involves both (affective) appreciation of a future desired state, and (cognitive) insight into the relationship between abstinence and future rewards.

When making decisions about the distant future, we often exhibit control and act consistently, although reconciling the cognitive and affective processes can be demanding. Many experience the urge to put off a decision.

In situations that require immediate decisions involving short-term rewards, however, the limbic system often overrides the pre-frontal cortex and demands immediate gratification. This is an automatic behavior, related to the urgent satisfaction of physiological needs, and displaces conscious control.

This may explain the failure to take account of risk when people settle in hurricane-prone areas or floodplains, or when they fail to build to proper specifications in earthquake zones, or to insure their properties. The immediate benefits (the attractiveness of the location, or the chance to consume more, rather than to pay an insurance premium), which are perceived by the automatic system, override more prudent behavior. Local authorities also often choose the revenue that will flow from extensive development in exposed coastal areas over more prudent policies that might avert subsequent disasters. These behaviors, which discount the importance of mitigating risk through insurance, or investment in higher construction standards, or stricter zoning requirements, are described as *myopic.*

How Can We Improve Our Performance?

Different preferences, experiences, and values lead humans to perceive, assess, and evaluate risk in many different ways. The dynamic interplay between reason and emotion and between controlled and automatic processes is complex and continuous, and varies under conditions of stress. Some responses may be gender specific,[45] perhaps because of the different consequences of sexual behavior for men and women and their different roles in child rearing.

Because the limbic processes that have allowed us to survive over millennia still shape our intuitive responses,[46] however, humans exhibit certain risk perception patterns that cut across cultures, gender and age groups. These include tendencies to

- Overestimate unfamiliar risks while underestimating those that we voluntarily assume
- Prioritize immediate gratification over delayed future benefits

In seeking to improve policy in averting and mitigating the effects of natural disasters, we must address four challenges:

1. The workings of the dynamic deterministic and stochastic[47] systems with which many such events confront us are not properly understood or modeled. We have not identified all the component elements, nor understood the core characteristics of the systems. Adequate mathematical models cannot be constructed, and the available approximations do not allow for reliable predictions. James Hansen of NASA's Goddard Institute for Space Studies noted in an article in *Nature* in April 2009, "Current models are inadequate and no paleoclimate analogue to the rapid human-made GHG [greenhouse gas] increase exists." In simpler terms, he notes that climate models are "our weakest tool" and that one "cannot trust their sensitivity in any of these key areas."[48]
2. Policy changes requiring (at least short-term) sacrifices[49] have to be justified in verbal terms, and the constraints that language imposes, coupled with the limits of human working memory, make it difficult to formulate arguments in ways that can persuade legislators or voters of the benefits of untested policies premised on high uncertainty and long time horizons. Furthermore, threats whose effects are distant in time, even if catastrophic consequences are probable at a (remote) future date, are sharply discounted by almost everyone.
3. The fact that different cost-bearers perceive complex systemic problems in different ways, whereas almost all oppose the postponement of immediate gratification for uncertain future benefits, exacerbates the *social goods problem* of matching the beneficiaries of mitigation to the bearers of the costs, especially when the costs must be incurred well before the (uncertain) benefits emerge.
4. Mistrust is an additional factor: Inaccurate characterizations of threats and predictions not borne out by experience[50] undermine already fragile trust and weaken the prospects of acceptance.

Leadership in the Face of Uncertainty

The task of a leader is to define a vision and a core strategy to achieve it and to communicate these persuasively so that others are encouraged and empowered to help realize them. As the current financial crisis has shown, crises focus the mind! Trillions of dollars were mobilized remarkably fast to bail out the banking system and provide fiscal stimuli to economies from China to the United States.

But success in a crisis demands more than money: The fear and negativity that the financial crisis evoked had to be managed skillfully to avert depression and restore growth. Calm and measured tones, a sense that policy makers knew what had to be done and were determined to do it, and unprecedented expenditure were needed to restore confidence. The experience of managing crisis in the financial markets may help us improve the prospects of more successful mitigation of natural disasters.

The rapid flow through from the collapse of the subprime mortgage market in August 2007 to a global financial crisis and economic contraction within a year shows that the linkages in our global systems can both *amplify the impact of harmful events,* or, as debt securitization was designed to do, *modulate and disperse their effects.* What we do in creating and modifying these linkages, in regulating and incentivizing behavior, and in adopting particular policies, is therefore of great importance.

There is rising evidence of extreme weather events due to climate change. Things may be worse than we have recognized. In *Nature,* James Hansen pointed to Arctic sea ice reaching record lows, many Greenland glaciers retreating, and the tropics expanding, and argued that halting the concentration of carbon in the atmosphere at 450 parts per million will not avoid catastrophe. Only by pulling CO_2 concentrations down to 350ppm, well below today's value, can we avert crisis, he argues.[51]

More broadly, the growing tension between a rising global population with expanding desires and the falling stock of *natural capital*—groundwater, marine life, biodiversity, crop and grazing land, and a healthy atmosphere—is not sustainable. Rising demands for "Western" lifestyles in the emerging economies may push us to an inflection point faster than we know. Climate change—and its impact on the other parts of the ecosystem—may create a systemic feedback loop that threatens survival. We must better align insights, expectations, policy, and action in addressing the challenge of averting and mitigating these effects.

Humans are not "rational," calculating machines, and policy will never be made (or grasped and sustained by the citizens, if it were) on the basis of statistical probability, sophisticated simulations, and mathematical precision. The excessive reliance in the financial system before August 2007 on mathematically complex models that claimed to hedge and distribute risk effectively, but took no account of systemic contagion or human fallibility, has also shown that it should not be.

But it is not enough to note that humans will not apply calculus consistently. Common cognitive biases—the product of the dominance of our limbic system over our cognition—give rise to dangerous inferences, and prompt behaviors that allowed individuals to survive before human society had urbanized and industrialized but which are ineffective and often dangerous today. The excessive consumption and waste that characterizes our most developed societies is a case in point.[52]

The mismatch between the complexity of the natural systems in which we are embedded and our limited capacity to understand their workings makes it difficult to devise sound policies. Our understanding of the systems and the responses we devise are limited by our rigid, reductionist mental models, which tend to attribute single causes to events. The policies we enact play out in a dynamic environment and lead to unintended consequences. Much policy that emerges from our legislative bodies is sullied with political compromises and trade-offs that contribute nothing to the purposes for which the laws were designed.[53] As a result, even well-conceived policies often give rise to perverse effects, breeding public cynicism, distrust, and resistance.

We need sophisticated tools to aid understanding of the complex circumstances we confront and to help overcome our limitations in comprehending them. Science, systems thinking, and mathematical simulations are essential, and we shall use them more extensively and in more sophisticated ways in the future. But we must align our continuous learning and the growing sophistication of our tools with humility about the human condition. To provide effective leadership in the context of natural disasters, therefore, we must do three things:

1. Clarify the issues as best we can and ensure that we do not contribute to confusion and irrational fears. Break down each issue into digestible and comprehensible elements that make it possible for people to understand the challenge and the need to address it.

2. Communicate openly and honestly. Share the information that is available while admitting what is not known, and define an agenda to advance the frontiers of understanding. Use language that can be understood and appreciated by the audiences—legislators, citizens, advocacy groups—for whom the messages are intended.
3. Focus the conversation on what must be done in terms of policy, pricing, and changed behavior to move constructively ahead. Seek and provide explanations for the sources of present challenges, but avoid attributing blame unnecessarily, and ensure that the energy is directed to creating the future.

We must compensate for our limited cognitive capability by continuing to design and develop models that help us better understand the complex, nonlinear systems we confront and have helped to create, while recognizing our weakness in responding sensibly to them. We must recognize that understanding of such systems is elusive, and that stylized assertion of the insights we have assembled at any point, in intellectual dogma, will not move large numbers of other people to abandon their biological habits and prejudices, sacrifice their short-term interests, and adopt new policies.

Democratic decision-making systems are often not the most effective means of translating new scientific insights into sound policy. Too many trade-offs, based on narrow sectional interests, are involved in the passage of most legislation. The common interest usually triumphs only—and not always—when imminent harm is widely perceived. Better policy in anticipating and mitigating the effects of natural disasters will thus only result from a judicious combination of scientific insight, appropriate humility, and effective leadership in the cultural context of each society. Policy advisors and political leaders alike need to understand their proper roles in this difficult task.

5

The Five Neglects: Risks Gone Amiss

Alan Berger, Massachusetts Institute of Technology

Case Brown, Project for Reclamation Excellence (P-REX), and Clemson University

Carolyn Kousky, Resources for the Future

Richard Zeckhauser, Harvard University

Overview

The economist's model of rational decision making in situations of risk is composed of five elements: (1) consideration of probability, (2) valuation of potential benefits and losses, (3) accurate use of (subjective) probability and statistics, (4) delineation and evaluation of all available alternatives, and (5) incorporation of all benefits and costs accruing to the decision maker.

Often, however, individuals fail to address one or more of these elements, giving rise to what we call the five neglects: (1) probability neglect, (2) consequence neglect, (3) statistical neglect, (4) solution neglect, and (5) external risk neglect. This chapter discusses when the five neglects are most likely to arise and how they may influence decision making. Two case studies of environmental risk provide a detailed description of their use in specific contexts.

Introduction

We must constantly make decisions in situations of risk. Should we undertake a potentially beneficial medical procedure that has a small probability of harmful complications? Should the local government allow development in the floodplain? How much money should Congress allocate to fighting terrorism?

Economists have developed a "rational choice" model for making decisions in these situations of risk, called expected utility (EU) theory. Under this approach, a utility value (utility being a measure of satisfaction or happiness) is first assigned to each potential outcome. These outcomes are then weighted by the probability that they will occur given a particular choice. The result is the expected utility reaped from that choice. All alternatives are evaluated in this way, and the one with the highest expected utility is chosen. When applied to societal-level decisions, often some metric of total benefits to the society is used in place of utility.

A rational choice approach to decision making is thus composed of five elements:

1. Consideration of probability
2. Valuation of potential benefits and losses
3. Accurate use of (subjective) probability and statistics
4. Delineation and evaluation of all available alternatives
5. Incorporation of all benefits and costs accruing to the decision maker

First, probabilities must be considered. In practice, there are only a few real-world situations in which objective probabilities are known. In all the other cases, individuals are required to form unbiased assessments of the probabilities, what are labeled *subjective probabilities*. For policy choices, decision makers often draw on models or historical data to generate such assessments. Subjective probabilities can be broadly interpreted as an individual's degree of belief in an outcome occurring. Comparing subjective probabilities to simple lotteries can often improve subjective estimates. For instance, an individual who assigns a 0.1 subjective probability to the likelihood that his property will be flooded in the coming year could recognize this is the same probability as a number 8 coming up on a roulette wheel with numbers 1 through 10.

Second, consideration must be given to the potential benefits and costs associated with an option. A common complexity here is that outcomes may be received only in the future. When they are, the utilities they offer are discounted. Outcomes in the future are discounted to reflect the fact that money invested today gains in value by tomorrow and also to reflect simple impatience and uncertainty. We'd rather have a dollar today than a dollar next year.

Third, the probabilities must reflect all available information and must not be biased. Further, calculations must also obey rules of probability. For instance, the probabilities of all potential outcomes from a choice must sum to one. This allows accurate calculations of the EU of each alternative. Making an optimal choice also requires that the fourth criteria be followed: All possible alternatives get appropriate attention. (In practice, some can be dismissed quickly.)

Finally, the decision maker must be sure to consider all costs and benefits an alternative will provide. Note that a choice that is rational for the decision maker will not be optimal for society at large unless the decision maker considers fully the benefits or costs imposed on others as well. These impacts on others are called externalities. To get a rational choice for society, therefore, requires replacing element 5 with 5a: Incorporation of all benefits and costs accruing to the decision maker and all external parties.

This process is more easily described than followed. Its effective use can be time intensive and may require sophisticated calculations. In everyday life, individuals are likely to deviate considerably from the rational model, often employing the use of mental shortcuts. That is, individuals are only boundedly rational.[1] The shortcuts they use can produce many systematic biases in decision making.[2]

Governments and businesses at times employ policy analyses or business plans to help make risky choices. These tools help tame biases. But such organizations fall prey to distinctive biases of their own due to efforts to claim credit or avoid blame, for example. And information often gets hidden in organizations by individuals pursuing parochial interests. These are examples of the so called *agency problem,* where a designated agent is making decisions for a principal and what is best for the agent may not be best for the principal.

This chapter focuses on the shortcomings of individuals making risk-related decisions, whether choosing for themselves or as agents for others or for institutions, including the institution of society at large. Individuals often fail to incorporate in their decision making the five elements we identified as critical for rational decisions. Failure to consider the five criteria give rise to what we label the *five neglects:*

1. Probability neglect
2. Consequence neglect
3. Statistical neglect
4. Solution neglect
5. External risk neglect

The following section introduces each of these five neglects. Each is illustrated largely through examples from decision making regarding environmental risks and natural disasters, although examples from national security or medical choices could easily be provided. After that, we discuss two brief case studies that describe the impact of several of our neglects in detail, and then end the chapter with some concluding remarks.

The Five Neglects

Probability Neglect

When making decisions under uncertainty, individuals may at times fail to consider the probability of an outcome occurring and focus entirely on the consequences. Cass Sunstein and others have labeled this phenomena probability neglect.[3] Such neglect is especially likely for emotionally charged risks. Sunstein and Zeckhauser demonstrate probability neglect in an experiment in which law school students are asked how much they would pay to eliminate a cancer risk from arsenic in drinking water. For some subjects, the risk was 1 in 100,000; for others, it was 1 in 1,000,000, or 10 times as great. When the risk of cancer death was described unemotionally, people paid more to eliminate a higher risk, as would be expected. However, when the death was described in gruesome and graphic terms, it did not matter which risk was faced; people were willing to pay about the same. The authors refer to this result of paying the same to reduce a very tiny risk or a much larger one an *emotion premium.*[4]

When individuals are neglecting probabilities, they will overreact to low-probability events. Love Canal provides a salient example. In this community in Niagara Falls, New York, homes and a school were built on top of a covered chemical waste site where tons of toxic waste had been disposed in an old canal. In the 1970s, the toxic chemicals began seeping into people's homes and yards. Alarmed residents and active media coverage built national concern about Love Canal and toxic waste sites more broadly. Eventually this forced the federal government to relocate the residents and spend massive amounts of money on cleaning toxic sites. However, there is no conclusive scientific evidence that the waste at Love Canal caused any enduring health problems to its residents, and the amount spent on removing those toxic wastes could have led to much greater risk reductions if targeted at other threats.[5] Probability neglect helps explain this outcome. It can lead, as it did here, to spending resources to achieve little relative to what they could achieve in risk reduction elsewhere. This is one of the reasons discussed by Zeckhauser and Viscusi that leads our risk-mitigation spending to often be severely cost-*in*effective.[6]

Consequence Neglect

Individuals can neglect the magnitude of outcomes, what we label consequence neglect, just as they neglect probabilities. Such neglect is most likely for nonsalient and difficult-to-imagine risks. These types of risk are often those that individuals have not experienced before nor thought much about; they are "virgin risks."[7] These are risks that are out of sight and out of mind. In most cases, however, consequence neglect will lead us to prepare insufficiently for very low-probability, but very high-consequence events. Because the risk is so small, individuals pay no attention to the consequences. If those consequences are extreme, however, some investment in prevention and protection would likely have a positive expected net value. Taking risk aversion into account, and looking at expected utility, such preventative expenditures would likely become even more valuable.

Richard Posner discusses the virgin risk example of asteroid collisions.[8] The probability of a sizeable asteroid—such as the one that might have wiped out the dinosaurs—colliding with the earth in any given year is very low: Posner uses a figure of 1 in 50 million to 1 in 100 million. This may be why we spend very little on asteroid-impact avoidance. Posner notes that with the small amount we are spending, NASA will not even finish mapping all the close, large asteroids for another decade. The small amount of attention spent on preventing an asteroid from hitting us could be due to consequence neglect. People focus on the probability, which appears almost infinitesimally small, and neglect the monumental consequence. Given that consequence, some form of cost-benefit analysis, à la Posner, would likely suggest we should spend more on assessing and possibly combating the risk than we do. One of the cases discussed later in this chapter further illustrates consequence neglect.

Statistical Neglect

Subjectively assessing small probabilities, and then continually updating them on the basis of new information, is difficult and time-consuming. Individuals may just skip the exercise of trying to make an informed probabilistic judgment altogether, perhaps using rules of thumb for estimating risks. Unfortunately, such rules can lead to systematic biases in decision making. Individuals have also been shown to misunderstand the basics of probability, and thus draw faulty statistical conclusions. Here we briefly discuss just four of many examples of statistical neglect that are well documented in the behavioral economics and psychology literature. The first two address the biased assessment and biased updating of probabilities. The second two represent fundamental misunderstandings individuals have about how probabilistic systems operate.

The availability heuristic refers to the fact that individuals tend to assess the likelihood of an event by how easily examples come to mind.[9] Individuals will thus overestimate the likelihood of risks that are particularly salient or have been experienced recently, and underweight risks that are difficult to envision. Threats will get undo attention right after a disaster and too little attention before a virgin disaster hits, or after the past disaster stretches into distant memory.[10] The availability heuristic can lead to too much ex-post spending and insufficient ex-ante spending on preparation and mitigation. The world reacted strongly to swine flu in 2009, despite considerable evidence that it would not be a massive killer. But the lessons of the 1918 epidemic that killed 50 million people worldwide had been long forgotten before the recent episodes of SARS and bird flu.

Similar to the availability heuristic, individuals are also likely, after an event occurs, to over-update their assessment of the risk if they had never experienced or thought about it before. On the other hand, if they did have previous experience with the risk, they are likely to ignore new evidence.[11] For example, flood risk can increase in communities as a watershed is developed and pervious surface area decreases, as development proceeds in areas at risk, or potentially as the climate changes. When communities have experience with flood risk, they may fail to appropriately update risk assessments in the face of such changes. A case study later in this chapter provides another example of failing to update.

Beyond neglecting and inaccurately estimating probabilities, individuals can misuse them. Individuals have been found to mistakenly assume that small samples are representative.[12] For instance, with only a century of data or less, we cannot accurately estimate the probability of hurricanes with a return frequency of, say, 1 in 50 years. Still, we often think we know, and after a few calm years, might assume the risk is lower than it is, and after a bad year, assume it is greater.

Individuals have also been shown to fall prone to the so-called gambler's fallacy, a related mistake, which refers to the belief that systems are self-correcting.[13] For example, after a coin has been tossed several times and come up heads each time, someone suffering from the gambler's fallacy would think a tail is more likely on the next toss. This might lead residents in disaster-prone areas to assume the risk has declined after a big event. This might be true for certain disasters, such as many earthquakes, where the quake relieves pressure on a fault; it is not true for most disasters.

Solution Neglect

Failure to consider all promising solutions to a problem represents a fourth neglect. An optimal alternative cannot be chosen if it is not even considered. To illustrate, a survey of homeowners in 100-year floodplains found that residents had a very narrow view of solutions to the flood problem. Most focused entirely on technological options and neglected to consider nonstructural approaches such as mitigation, changes in land use, insurance, or the use of warning systems.[14] One of these alternative solutions might offer higher net benefits but would not be undertaken because it was not considered. The two case studies below provide detailed examples of solution neglect.

We hypothesize three possible explanations of this phenomenon. First, individuals have been found to have an undue preference for sticking with their current choice, or the current policy, a propensity termed *status quo bias.*[15] Given this, solutions that are not currently being implemented get too little consideration, and possibly complete neglect. Second, approaches to problems build up political capital the longer they are in existence. This makes it difficult to consider, or even envision, new solutions. Finally, decision makers have limited time and attention to seek out all promising responses to a risk. Given the costs required to get a solution recognized as a possibility in the political arena, some superior solutions will never get considered.

We highlight two classes of solution neglect related to environmental risks: *natural capital neglect* and *remediation neglect.* Natural systems can produce value. Thus, environmental economists have extended the notion of capital to ecosystems, referring to them as natural capital. When natural capital gets neglected, society fails to consider the fact that natural systems can substantially reduce risks. For instance, wetlands act like a sponge, storing floodwaters, and coastal vegetation, such as mangroves, can buffer storm surge. Often, only built structures, such as levees and dams, are considered for such tasks.

The few cases where natural capital has been considered as a solution make clear the need to have a vocal advocate for the option to be put on the table. One example comes from Napa, California.

Napa had long suffered from floods along the Napa River, but the community rejected U.S. Army Corps of Engineers proposals for a traditional engineering approach to flood control. In the 1990s, a community coalition developed a "living river" design for the Napa River to protect the community from 100-year flood levels. The project removed levees and restored more than 650 acres of tidal wetlands to absorb flood flows.[16] The Corps ignored natural capital, the coalition introduced that option; the option won and proved successful.

Remediation neglect refers to the fact that we often fail to consider that fixing what is broken can sometimes be the best way to mitigate a risk. Such neglect arises because restoration may appear to be going "backward" instead of "forward." But fixing mistakes may be better than letting risky situations lay untouched for long periods of time. This form of solution neglect may be coupled with consequence neglect in situations where a longstanding activity continually creates a small risk of a catastrophe, assuring that a bomb is always ticking. In such cases, remediation is a promising, but frequently neglected, alternative. We discuss an example in our next case study. Another is the failure to improve the levees in New Orleans before Hurricane Katrina struck.

External Risk Neglect

When making decisions, individuals or groups, following self-interest, tend to consider only the benefits and costs that accrue to them and ignore benefits or costs imposed on others. This is rational behavior, but when externalities are great it leads to outcomes that are far from socially optimal. Here, we are mostly concerned with negative externalities, or costs that are imposed on others.

External risk neglect refers to a particular type of negative externality—raising risk levels others face. This is a type of JARring action, discussed by Kousky and Zeckhauser, where costs are imposed on others that are spatially or temporally distant.[17] When such risk impositions are not considered in decision making, we refer to it as external risk neglect. A prime example of such neglect comes from the "levee wars" in St. Louis, Missouri. St. Louis, located between the Missouri and Mississippi Rivers, constantly faces the threat of floods. Communities adjacent to the river seek protection of their floodplains by building levees. Although providing some degree of protection for their own residents, the levees push the floodwaters onto neighboring communities. This leads to the escalating levee wars. One community's decision to build a levee causes its neighbors to do so, too. When a community decides to build a levee, it neglects the risk this levee imposes on others. The socially optimal level and configuration of protection for the region will have much less of a walled river than results when communities take self-interested actions.

The three standard mechanisms to deal with externality problems—bargaining, tort liability, and regulation—encounter difficulties when the externality is an elevation in risk. First, changes in risk levels are not readily visible and might be hard to detect and trace to a source. Second, risk impositions are often created by many and imposed by many. Greenhouse gas emissions are a stellar example. When the creators and recipients are many, there can be collective action problems, and high transactions costs can impede both bargaining and tort solutions. Third, those creating the risk are often in a different political jurisdiction from those injured, inhibiting direct regulation. Finally, there will be many cases where current generations increase risks for future generations. Those politicians who pass regulations are elected by present citizens. Those receiving the externality are represented only by the altruism of current systems. Regulation is likely to be too lax.

Case Studies

We have employed logic and anecdotes to argue that our five neglects frequently lead to risks gone amiss. That is, as a society and as individuals, we routinely devote resources to risk reduction where they do little good and neglect substantial risks that could have been curtailed at prices worth paying. We now turn to two case studies that explore in greater detail the problems associated with some of these risk neglects.

Both cases are examples where there is a compounding of past failures to address risk and multiple forms of neglect commingle. Both cases also demonstrate a larger, all too common problem: failure to think about a risk in any capacity, or simply generalized risk neglect. Warning signs are too often waved aside, because many of us are imprisoned with an "it can't happen to me" mentality. "Let sleeping dogs lie" may be wise advice for dealing with conflicts, its intended area of application, or for canine management. But it can be a disastrous strategy for risk management, as the world learned to its sorrow with the 2008 financial meltdown, the 2004 tsunami due to the Sumatra earthquake, and the terror attack of September 11, 2001. To be sure, specific neglects played a role in these disasters: External risks were neglected by financial institutions before the meltdown, potential solutions were ignored by decision makers, and probabilities severely miscalibrated. In this section, we take two lesser-known cases to explore in detail how such risk neglects operate and their resulting consequences.

The Pontine Marshes

The Pontine Marshes comprise an area measuring 980 square kilometers (378 square miles) just south of Rome on the shore of the Mediterranean. For more than two millennia, popes, emperors, and famed hydraulic engineers from around the world attempted to drain this malarial, marshy plain by building canals. Now vast tracks of reclaimed land, the Pontine Marshes are heavily polluted. The Province of Latina's governmental data reveal that nine out of ten macro-basins in the plain are more than 50 percent polluted.[18] The vast majority of the surface and ground waters in the Pontine plain contain high levels of nitrates and phosphorous, not to mention undetermined amounts of hazardous industrial waste pollutants. Contaminated plumes flow from the canals directly into to the Mediterranean Sea. Further, groundwater pumping threatens agriculture with saltwater intrusion. These problems arose primarily from solution and external risk neglect.

Drainage of the marshes began in the thirteenth century. Drainage was not completed until 1934, however, when Benito Mussolini was able to combine rational planning and mapping techniques, a nationalistic fascist agenda, and modern dredging and pumping machinery. Drainage was a great feat not merely of civil engineering, but of human mobilization. From 1928 to 1935, 80,000 people were brought in, mostly from the north of Italy, to drain 145,000 hectares (358,000 acres, 600 square miles) of the Pontine Marshes and adjacent provincial areas. Over the 700 years that passed between the first attempts at settlement and Mussolini's project, no alternatives apart from canal building were considered, an example of extremely long-term solution neglect.[19]

This myopic focus has been coupled with external risk neglect. Relatively clean water drains from the Lepini Mountains, but after 1 kilometer of flow through agricultural and industrial operations, it becomes contaminated. This polluted water creates health risks for the greater seaward population and imposes risks for marine ecosystems. These risks are created by farmers who heavily use fertilizer, polluting industries, and regulators who curb neither activity. Thus, individual decision makers do not consider the risks they impose on others. Furthermore, farmers, attempting to avoid the polluted canals, increasingly turn to illegal wells to pump groundwater for their irrigation needs. As a result, 24,000 illegal wells dot the coastal plain. They weaken the hydrostatic pressures that form a bulwark meniscus against the saltwater intrusion that increasingly threatens agriculturally productive portions of the plain. Thus, external risk neglect results in compounding risks "downstream" in a series of risk-producing byproducts.

Years of solution neglect have the potential to be overcome by the entrepreneurial efforts of the Project for Reclamation Excellence (P-REX), which identified and reached out to help deal with the current risk situation. P-REX is introducing the combined use of natural capital and new ideas for remediation to lower current risk levels.[20] Pumps and canals cannot do enough. Indeed, they are part of the problem. Paradoxically, the drained wetlands would provide precisely the services needed to increase freshwater quality. Extensive fieldwork, provincial cooperation, and regional analyses enabled P-REX to formulate a basic strategy to reclaim portions of the marshes as filtering wetland "machines." Combining properties of industrial efficiency and natural wetland filtering/sequestering, the strategy collects canal water, distributes it across a wetland system to remove the pollutant load, and then outputs the treated water to the canals, groundwater, and sea. The wetlands are capable of treating water at modest costs for both construction and long-term maintenance. In addition, they provide benefits in the form of bird, amphibian, and fish habitats, better recreational options, and groundwater recharge potential. Natural capital is an asset to be mobilized, not neglected. Similar forms of pollution conditions due to the neglect of natural capital and external risks are found in agricultural basins worldwide.

Mining Reclamation in the American West

There are more than 600,000 inactive and abandoned mine sites in the United States, heavily concentrated in the western states. These abandoned mines pose numerous risks in the form of potential dam breaks, landslides, or structure collapses. They also represent physical hazards, with 33 people dying at these sites between 1999 and 2007. One of the most significant risks from inactive mines, however, is hazardous chemicals leaching into water systems and spreading into watersheds.

First and foremost, these abandoned mines are an example of external risk neglect. Mining companies did not consider the risks their activities imposed on others living near their operations. The Summitville Mine in Colorado well illustrates this neglect. More than 500 acres of natural landscape were sullied in Summitville. Underground and surface drainage from the mined areas produces heavy metal-laden, acidic water that laces the Alamosa River and its tributaries with arsenic, iron, copper, aluminum, and zinc.[21] These metals and acidic conditions are known to be toxic in very small concentrations to many forms of aquatic life. Over time, reservoirs holding toxic water from the cyanide heap-leach pad operation (gold mining) leaked into neighboring streams and ultimately proved disastrous for the downstream ecologies. Due to several forms of reclamation, including revegetation, mineshaft plugging, and building water-treatment plants, the U.S. government spent more than $175 million on this single site.[22] It is unlikely that the total mined gold and silver amounts to an equal value on a discounted basis, undermining the original logic of the resource extraction.[23] If firms had internalized the damages mining caused to external parties—including some not showing up for many years—instead of engaging in external risk neglect, much of the polluting activity would likely have been curbed.

Another example is the largest collective Superfund cluster: the Clark Fork Basin Sites, a collection of former mining operations across southwestern Montana. The area includes 500 underground mines, 3,000 miles of underground workings, and 4 open-pit mines, including the Berkeley Pit.[24] The Berkeley Pit, a tremendous mile-wide pit lake, contains metal concentrations at levels 18,000 times the concentrations that affect aquatic life.[25] The pit is infamous for a 2005 incident involving 342 snow geese that landed on the pit lake and died soon thereafter, a mega-metaphor relative to the canary in the coal mine. This is an example also of statistical neglect, particularly the availability heuristic, because after the event, the risk became salient, and some remediation action began.

The pit's major risk to humans involves the rising lake level due to lack of costly and aggressive pumping of groundwater feeding into the area from underground fissures and mine workings. Above a certain level, the lake will begin to contaminate a local aquifer from which humans partake through both natural and mining-induced underground rock fissures. A water-treatment plant has been constructed to eliminate this risk once lake levels achieve a certain depth. However, it is unclear at this juncture whether that measure will suffice.

Today, these abandoned mines are an example of consequence neglect. The risks from mines are not salient for most of the population, and the costs of remediating the sites are very high, leading to a neglect of the consequences should nothing be done. This situation is further exacerbated by the fact that many of the original owners and operators are long gone.

Should these mine sites be cleaned up, and if so, which ones and to what level? The answer is surely that some, perhaps most, merit significant cleanup, but unless the costs and benefits are assessed carefully, we will never know. Significant dollars will be required. But how many? The answer is debated. The Bureau of Land Management, the agency that oversees the abandoned mine lands program, estimates a mere $130 million in tax dollars will be needed to fund the cleanup of *all* high-priority sites through 2013. Meanwhile, an inspector general report found that a single district in California will require more than $170 million in cleanup funds alone.[26] There is thus wide disagreement on the cost of cleanup. Some estimates by the U.S. Department of the Interior actually place the cost of repairing all dangerous abandoned mine sites conservatively around $3 billion.[27] The Abandoned Mine Land Fund, collected by the government through taxes on coal companies, currently holds almost $2 billion but remains notoriously strangled by budget battles and bureaucratic barriers. These funds must be used to clean up coal-mined sites first, before being reallocated to other types of mines on a state-by-state determination. Furthermore, the federal fund is "on budget," requiring its allocation to be held back to lower overall budget deficits.

The abandoned mines also represent remediation neglect. As is the case with Summitville, most abandoned mine reclamation proceeds in a stopgap fashion—attempting to remedy former mistakes but never fully addressing the risk-inducing conditions. Thus, in the Clark Fork Basin case, a century of smelting, concentrating, and waste-accumulating operations has produced heavy metal contaminated surface water, groundwater, and soil. Piecemeal repair of sites will not end the accumulated contamination. The metals are distributed along the stream banks, behind dams, in ponds, and in various soil deposits across a 100-mile expanse. Part of the damage is currently being addressed. The EPA, in coordination with ARCO mining company, is spending more than $120 million on the site. Authorities have removed a pollution-collecting dam, reestablished the open flow of the river confluence, and transported the contaminated sediments to another Superfund site. Yet, considering the numerous potential risks the Clark Fork Basin Sites impose, this major operation could simply open the flow of upstream pollutants to downstream sites. Only a full-scale, comprehensive reclamation effort will lower the combination of the probability and the cost of severe environmental consequences.

Finally, the abandoned mines problem provides an example of statistical neglect. Across the United States, residential developments are creeping closer to the lands and natural systems affected by mine pollution. This changing proximity requires updating assessments of the potential risks. As Summitville nears reclamation "completion," it is noteworthy that the EPA still describes the site's remoteness as part of its logic for not going beyond a certain level of risk mitigation. As remoteness of the site and its downstream effects diminish with changes in residential land-use patterns, will the risk assessments be adjusted accordingly?

Conclusion

What basic strategies might stem the five neglects? A conscientious assessment of current risk conditions would be a good start. With the Pontine Marshes, remapping the data across the basins and sub-basins showed the pervasive but under-recognized extent of the pollution. Some reeducation on environmental systems can help public officials understand risk phenomena. Italian officials detested the very word for marshes (*paludes*). However, they gradually warmed to the idea that these new environments would add both recreational and ecological value in addition to their treatment function (something a traditional treatment plant cannot achieve). Risk deliberations, such as those on the marshes, involve political, economic, and technical knowledge. Thus, a diverse, workable team of interdisciplinary individuals are critical to craft a vision of proper scale and breadth. Finally, most risk-reducing strategies require a structural shift in mindset from the short-term political timescale to the long-term environmental and economic timescale.

Our two case studies focus on the environment. However, the five neglects are commonly found across broad classes of societal risks, including natural disasters, terrorism, and financial crises. For example, better representation of current knowledge of the active faults in Sichuan Province could have easily justified reinforced building codes in the area before the massive 2008 quake occurred. A long-term perspective would have shown that the consequences of 50,000 dead, millions homeless, and tens of billions of dollars in damages—even if an unlikely outcome—would vastly outweigh any savings reaped by building with cheap, unreinforced brick.

Despite the 1998 attacks on our embassies in East Africa by followers of Bin Laden, which killed hundreds, the nation rested comfortably as the twenty-first century began. Potential terror attacks on our shores received little media or government attention until we were wrenched from our lethargy on September 11, 2001. Massive expenditures and wars followed.

Careful assessment of risk levels in financial markets in 2006 and 2007, particularly those imposed on external parties through unintelligible derivatives or excessive leverage, could have been undertaken by academics, regulators, or financial institutions. Instead, nearly all parties engaged in happy neglect of both the probabilities and consequences of a meltdown. Trillions of dollars to both investors and the economy might have been saved.

We are good at fighting yesterday's fires. But new risks—avian flu, groundbreaking financial crises, pollutants long ignored, climate change—continuously emerge, and old risks wax and wane. Unfortunately, collectively and individually, we have the penchant for neglecting important elements of risks, including determining which ones are important. For that sin, we suffer both higher risks and higher costs.

6

Can Poor Countries Afford to Prepare for Low-Probability Risks?

Michele McNabb, Freeplay Energy
Kristine Pearson, Freeplay Foundation

Overview

This chapter examines how less-developed countries can prepare for low-probability risks in the face of so many other pressing needs such as health care, education, clean water, and roads. The case of Cyclone Nargis in Myanmar (Burma) is examined, among other recent disasters. Although it would be easy to vilify the globally unpopular government of Myanmar and blame it for the deaths of 130,000 people, the truth is more complex. Cyclone Nargis hit a part of the country with a low probability of cyclones. Can poor countries like Myanmar build comprehensive cyclone warning systems for areas that might not face another cyclone for decades or even centuries? What good is a warning system if the people are too poor to evacuate and roads are nearly nonexistent? With global climate change, anomalistic weather is projected to increase, meaning extreme weather events are likely to impact areas previously unaffected. How can early-warning systems be created for every potential disaster in every region? The authors argue that developing countries cannot afford to build individual early-warning systems for low-probability disasters, so they must rely on (1) multihazard warning systems, (2) disaster risk-reduction education and training, (3) low-cost/low-technology solutions, and (4) multiuse communication structures that can serve general development and early-warning purposes.

Can Poor Countries Afford to Prepare for Low-Probability Risks?

Natural disasters don't discriminate between rich people and poor people. Whether over shacks or mansions, floodwaters rise evenly, and hurricane winds blow with the same intensity. Yet the poor, the disenfranchised, and the weak usually suffer the greatest loss of life and lose a greater proportion of their livelihoods in disasters. The reasons disasters have such disproportional effects on the poor are clear: They have less ability to prepare for and mitigate the effects of disasters. They live in flimsy houses. They are likely to hold any wealth in assets like cattle or jewelry instead of in banks. They don't have insurance. Their jobs often depend on the land. They lack vehicles or money to evacuate quickly. They may lack means of communication to learn of an impending disaster or to plan an escape.

In rich countries, governments normally accept the responsibility to provide extra assistance to vulnerable groups when a disaster strikes. When the world's richest country failed to protect its most vulnerable citizens as Hurricane Katrina hit New Orleans, the entire moral fiber of the country was shaken. Stories of old people abandoned by their caregivers and the obvious racial and socioeconomic composition of people crowded on roof tops and in sports stadiums caused countless editorials and deep questioning about government's duty to protect its own most vulnerable citizens. Barack Obama highlighted the moral responsibility of governments when he accepted the Democratic nomination for president, saying "We are more compassionate than a government...that sits on its hands while a major American city drowns before our eyes."[1]

However, what about the governments of poor countries? Do they not have the same moral responsibility to protect their citizens? Cyclone Nargis killed 130,000 people in 2008 in Myanmar (Burma). Although it would be easy to vilify the globally unpopular military government of Myanmar and blame it for the atrocities, the reality is much more complicated. The government clearly impeded relief operations in the first days after the storm due to a combination of bureaucracy, paranoia, and paralysis; however, many other factors suggest that blaming the Myanmar government alone would be simplistic.

First, the government's meteorological department did issue cyclone warnings, and the excellent international tropical cyclone warning system functioned well, tracking the storm at sea for 6 days and sending warnings from the regional center in India to Myanmar 48 hours in advance. It is unclear how many people living in the Irrawaddy Delta actually received the warnings, but even if they had received them, the poor roads, lack of transport, and extreme poverty in the region would have prevented a mass evacuation. If a government cannot afford schools, roads, or hospitals, how it is supposed to protect its citizens from the ravages of nature?

Second, Cyclone Nargis was a highly unusual event, hitting a part of the country that had not experienced cyclones for decades.[2] Parts of Myanmar regularly experience cyclones, but the wide flat floodplains along the Irrawaddy Delta had not faced a cyclone in more than 40 years—indeed, the director of a U.S.-based weather service called Nargis "one of those once-in-every-500-years kind of things."[3] The storm surge quickly flooded the vast flat plains where most of the population lives. Although there had been investment in early warning for high-probability areas, similar investments were not made in the delta because of the low probability of cyclones. So how can a poor country prepare itself for events that might not recur for decades?

Third, some experts claim the unusual trajectory and intensity of Cyclone Nargis resulted from climate change. The Centre for Science and Environment in India claimed that Nargis was "not just a natural disaster, but a human-made disaster caused by climate change."[4] Although most scientists warn again labeling a single event a "sign" of climate change (extreme, anomalistic events have always occurred), clear consensus exists that the intensity of severe weather will increase and that areas previously unaccustomed to cyclones, floods, heat waves, and so on will face these threats.[5] So, does the moral responsibility for preparing a poor country like Myanmar from climate-change-induced hazards lie with the poor country or with the countries that created the greenhouse gases and caused climate change?

Finally, some environmentalists pin Nargis's high death toll on the destruction of mangrove swamps for rice and shrimp farming; whereas other experts say years of Western sanctions against the military regime had only exacerbated poverty and driven the environmental destruction as millions of desperately poor struggled to survive. Therefore, protecting the most vulnerable from disasters—especially low-probability disasters—is exceedingly complex.

State of Early Warning in Developing Countries: High-Probability Events

Over the past 30 years, significant investment has been made in early warning throughout the world. Advances in technology have greatly increased our ability to predict many types of natural hazards. Scientists have a much greater understanding of the earth's weather systems thanks to satellites, sensors, radar, and computer modeling. Global cooperation has led to major improvements in short- and long-term forecasting, with rich and poor countries working together to share resources and knowledge. The global tropical cyclone[6] warning system described next is perhaps the best example of the benefits of global technical and scientific collaboration in early warning.

Although there is room for improvement in nearly every early-warning system, most countries have at least rudimentary ability to provide warnings for *high-probability events*—events that have happened regularly in the past and are expected to continue. Many flood-prone countries operate flood early-warning systems; most cyclone-prone countries have strong early-warning systems in place; and drought prone countries in Africa monitor rainfall and crop conditions to sense the onset of drought before conditions lead to food insecurity or famine.

For example, Bangladesh, Cuba, and Mozambique, although some of the world's poorest countries, have good early-warning systems to cope with cyclones, which hit all three countries nearly every year. Each of the three countries has adopted cyclone-warning systems tailored to their specific geographic, cultural, and political situation. In all cases, the strength of their systems is based not only on expensive technologies but also on the involvement of the vulnerable populations themselves. Scientific knowledge that a cyclone is developing in the ocean is meaningless unless there are also systems to get the warnings out to at-risk populations. But even that is not enough; vulnerable groups must have options available to protect themselves when they receive the warning.

One of the reasons Bangladesh's cyclone-warning system is widely lauded is that it not only provides official warnings from authorities and includes an extensive network of volunteers who communicate down to the village level, but the country has also built several thousand cyclone shelters. The raised shelters provide emergency accommodation in safe durable buildings not far from people's homes. Thousands of the poorest people in the poor nation of Bangladesh now have a place to go when a cyclone hits. When the massive Cyclone Sidr struck in November 2007, 3,400 people still died, but an estimated 1.5 million people sought refuge in 2,168 cyclone shelters.[7] The death of more than 3,000 people is a terrible tragedy, the number of shelters is still woefully inadequate, and maintenance is a perpetual challenge, but without the option offered by the shelters, the death toll would have been much higher.[8]

The cyclone early-warning systems in many other countries lack this last component—options of last resort, especially for people who do not have the means to evacuate or live in poor communities with no sturdy buildings able to withstand the wind and rain of cyclones. To advise people to evacuate when they have no vehicles, to take shelter when they have no permanent buildings, or to seek higher ground on a flat flood plain is of little value.

For high-probability events, successful models exist, and most countries have implemented early-warning systems. Regional and global collaboration assist governments with the information, resources, and tools to build and continuously improve these systems. If this is true, then how could more than 200,000 people perish in the Indian Ocean tsunami? The answer is simple: The tsunami was a low-probability event.

This chapter argues *against* spending resources to establish early-warning systems for low-probability events. Highly anomalistic events will continue to happen, and it is impossible to be fully prepared for every event that might happen once in 50 or 100 or 1,000 years. It is a poor use of scarce development resources to set up a tsunami early-warning system in Somalia, Kenya, Tanzania, or Madagascar—all of which suffered minor impacts in the Indian Ocean tsunami. It is well documented that early-warning systems that are not activated regularly lose effectiveness and fall into disrepair.[9,10]

State of Early Warning in Developing Countries: Low-Probability Events

The challenges poor countries face in protecting their poorest citizens from high-probability events are magnified in the case of low-probability events. If Mozambique struggles to create and maintain flood and cyclone early-warning systems despite the fact that it faces an average of 3 cyclones every season and it has 11 international rivers flowing through its soil, how can it possibly prepare for a tsunami that might not occur in a lifetime? Should it use scarce resources to educate its citizens about tsunamis or other low-probability events that may not strike for decades or even centuries?

The tsunami early-warning system for the Pacific Ocean is more than 40 years old. One of the drivers of the system was the 1960 Chilean earthquake, the most powerful instrumentally recorded in history. The resulting tsunami affected Chile, Hawaii, the Aleutian Islands in Alaska, California, Samoa, Japan, the Philippines, New Zealand, and Australia. Hilo, Hawaii, was one of the worst effected cities, where waves as high as 35 feet were recorded.

Based outside of Honolulu, Hawaii, the Pacific Tsunami Warning Center has provided dozens warnings for the Pacific Ocean countries. Scientists continuously improve the system, tracking the effects of underwater earthquakes and landslides to model the potential occurrence of tsunamis. But no system was in place in the Indian Ocean because tsunamis are relatively rare in that basin. In fact, as millions of dollars were rushed into creating a tsunami early-warning system for the Indian Ocean after the fact, some experts were suggesting the money would be better spent creating a system for the Mediterranean Sea—statistically more vulnerable to tsunamis than the Indian Ocean, with 140 million people living near the shoreline, plus millions of tourists visiting at any given moment. Some basic work has gone into the Mediterranean tsunami early-warning system, mainly in terms of data collection through ocean buoys, but little public outreach or education has taken place.[11] A large undersea earthquake triggering a tsunami in the Mediterranean today could kill tens of thousands. Based on probabilities and risk, additional investment in public education about tsunamis in the Mediterranean is urgently needed.[12]

After a mega-disaster, there is a strong desire to "do something." Immediately after the Indian Ocean disaster, money was put into tsunami early warning in Tanzania and other East African countries that suffered only minor losses during the event and had never experienced a tsunami before. More than $10 million was requested for tsunami-related activities in Somalia, for example. Such a reaction, although understandable, is misguided. Money spent on single hazard early-warning systems for low-probability events in poor countries could be better spent on general development activities that can contribute to disaster preparedness: improved communications, roads, education, building codes, and so forth.

High or Low Probability: How Climate Change Is Changing the Nature of Risk

Risk assessment is considered the first step in risk management. These risk calculations are often based on available historical data. The most common type of probability calculations are "return periods" on flooding—calculations of how often a specific size of flood occurs, based on data from the past 100 or more years. A rigorous analysis of data can allow experts to classify floods as a "1 in 100-year event" or a "1 in 10-year event" with some degree of confidence.

However, it is widely agreed that climate change is making forecasts based on historical data less relevant (although how much less relevant remains unknown). The past is no longer an accurate predictor of future events—floods are occurring more frequently and impacting areas previously unaffected. Changes in temperature mean that vector borne diseases such as malaria may spread to areas previously free from the disease, unusual heat waves are affecting Europe, and Australia is suffering severe drought and wild fires, for example.

Climate change means risk-assessment methodologies must factor in a greater degree of uncertainty than simply an analysis of historical data. Increased uncertainty makes it that much more difficult to label an event "high probability" or "low probability." Some high-probability events will become more extreme meaning an even higher level of preparedness is needed. Some low-probability events may happen more frequently or affect new areas, blurring the line between high- and low-probability events.

Who Should Pay for Early Warning?

Just as natural hazards don't discriminate between rich and poor, they know no borders. The same hurricanes threaten Cuba, the United States, and Mexico. Ashes from a volcano eruption in the Philippines affect rainfall and weather patterns around the world. Droughts in Africa cause people to cross borders in search of water and food. Heavy rainfall in landlocked countries floods coastal communities thousands of miles away. So while the state bears primary role for early warning, responsibility and funding is rightly shared from the global to the household level.

Arguably the best example of integrated early-warning system with collaboration from the international to the household level is the global cyclone early-warning system. The World Meteorological Organization's global operational network enables continuous observation, data exchange, and regional forecasting. Six regional specialized meteorological centers around the globe provide forecasts, alerts, and bulletins to national meteorological services to all countries at risk with lead times of 24 to 72 hours. The national services then issue warnings to government, media, and the general public according to national protocols. Historical risk areas are well established (although historical patterns are becoming a less reliable predictor, as demonstrated in the case of Myanmar), and five Regional Tropical Cyclone Committees work continuously to enhance forecasting skills of all members. Costs and responsibilities are shared and the system works extremely well.

Global Collaboration

Global collaboration in early warning has been driven by both humanitarian imperatives and self-interest. Often, the two are entangled and difficult to separate. More technologically advanced countries may support enhanced flood or tsunami warning systems, but they also sell river gauge or ocean-monitoring equipment, sophisticated computer modeling capacity, and so on.

There is nothing inherently wrong with self-interest playing a role in global collaboration on disasters—in fact, a greater recognition of the potential benefits to richer countries can help increase investment in early warning and disaster risk reduction in poor countries. Unmitigated disasters often lead to a downward spiral of poverty, increased social inequities and tensions, and even migration. For example, families lose their homes and assets in a hurricane or earthquake; they are forced to send family members on difficult and dangerous journeys to find work abroad; and unskilled and uneducated migrants may fail to find work and end up relying on social programs in the host country or turning to illegal activities to survive and support family at home. Disaster risk-reduction and -mitigation efforts can reduce this downward spiral.

Modeling of the global climate system has lead to significant advances in understanding how sea surface temperatures (El Niño and La Niña) affect seasonal weather patterns, which, in turn, has important implications for drought, flood, and malaria early warning in developing countries. Satellites launched into orbit for weather-monitoring purposes in developed countries were inadvertently discovered to have the capacity to monitor vegetative vigor on the ground—which has become a key indicator for drought early warning in Africa. River systems modeling developed in Japan and the United States has been shared with developing countries where the understanding of rivers and flooding was nonexistent or rudimentary.

Regional Collaboration

Regional collaboration in early warning is generally weak, especially in the developing world. There are a few examples of regional bodies that successfully share information and resources, leading to better early warning, such as CILSS (Comite Permanent Inter-Etats de Lutte Contre la Secheresse) for drought in West Africa and the Mekong Delta River Authority for flooding in Southeast Asia. But there are many more cases where regional cooperation is ineffective.

Flood monitoring in sub-Saharan Africa offers an example of how the weaknesses in regional collaboration negatively impacts early-warning efforts and increases people's vulnerability. Many of Africa's river basins are international—meaning that rain falling in one country will eventually find its way into rivers that pass through other countries, potentially causing flooding downstream even if there is no rain locally. It is imperative for downstream communities to know how much rain is falling upstream and how fast the rivers are rising, yet in many cases, the information is not readily shared. Linking upstream information with downstream communities can provide 48 to 72 hours' warning of an impending flood and enough time to evacuate their assets and move to higher ground. These types of upstream-to-downstream linkages have been created in some places, notably in Central America, but examples of multicountry collaboration in contributing to regional early warning are few.

One reason regional collaboration is weak may be a lack of perceived self-interest. Using the flood early-warning example, four Southern African countries share the Limpopo river basin, yet all of the water eventually flows through Mozambique into the Indian Ocean, presenting regular flood risks to communities living near the river's mouth. Even though the flood risk is only in Mozambique, most of the catchment area is in South Africa, with small parts in Botswana and Zimbabwe.[13] For South Africa, heavy rainfall in the high elevation catchment areas has little national impact and only limited local impact. South Africa may accept it has a humanitarian imperative to help its poorer neighbor (its military has dispatched helicopters to rescue Mozambicans stranded by floodwaters in 2000), but when South Africa itself has countless internal demands for improved housing, health care, and schools, should it prioritize the establishment of an extensive network of rainfall gauges for the main benefit of its neighbor?

State's Responsibility

The World Conference on Disaster Reduction in Kobe, Japan, in January 2005 released the *Hyogo Framework for Action 2005-2015: Building the Resilience of Nations and Communities* (HFA).[14] The HFA placed the primary responsibility for implementation of early warning and disaster risk reduction on national governments. Ensuring its citizens' safety is a primary responsibility of government, and national leadership and ownership are keys to effective early warning and early action.

Even poor countries can mount effective early-warning systems for high-probability events. The example of Cuba's hurricane early-warning system illustrates this clearly. The country is hit by hurricanes nearly every year, yet the fatalities in storms are usually far fewer than on neighboring islands. A combination of effective government planning, annual simulation exercises, and citizen responsibility ensures everyone is aware of a storm's approach and knows exactly how to respond.[15] Yet nearby Haiti suffers immensely from storms, and its government is ill equipped to protect its citizens. The lack of government preparedness coupled with decades of deforestation has resulted in uncontrolled landslides and flooding, further exacerbating the problem and making its population even poorer (in fact, the poorest in the Western Hemisphere).

When a state lacks human or financial resources to protect its citizens or lacks the commitment, what can and should the global community do to protect the most vulnerable? This issue is addressed in the final section.

Community Responsibility

In the last decade, significant advances have been made in recognizing a community's responsibility for protecting themselves from disasters. Even the most vulnerable communities should not be seen as helpless victims of a natural disaster but as the group with the largest vested interest in early warning and early action.

Empowering communities to help themselves prevent and mitigate disasters is many times more effective than any other form of risk reduction.

Initial advances in early warning had a strongly scientific bias. Investments were made in technological solutions without much practical thought about how communities would be warned and how they would react to warnings. This mistake is still being made as evidenced by the lack of progress over the past few years in building a tsunami early-warning system for the Mediterranean. Almost no resources have been devoted to educating the millions of people who live near the shores of the Mediterranean about how to recognize a tsunami and what actions to take. This is a disaster waiting to happen—the threat exists, and little has been done to mitigate the risks for the vulnerable people.

Community involvement in early warning and early action must incorporate three levels of preparedness:

1. **Communities need to understand their risks.** All people, not just those in developing countries, misjudge their risks because they don't have an objective basis for assessing them over a long time frame. When a catastrophic, low-probability hazard occurs, like the Indian Ocean tsunami, people along coastlines worldwide overestimate their risk of another event. Communities living in floodplains generally have a good conception of how often small, medium, or large floods occur—but if a large devastating flood occurred recently, they often overestimate their risks.

   It has been believed that bringing scientific data on historical disaster patterns (100-year records of rainfall or cyclone tracks) together with local knowledge about past events gathered from older residents or collective memory was the best way to assess risks. However, with climate change, there is a new challenge: Those historical records or stories passed down over generations may no longer predict future frequency or intensity. There is evidence in the Mozambique floods of 2000, for example, that people were warned on radio the impending floods would be "a major flood," which community elders interpreted to mean similar in magnitude to the floods experienced in the early 1900s.[16]

However, the floods vastly exceeded floods in anyone's living memory.

It is essential that communities map their own knowledge of prior events, incorporate any available data on historical events, but also understand that climate change adds a level of uncertainty never before experienced. The past is no longer an accurate guide to the future of disaster events.

2. **Communities need to understand warnings from outside, and their local knowledge needs to be shared and assessed scientifically.** Warnings may be shared from national authorities down to community level, but insufficient analysis has been carried out on how the messages are perceived. In some cases, messages may lack specificity ("floods are likely along the Mekong") or be overly technical ("a Category 3 cyclone with maximum sustained winds of 150km/hour will hit between 2100 and 2300 hours tomorrow"). Although these messages provide a basic level of alert, they are unlikely to engender any actions from the vulnerable populations—unless they have confirming evidence from traditional warning indicators.

   Almost all communities have "traditional" hazard warnings embedded in their culture. In developing countries, many of these warning signs are based on animal behavior including birds singing at unusual times of day, monkeys or small animals fleeing an area, or livestock refusing to approach shorelines.[17] In the past, local knowledge about early warning signs has been largely dismissed as unscientific, but it is increasingly clear that local knowledge can complement technical warnings. For example, in Mozambique, downstream communities watch the color of the river water and the size and type of debris floating down to judge the magnitude of a potential flood.

   In Simeuleu, an island off the coast of Indonesia only about 100 kilometers from the epicenter of the earthquake that triggered the tsunami, only 7 people of a total population of 83,000 were killed. The island had suffered from a tsunami in 1907 and knowledge of the warning signs—especially the ocean receding after an earthquake—had been passed from generation to generation through songs and poems. Instead of dismissing this local knowledge, it should be studied and integrated into warning systems as appropriate.

3. **Communities need to have options if a warning is sounded.** Although this step sounds obvious, it has received remarkably little attention by practitioners and is a missing link in many early-warning systems in developing countries. In the case of Cyclone Nargis, for example, even if risk assessments had been carried out and warnings had been received by all people living in the Irrawaddy Delta, there would have been little concrete action they could have taken to escape the devastation. The roads were insufficient to handle a mass evacuation, the population lacked means of transport, and people were unwilling to leave their assets behind for fear of theft.

   The Bangladesh cyclone early-warning system presents one of the few examples of warning systems that have found ways to increase communities' options for responding to a warning. Poor populations in Bangladesh face almost the same challenges that affected the residents of the Irrawaddy Delta. With few durable buildings, options to shelter from cyclonic winds were few, and even robustly constructed buildings could be flooded by the heavy rains accompanying the cyclone. But Bangladesh has built a series of more than 2,000 raised cyclone shelters, near the at-risk areas. People no longer have to choose between leaving all of their belongings and livestock and fleeing long distances.

   Understanding and supporting traditional means of self-protection can be an important step. For example, much global attention was paid to the birth of Baby Rosita in a tree in Mozambique during the massive floods of 2000. Press reports created images of a pregnant woman suddenly stranded in a tree. Almost no acknowledgment of the full story took place—Rosita's family began constructing a platform shelter in a tree several days before the big floods came and storing critical supplies there, following traditional practices. In the low-lying floodplains of southern Mozambique, there is nearly no high ground. A few trees are the only thing standing a few meters above the waterline, and so the idea of building shelters in trees is perfectly rational. Efforts to provide options for reacting to a disaster could involve developing improved techniques for building tree shelters, providing durable construction materials, and advising on sanitation during an extended period in the tree shelter.

Options for Early Warning for Devastating Low-Probability Events in Poor Countries

Can poor countries ever be prepared for catastrophic, low-probability events? Should they allocate scarce resources to an event that may not happen for decades or even centuries when they have critical needs for investment in education, health, and infrastructure? Or does the industrialized world have a responsibility, given its contribution to climate change, for funding early warning for low-probability, high-impact events in developing countries?

The solution to these difficult challenges isn't fatalism or inaction. A combination of four actions can help mitigate the effects of anomalistic events and also can contribute to general development:

1. Multihazard early-warning systems
2. Disaster risk-reduction education
3. Low-cost/low-technology solutions
4. Multiuse communication structures

Multihazard Early-Warning Systems

The concept of multihazard early-warning systems is gaining favor around the world, especially for places that face numerous, fairly low-probability events. In many cases, high-probability events need their own early-warning systems because every part of the hazard is unique, from data collection to response options. For example, an area might face high risks of both volcanoes and droughts. But the chain of information flow and action is completely different between a volcano early-warning system and a drought early-warning system, for example, so separate systems make sense.

Multihazard early warning does not advocate for the creation of a mega-early-warning system but for grouping low-probability hazards and for sharing data and structures among all systems when it makes sense. One notable effort is the Global Earth Observation System of Systems (GEOSS) initiated by the Group on Earth Observation, which intends to build on existing information systems such as the Global Telecommunications System and add new initiatives to create timely, accurate, and interoperable data on all aspects of the earth, for use in early warning, risk reduction, and other endeavors.

For poor countries facing multiple low-probability hazards, a multihazard system can increase efficiency and reduce costs. Grouping hazards also increases the likelihood that the system will be triggered more frequently—which is absolutely essential for early-warning systems to improve over time.

Shanghai, China, has pioneered efforts to build a multihazard early-warning system that can be a useful model for mega-cities in the developing world. The approach grouped together the many hazards faced by the 17 million residents—typhoons, tornados, strong winds, and floods and also chemical spills, nuclear accidents, public health emergencies, and so on. The Shanghai system has integrated a "top-down" approach with unified policies, data collection systems, and multiagency command structures with a "bottom-up" approach that ensures the community is aware of the risks, understands appropriate responses, and can channel information upward to emergency response authorities and receive information transmitted from authorities.[18]

Similar principles can be applied to nonurban settings, too, with the focus on disaster risk-reduction education and low-technology solutions, and on multiuse communications systems.

Disaster Risk-Reduction Education

Education plays a fundamental role in reducing disaster risks, whether for high-probability or low-probability events. It could be argued that education is even more important for low-probability events because people will have their own firsthand knowledge and experience with high-probability events, whereas for low-probability events, this personal experience will be missing.

This was compellingly illustrated by 11-year-old Tilly Smith during the Indian Ocean tsunami. The British schoolgirl was vacationing in Phuket, Thailand, with her family when she saw an event exactly as her geography teacher had described to her in England a few weeks earlier. The ocean was bubbling "like the foam on a beer," said Tilly, and receding—the signs of an impending tsunami. She warned her family and dozens of other hotel guests on the beach, all of whom escaped to safety.[19] Initially, her mother did not believe her and nearly refused to leave the beach, because she had never heard the word *tsunami* and didn't understand the risks. If all the local and visiting schoolchildren in Phuket had studied the same lesson, the death toll could have been greatly reduced.

Educational programs also teach people about general safety improvements they can make to their homes to become better prepared for many types of hazards. Various low-cost/low-technology solutions can help prepare people for many types of disasters.

Low-Cost/Technology Solutions

Preparedness for low-probability events does not have to be expensive. It can involve "normal" development interventions that have additional benefits if a low-probability event strikes. Supporting the development of small-scale savings programs, where poor people trust banks and begin to accumulate money in cash rather than assets, can play a big role in recovery after a disaster. Improving construction practices in "nonengineered," traditionally constructed buildings similarly can provide better, safer, and more comfortable living conditions, but also can enhance resilience to disaster events.

Many governments have tightened building codes to stop the construction of flimsy housing that easily collapses in an earthquake, cyclone, or flood. After the Bam earthquake in 2003 killed more than a quarter of the town's 100,000 people, Iranian authorities banned traditional mud and adobe houses and prevented the building of dome structures.[20]

Avalanches are becoming more common in parts of the Alps, perhaps due to climate change. The Swiss government operates sophisticated detection and early-warning systems, but local residents near

Davos have taken their protection into their own hands with low-technology solutions. Every year, they trek up the mountains to install snow fences to impede avalanches. At the same time, they have planted thousands of trees. When the trees grow to full size in 40 to 50 years, they will replace the fences and break the movement of avalanches.

Although insurance is scarce in developing countries in general, and insurance against low-probability events even more unlikely, households can be encouraged to take actions to protect themselves from future disasters. With climate change, farmers who traditionally counted on one moderate drought every three years and one major drought every decade may suddenly face a major drought every three years. This means that farmers must be encouraged to adapt to the reality that the future may be even harder to predict than the past. Engaging farmers in climate change adaptation discussions is essential. Radio programs, extension messages, and SMS/cell phone text messaging technologies can help inform farmers about how climate change may impact the predictability of the seasons and require changes in farming practices.

Thorough risk assessments at the community level can help identify mechanisms through which the community can become more resilient.

Multiuse Communications Systems

Communication saves lives during a disaster. Communications are also an essential component of a nation's development. How can authorities in the national or regional capital get information to the community level? And how can receivers of information at a community level get it out to the most remote members of community—the so-called last mile? And how can communications flow from the remote members of the community upward to national authorities, in the case of a disease outbreak, for example? A communications assessment can reveal gaps in the ability to reach certain groups of people. For example, cell phones are becoming common throughout the developing world. Many communities have cell phone coverage and at least a few residents own cell phones. Cell phone text messages about an impending disaster might reach the residents with cell phones. But how do those residents spread the word to others who are less likely to own cell phones such as child-headed households, rural women, elderly, or disabled? Redundancy in communications structures is essential, too. What happens if the cell phone network is damaged in an earthquake, for example?

Special attention needs to be paid to the vulnerability of groups such as women, children (especially girls), and the disabled and ill. The groups may fall outside the normal flow of information in a community—HIV/AIDS widows or orphans may be shunned by the community and have no regular or reliable access to information flowing into the area. Vulnerable groups have less money to buy cell phones or radio batteries, so they may live on the margins of the community. Enhancements to communications systems need to focus on these traditionally neglected groups.

Various options for "last mile" communications are being tested around the developing world.[21] Cell phone broadcasting of warnings has potential applications, but with the limitations previously described. In some densely populated places, volunteers with megaphones and whistles can pass through the community sounding an alarm. In many places in the developing world, radio broadcasts remain the most effective means to reach large numbers of people, even when they are dispersed widely. Local community radio stations that broadcast in local languages can receive and rebroadcast warnings effectively, provided they have not been damaged by the event.

The RANET project[22] has created models to disseminate information via satellite to community radio stations, which then broadcast them over FM frequencies to local populations. In places where radio ownership is limited by poverty, or where people cannot afford to buy disposable batteries every few weeks, windup and solar-powered radios, like the Freeplay Lifeline radio, provide a low-technology, low-cost solution. If community radio stations are damaged, these radios can receive warnings broadcast over regional, national, or shortwave frequencies.

Ensuring communications to at-risk populations has many other benefits. When no disaster threatens, radios can broadcast health, agriculture, and educational programming, for example. The RANET stations described above educate farmers about seasonal forecasts as well as planting techniques and market prices. Communications systems put in place for early warning can help medical staff evacuate injured or ill patients from remote areas.

Conclusion

The world is confronted by almost limitless natural hazards, some regular and fairly predictable and others extremely rare and unpredictable. Although it is reasonable to expect all countries to protect their citizens from disasters that occur regularly, it is difficult, even for rich countries, to prepare for low-probability events. Although there are many remaining uncertainties about global climate change, there is consensus that the number, location, and intensity of natural hazards will become less predictable. For poor countries, with critical needs for investment in health, education, and infrastructure, investments in single-hazard early-warning systems for low-probability events are unwise.

Following a mega-disaster like the Indian Ocean tsunami, it is understandable that the world would want to help not only the countries devastated by the tsunami (for example, Indonesia and Sri Lanka), but also countries that suffered only slightly from the disaster (for example, Tanzania and Somalia). This chapter has argued that investments in tsunami early warning in East Africa could be much more wisely made in multihazard early-warning systems, disaster risk-reduction education, or even general development activities that contribute to risk reduction such as improved building codes or better communications. If emotion were completely removed from the risk-assessment process, post-tsunami investment may have prioritized the creation of a tsunami early-warning system in the Mediterranean Sea rather than in the Indian Ocean, given the fact that it is statistically more vulnerable.

Global collaboration, national government commitment, and community involvement have created excellent early-warning systems for high-probability disasters even in some of the world's poorest countries. Yet for low-probability events, a different model is needed—one that emphasizes not the hypothetical hazard but the underlying vulnerabilities.

7

The Role of Risk Regulation in Mitigating Natural Disasters

Bridget M. Hutter
London School of Economics and Political Science

Overview

Mitigating the damaging effects of natural disasters is a global priority. Risk mitigation can help minimize the great human and financial costs associated with disasters. Various generic forms of mitigation can prove useful in reducing the damage that may be caused by natural disasters. This chapter focuses on the role of risk regulation. It considers the situations for which risk regulation is best suited and circumstances that might limit its effectiveness. One consideration is the importance of balancing anticipation and resilience—putting in place firmer emergency plans and capacities where one can realistically anticipate and act constructively, and focusing on resilience in less-certain areas. The chapter also considers a broad view of risk regulation regimes to incorporate transnational and governmental regulation and also regulation involving business and civil society organizations.

In May 2009, the United Nations *2009 Global Assessment Report on Disaster Risk Reduction* underlined that the risk of natural disasters is increasing across the world, partly as a result of climate change, environmental degradation, and poor urban planning.[1] It urged governments to invest in risk reduction, emphasizing the cost-effectiveness of such measures and citing the example of Japan and the Philippines to illustrate how investment can result in significant risk reduction.

The report explains that both countries are exposed to frequent cyclones, but the estimated annual death toll from cyclones in the Philippines is almost 17 times greater than that of Japan. Focusing on the mitigation of natural disasters is clearly a key global priority.

The concept of mitigation implies that disasters are inevitable. For instance, there is an acceptance in many official documents that natural events cannot be prevented. The U.K. Parliamentary Office of Science and Technology warns that natural disasters "can strike in minutes" and cannot be prevented.[2] This emphasis on planning for contingency and recovery conveys messages of probability and inevitability that risk events will occur. In the private sector, this is exemplified by the emergence of business-continuity management that focuses on post-event recovery. The key message is that it may be possible with forward planning, such as risk identification, mitigation strategies, and predisaster emergency and recovery planning, to substantially reduce the damage that may be caused by a natural disaster, or indeed others sorts of disasters. Likewise, the recent financial crisis has led to calls for measures to be introduced that will improve the resilience of the financial system in the event of the failure of a financial institution. For example, financial institutions will be subject to greater routine "stress testing" to see whether they could cope should there be a dramatic downturn in the economy. In addition, greater attention is being paid to how failed financial institutions could be unwound in a more orderly manner (following the difficulties arising from the winding down of Lehman Brothers); how national and international authorities should work together to resolve a crisis (following the difficulties arising from the overseas branches and subsidiaries of Icelandic banks); and how depositors in banks could benefit from higher levels of deposit insurance and from more rapid payouts of compensation if failure occurs (following the problems with Northern Rock).

Various forms of mitigation can prove useful in reducing the damage that may be caused by natural disasters. For example, avoiding land use in known hazardous areas and establishing and enforcing building codes to prevent the collapse of poorly designed and constructed buildings can help us avoid the considerable costs that may be associated with disaster recovery and in turn save lives and prevent injury. Understanding these benefits can also encourage longer-term thinking and investment in mitigating disasters that may otherwise be perceived and uncertain and even improbable. This chapter focuses specifically on the role of risk regulation, part of a governance system that can prove so vital in risk mitigation. It also emphasizes the need for these processes and measures to involve the public, private, and civil sectors.

Regulating Risk

Risk regulation refers to the governance, accountability, and processing of risks, both within public-and private-sector organizations as part of their risk management and compliance with government laws. Risk regulation is inherently about the anticipation of risk and preventing its realization: It is forward looking, trying to be preventive rather than reactive in its outlook. Social commentators associate these governance regimes with a new modern worldview in which risks are conceptualized as manageable. The prominent social theorist Anthony Giddens[3] argues that there is a growing preoccupation with the future. He maintains that there is no longer a belief in fate but an "aspiration to control" the future. This is partly attributed to the growth of science, a theme pursued by another commentator on risk, Ulrich Beck,[4] who believes that there has been a growing belief in science, rationality, and calculability. Beck argues that our belief in our ability to manage risks is so great that "even natural hazards appear less random than they used to."[5] So he argues that there is a growing belief that we are more able to forecast and manage natural disasters in ways hitherto unseen. The expectation is that the occurrence of natural disasters may be anticipated and how to react to them determined through emergency planning. Risk regulation is thus very much part of a modern effort of anticipating risks and acting to prevent them or failing that, having in place plans to cope with the harmful effects of risks that have materialized as disasters.

Traditional modes of governing risk have typically been public-sector centered.[6] The best known form of public-sector regulation has been "command and control regulation," through the command of the law backed by the legal authority of the state. Alternatively government has regulated activities through policies designed to influence economic life (for example, through taxation or broad economic policy). Over the past two decades, concerns about the limits of state activities led to changes involving a move from public ownership and centralized control to privatized institutions and the encouragement of competition. This led to a broadening conceptualization of regulation so that it is no longer regarded as the exclusive domain of the state, and the role of nonstate actors in regulation is now widely acknowledged. Many of the sources of regulation are well established; they have existed for a long time in one form or another. What is new is the growing recognition of these alternative sources as regulation, their formal cooption by the state, and an increasing coordination of activities between various regulatory sources. Typical examples here include insurance companies, professional organizations, and civil society organizations such as nongovernmental organizations (NGOs) and charities. These developments prompted policy discussions that advocated a regulatory mix in which the state harnesses sources of regulation beyond the state.

This chapter focuses especially on the role of state-backed risk regulation involving local and national governments and also regulatory hybrids involving the state, such as forms of third-party delegation (for example, to insurance companies and charities). It focuses primarily on pre-event mitigation measures such as land-use regulations and building codes that have received less attention than ex-post recovery actions such as disaster relief. Indeed, the Stanford economist Roger Noll has argued that policy makers have a tendency to underinvest in prevention and overinvest in response. Other research (for example, the U.N. comparison of the Philippines and Japan cited earlier),[7] suggests that taking ex-ante measures can significantly reduce ex post expenditures. This chapter focuses on those situations for which risk regulation is best suited and circumstances that might limit its effectiveness. It argues that risk regulation is most effective where it is based on solid risk information, where there is provision for an effective enforcement apparatus and where there is a broad base of support for regulatory objectives. Its effectiveness will be limited by high levels of uncertainty, poor enforcement, and where central governments have not secured broader cooperation for risk-mitigation measures. One important consideration is balancing anticipation and resilience—putting in place firmer emergency plans and capacities where one can realistically anticipate and act and focusing on resilience in less-certain areas.

The Importance of Information

Risk regulation policy decisions depend on information about the likelihood of a natural disaster occurring and information about the extent of probable damage should a disaster occur. The knowledge base on which policy is formulated is crucial. It is vital that we have a knowledge base of the risks, their probabilities, and what preventable measures are possible and effective and in what circumstances. Indeed, the U.N. 2009 Report called for countries to consider in much more local detail how climate change will affect their towns and cities.[8] The *Lancet* medical journal also urged public health services to give much more pressing and detailed consideration to the ways that climate change might affect health and to develop policies to cope with this.[9]

But we also need to be aware of the limitations of the data we have. The past is not always a good predictor of the future; we need to be realistic about the reliability of the available information.[10] The importance of this is highlighted by the recent financial crisis that revealed how the risk models used by the financial markets in the previous decades were colored by a climate of optimism that encouraged mistaken assumptions about risk and the ability of markets to regulate themselves. In the case of disasters, historic data is insufficient because climate change may be increasing the incidence and patterns of natural disasters and thus exposing larger populations to the possibility of natural disasters. There are additional concerns that urban areas are particularly and increasingly vulnerable to natural disasters as natural and technological disasters are colocated and interact more and more.[11] Charles Perrow[12] discusses the problem with respect to the United States, where a growing concentration of economic power, hazards, and populations makes disasters more consequential. He cites the example of Hurricane Katrina, which caused such damage in New Orleans, Louisiana, an area of high population proximate to accumulations of hazardous material. China is another area prone to natural disasters and has particular problems as it rapidly urbanizes and witnesses increasing urban concentrations of people and industrial sites in close proximity.

The focus of this volume is on low-probability, high-consequence events, and even in these cases there may be much less information than might be supposed depending on the particular disaster involved. Generally, there is some certainty about the area at risk, but the precision of this varies widely. For example, whereas there may be some confidence with respect to volcanoes and flooding, it may be difficult to locate with much certainty the precise location of earthquakes, hurricanes, and wild fires. This is well illustrated by Hurricane Gustav in 2008. The trajectory and force of the hurricane proved difficult to predict, and nearly 2 million people fled the Louisiana coast in anticipation of a Category 3–4 hurricane, but by the time it reached Louisiana it had downgraded to Category 2. This does, of course, raise the question of how seriously the next hurricane warnings in Louisiana will be taken; there is a danger that they might be ignored. It may well be that broad areas are at risk such as happened in the 2009 Australian wildfires. These exemplified the unpredictability of these fires and the dangers of relying on past data. The state of Victoria experienced unprecedented conditions—a severe heat wave, low humidity, and strong and unpredictable winds—and this led to the worst bushfires on record in Australia. It is important in such changing conditions to collect available information and to invest in a public body with responsibility for collating, analyzing, and storing this information and ensuring that possible policy decision are considered.[13] The types of information might include data regarding seismic activity, the incidence of natural disasters, and any knowledge about the effectiveness of development planning and building codes in disaster situations. Just as the available data may not always be as comprehensive and certain as we would like, so too are early-warning systems often unreliable. It is important to have up-to-date information about the availability and accuracy of these systems and the amount of warning they do give before deciding whether early-warning systems are indeed worth mandating, should this be a financial or political option. This may demand investment in research and development and keeping up-to-date with the available information and knowledge. Transnational organizations such as the United Nations can play an important role as purveyors of such information. Likewise, states and NGOs may play an important coordinating role for research and development.

In a number of mitigation strategies, using risk regulation may be helpful. Murat Balamir[14] distinguishes between three strategies in the pre-event risk-management stage: risk avoidance, risk minimization, and risk sharing. He suggests that there is a "logical sequence" to these measures, and so land use is a priority; building controls are available for where development cannot be avoided; and risk sharing provides for those cases and occasions when risk cannot be eliminated. Let us consider the role risk regulation may play in each of these stages and the advantages and limitations they present us with. For example, we need to consider where information regarding the location of hazards is sufficiently reliable to inform land-use planning; how feasible it is to implement building codes with respect to new builds and also retroactively; and how one might encourage public private partnerships to share the burdens of risk events and where possible to encourage transnational cooperation whereby impoverished areas of the world are helped to cope with disaster planning and recovery by those with more resources.

Risk-Avoidance Strategies

Risk-avoidance strategies focus primarily on land-use policies and most particularly the delineation of areas where settlements are regulated. These range from hazard zones where no urban development or planning is permitted through to development laws, such as have been established in earthquake zones in Turkey, whereby permission to build has to be sought and this involves consideration of a geological survey report.[15] The State of California has enacted legislation that requires that a Natural Hazard Disclosure Statement is provided by those selling property that falls within one or more state-mapped hazard areas, including a seismic hazard zone, areas prone to landslides, tsunamis, and wildfires. In Japan, hazard zones have been created in areas prone to sediment related disasters such as landslides, especially in the vicinity of major cities. Since 2001, new building developments in hazard zones have been restricted, relocation and the development of early-warning systems encouraged, and public awareness raised about possible disasters. In the most hazardous areas, licenses are required for land development and certifications required for buildings. The effectiveness of such regulation depends on them being fully enforced. It also relies on the risks being understood. These are exemplified in the negative by the Californian example, where there is evidence that disclosure by real estate agents occurred late in the transaction process and that its importance was not always appreciated by purchasers.[16]

There are a number of other limiting factors for such forms of risk regulation. First is a reliance on the accuracy of the available data. Determining land-use plans on floodplains is possible, but doing this in earthquake and a hurricane area is less feasible.[17] In some countries, large areas may be vulnerable to natural disaster, thus making it particularly difficult to implement avoidance strategies. Bangladesh, with its dense population and vulnerability to monsoon floods and cyclones, is a clear example. Second, local politics may couple with financial needs to lessen the inclination of local government to introduce and then enforce such zones. These measures may render parts of a local area uninhabitable, and this may lessen tax revenues and depress business activity in the area. These effects depend on local financial needs. The hazard areas around Mount Vesuvius in Italy are densely populated, and one explanation of this is that the local community privileges economic interests such as the fertile soil, climate, and tourism opportunities above the volcanic risks involved in living there. Third, some may regard the declaration of hazard zones as areas that cannot be developed as an infringement of the right to choose where to live and work. Factors such as these may mean that hazardous areas will inevitably be developed, and therefore risk-avoidance strategies need to be supplemented by other risk-management strategies.

Risk-Reduction Strategies

The best-known risk-reduction strategies are building codes, especially in earthquake and flooding zones, where damage is primarily to buildings and infrastructure. Where building codes do not exist or are not enforced, the loss of life may be considerable. It is probable that many of those who died in the 1999 Turkish earthquake and 2008 Chinese earthquake would have survived had construction standards been vastly improved or enforced. Building controls embrace a variety of risk-regulation tools (for example, design and engineering standards, construction standards, and the monitoring of compliance with these standards). These standards are often in the form of codes that are flexible and open to updating.

New building codes are commonplace and found to be highly effective, especially where they incorporate learning from previous disasters. Robin Spence[18] reports the benefit-cost ratio to be high because the cost of incorporating the requirements of building controls are relatively small compared to the overall building costs, especially when one takes into account the reduction in damage that may be effected and the lives such improvements can save. Retrospective building upgrades involve strengthening programs for existing buildings in areas of natural disaster. These are less common than new building programs, partly because they can be so costly. But they do exist. For example, Mexico City introduced a major program of retroactive strengthening following the 1985 earthquake, as did California following the 1994 Northridge earthquake. Florida also enforced their building codes following Hurricane Andrew in 1992. Howard Kunreuther and his colleagues[19] discuss how this disaster led to a revamping of the codes. Programs such as these could be mandatory, but they also need to be accompanied by funding programs to enable their realization and incentivize compliance.

Another form of engineering and construction that falls into the risk-minimization category is the building of flood defenses, such as dykes, levees, or coastal defense projects. Levees control the water flow into flood-prone areas, and ideally they prevent flooding. There are a number of major examples, including the Netherlands, where much of the country is actually below sea level and highly vulnerable to flooding from rivers and sea surges. This led the Dutch government to invest in the Delta Works project comprising a series of constructions of dams and barriers to protect the southwest of the Netherlands starting in the 1950s and continuing to 1997. Another prominent levees project involves those protecting New Orleans from the Mississippi River.

There are limiting factors for risk-minimization programs. It is first vital that any regulations and codes that are produced are adopted and enforced. Indeed, an overriding message of regulation research is that enforcement mechanisms, whether they be public-sector or private-sector third-party inspections, are crucial to the implementation of risk-regulation policies. There needs to be a clear allocation of responsibilities and liability and also sanctions for non-compliance. Burby[20] cites such factors as essential to the successful implementation of public and private flood-insurance programs. Moreover, it is essential that there is a demonstrable preparedness to use sanctions; otherwise, they can become merely symbolic and rendered ineffective.

It is vital that the personnel involved in these schemes are proficient to design, to construct, and to inspect. Concerns about this may lead to regulation in the form of professional registration and regulations that demand only registered people be permitted to undertake these roles. Such a system was instituted in Turkey following the 1999 earthquake, when a professional proficiency requirement was decreed. This required inspectors to have a minimum of five years of practice in engineering and architecture, to attend training courses, and to take technical exams.[21] Similarly, the OECD has recommendations for standards of educational buildings in earthquake zones.[22] Establishing and implementing such structures is no mean task, and developing countries may struggle to find the capacity for this.[23] Indeed, there may be financial and political obstacles to risk-minimization schemes, especially those involving building upgrading where the allocation of funds to aid improvements may also pose distributional problems in terms of local politics. Spence[24] cites a number of examples where this has been a difficulty (for example, in Turkey prior to the 1999 earthquake and Southern California following the 1933 Long Beach earthquake, where is took some 39 to 48 years for local communities to agree to earthquake mitigation legislation).

Another difficulty with risk-minimization schemes is the danger that they can lull people into a false sense of security that means that they do not take the hazard as seriously as they should and fail to prepare for what to do should a disaster materialize. Indeed, some fear that incentivizing schemes to adopt building controls in hazardous areas may even stimulate the development of such areas and thus increase the risks of damage.[25] In other words, risk-minimization matters may even increase vulnerability.[26] This happened in New Orleans in 2005 when Hurricane Katrina breeched the levees in multiple places and led to very serious flooding of the city (approximately 80 percent of the city was flooded) and multiple deaths. (Estimates vary, but well over 1,000 deaths represents consensus thinking.)

Risk-Sharing Strategies

Part of pre-event planning includes precautionary decision making about how to deal with a natural disaster when it happens and in its aftermath. This anticipatory planning may cover short-term contingency planning and longer-term repair planning. This may involve the state and the market burden sharing at local and national levels.[27] Risk sharing includes predisaster risk transfer through insurance or other hedging instruments such as catastrophe bonds or weather derivatives, or collective loss sharing post-disaster that may take place nationally or globally through charitable donations. Globally this entails richer countries assuming some responsibility for losses in less-developed countries.

Insurance has become an important form of risk sharing in a variety of contexts. Governments try to ensure that insurance is available and linked to risk-regulation strategies in a number of ways. Insurance can play an important role in persuading individuals to invest in mitigation measures, especially if there are reductions in premiums to incentivize this.[28] A major route is for governments to enter into partnerships with commercial companies. A key decision is whether to make insurance mandatory: It could be mandatory for commercial firms to provide insurance for natural disaster situations[29] and also for domestic and commercial occupiers of premises to have insurance. Beyond this, insurance may regulate risk minimization or reparation payments through differential premiums depending on compliance with building codes.[30] These are forms of delegated regulation or regulatory mix. Insurance companies may be delegated responsibility for inspection and compliance checking such as ensuring that building codes have been complied with. Alternatively, the state and insurance industry may be joint providers in which case there may be government insurance schemes or the state may offer reinsurance facilities to commercial insurers.

There are a variety of national insurance schemes in operation and addressing different types of natural disaster. The U.S. National Flood Insurance Program is a well-established scheme, originating in 1968. It provides flood insurance to communities that adopt loss-reduction measures such as floodplain management and promoting the awareness of flood insurance. Two types of policy are available. One covers the cost of repair for flood damage, and the other provides for buildings that have been substantially or repeatedly damaged and funds either retroactive building mitigation or relocation.[31] New Zealand has provided a government-backed insurance scheme for earthquake damage since 1993. This coverage is compulsory.[32] In 1982, France established a national system that requires commercial firms to offer catastrophe insurance that is bundled with property insurance. The government delineates the areas covered and finances the reinsurance of the program. The program offers decreasing compensation to those in high-risk areas, encouraging relocation or the adoption of loss-reduction measures.[33] The Turkish Catastrophe Insurance Pool, established in 2000, is a joint venture between the World Bank and Turkish Government. The scheme mandates those in urban areas to have insurance and aims to incentivize other risk-mitigation measures such as retrospective building controls.

Each of these schemes is interesting as to varying degrees they substitute for private insurance programs. They also all build in incentives to take other risk mitigation action, such as relating premiums to actions taken by property owners (such as retrofits, compliance with new building standards) and also by specifying education and awareness building campaigns for the local community.[34] These methods are important in mitigating some of the major risks associated with public-private insurance schemes.[35] There are concerns that government based schemes can create moral hazards as their risk classification is not always as developed as it would be in commercial schemes. Particular problems can arise with insurance when risks are pooled rather than individually calibrated. To avoid this problem, it is important to adjust premiums to take into account other risk-mitigation measures, such as compliance with risk regulation or penalizing repeated claims. But even when these measures are in place, there is another major source of moral hazard, namely the political reality that it is almost impossible not to provide post-disaster aid for those without insurance. This fact underlines the desirability of mandatory insurance schemes.

Important Considerations and Constraints

Many of the limitations we have discussed with respect to risk avoidance, risk minimization, and risk sharing are encountered in all societies, but they are undoubtedly exacerbated in poorer developing countries where the prerequisites of stable governments and good governance systems may not be met. Indeed, these societies are especially, but not exclusively, vulnerable to concerns about the solvency and sustainability of such schemes given the increasing incidence and severity of natural disasters caused by climate change.

A number of general factors can influence the efficacy of risk regulation strategies. An important *cultural* influence is how anticipatory or fatalistic a culture is. This can be key in securing buy-in to mitigation policies. Fatalistic attitudes can be a significant obstacle to risk regulation.[36] It may be a regional characteristic, as Murat Balamir[37] suggests used to be the case in Turkey until the 1999 earthquake, when there was a significant move to change attitudes to disaster policy and become anticipatory, or it may be more localized. Local communities may view natural hazards as "facts of life" that cannot be avoided. And this may be a view shared by planners who do not believe risk-minimization efforts will be successful.[38] It has been suggested that such views can be changed by the ways in which public agencies and the news media report information: They can help to change attitudes by conveying the message that damage is preventable.[39] Public awareness of the risks posed in local areas and the mitigation efforts in place are also important to the success of mitigation efforts.[40]

Central-local government relations are crucial to the success of risk regulation, as so often these measures emanate from central government, but the implementation of risk regulation measures such as planning laws, building controls, and hazard zones is local. This can easily lead to difficulties and inconsistencies because of intergovernmental tensions and the existence of obstacles to local hazard risk regulation. These center on local willingness and local capacity to implement central policies.[41] Local government may simply decide not to prioritize hazard-mitigation measures. This may be for a variety of reasons. (For instance, the local population may not be interested, perhaps because of fatalistic views about the possibility of averting or mitigating natural disasters.) Alternatively local resources may be scarce and other probable events appear more pressing (for example, local health, education, or crime issues).[42] There may also be confusion about the shared responsibilities of central and local governments. Robert Wolensky and Kenneth Wolensky[43] report that there is often a lack of shared governance in federal and state priorities in the United States.

Clearly, it is vital that central governments secure local government buy-in to risk mitigation through education, discussion, and efforts to co-opt local support and participation in disaster mitigation. Commentators stress the importance of strong state mandates for hazard mitigation, acknowledging that voluntary arrangements are less likely to be effective. But this needs to be coupled with efforts to secure local support and commitment. One U.S. state where federal mitigation policies are especially advanced is California. New construction is subject to earthquake-level building codes. But there is great variability with respect to retrospective building requirements. Mary Comerio[44] explains that one reason for the variability between cities is the cost and hence resistance from residents. One exception is Berkeley, where tax rebates were introduced for this work. In 2004, 38 percent of homes in this area had such improvements, which Comerio attributes to high levels of income and education and active campaigning by the local population.

One danger of too much central government control manifests itself in the post-recovery sphere when local initiatives may be hindered by central government. Emily Chamlee-Wright,[45] referring to the effects of Hurricane Katrina, argues local governments, businesses, and civil groups need to be given space to decide how to recover. This is also a principle of integrated disaster-management schemes. The Japanese-integrated management frameworks following the 2000 Takai floods included strengthening the capacity of local communities to make their own management choices and promoted their participation in risk management.[46] The Turkish earthquake management experience has also underlined the importance of stakeholder involvement to secure compliance with mandatory schemes.[47] The message is that there are limits to what central government can do, and it is crucial to enhance local capabilities and ensure that political affiliation does not bias decisions and implementation.[48]

Corruption is another major obstacle to the effective implementation of regulation and also the distribution of large aid packages.[49] Corruption is cited as a major factor in the high loss of life in the Turkish earthquake of 1999, and there are suspicions that it may have been a factor in the high number of fatalities in the Chinese earthquake in Sichuan in 2008. In the Turkish case, corruption meant that planning and construction codes were not enforced. Moreover, construction amnesties were granted in some areas.[50] Again, this underlines the need for good governance systems and the prerequisites of stable governance structures. Encouraging these is important for the handling of any kind of disaster, natural or otherwise.

Discussion: Lessons and Recommendations

Using risk regulation in the mitigation of natural and other disasters can contribute significantly to reducing the risks and costs associated with these disasters. However, these measures need to be used strategically. Absolutely crucial in deciding policy options are the quality and accuracy of the information available about the levels and the location of risks. Working locally to enhance sustainability and resilience is important in all areas vulnerable to extreme events. Where levels of certainly are high, then, more detailed risk-regulation measures and planning are also possible.

The reasons for this are explained by Aaron Wildavsky,[51] who urged caution in the use of anticipatory strategies and advocated enhancing resilience (that is, the ability to learn from experience and cope with surprises). He argued that anticipation can lead to a great deal of unnecessarily wasted effort and resources because of the high volume of hypothesized risks, many of which are exaggerated or are false predictions. Anticipatory strategies, argues Wildavsky, reduce the ability of organizations and societies to cope with the unexpected. Indeed, many preventive programs have their own unexpected risks attaching to them. It is only where information about vulnerable areas is fairly precise and accurate that specific, targeted risk-regulation measures and investment are so valuable. This is especially true of risk-avoidance measures that are not only reliant on accurate information but also reliant on a willingness to implement and enforce at the local level.

Where risk-avoidance strategies are not possible, for either informational or sociopolitical reasons, risk-mitigation strategies may be optimal. To be successful, these are reliant on enforcement mechanisms and a readiness to use sanctions. Retrofit measures may also require financial incentives. But these need to be handled carefully so as to avoid the danger of offering false assurance that they mitigate all eventualities. In reality, these measures may still be insufficient to protect against extreme events, and then there has to be awareness of this and of alternative strategies.

Recovery strategies are therefore advisable in all areas of high risk. There may be dangers of moral hazard attaching to these processes. It is alleged that there is some evidence that where governments provide for recovery individuals are less likely to be proactive providing for their own recovery. In this case, the dangers of moral hazard need to be avoided if at all possible. And the optimal way of doing this seems to be building in incentives to adopt other mitigation strategies and if possible making such insurance mandatory.

It is common in risk-regulation discussions to advocate a regulatory mix in which the state harnesses sources of regulation beyond the state so as to empower different participants in the regulatory process. This includes national and local governments, businesses, and local communities. In the private sector, insurance companies are especially important. A mix of sources of information and support helps to maximize the promotion and achievement of risk-management objectives. It is also recommended that a mix of different types of regulation be established, involving a mixture of sanctions and incentives. The state can play a crucial role in this by mandating mitigating measures but as we have seen these rest on a variety of prerequisites. A key condition is the presence of strong enforcement mechanisms to ensure that any measures put in place are adopted and implemented by local government, whose support is, again, decisive. Indeed, buy-in from the local community is important to the success of sustainable and workable schemes. Likewise, stable and noncorrupt local infrastructures are necessary.

It is essential to acknowledge that there are likely to be local variations influencing the effectiveness or even possibility of using some forms of mitigation. This needs to be dealt with by providing regulations that can be tailored to local circumstances. Such regulations are typically principles rather than rules based, allowing for flexibility and discretion in implementing them in varying situations. There will be variable levels of regulatory enforcement between countries and even within countries. In other cases, culturally sensitive and practically possible means of communication need to be developed, because mitigation plans and hardware may not easily travel.

NGOs can be especially helpful here, particularly in developing countries. They can help to secure local-level cooperation in disaster mitigation and preparedness, through environmental management and long-term sustainability efforts. The Red Cross has long been involved in disaster-preparedness programs that focus on ecological management in the hope that disasters may be prevented through a focus on long-term sustainable development.

Transnationally, the United Nations can play an important role, most especially through its International Strategy for Disaster Reduction, which aims to play a facilitating role with respect to research and information sharing and stimulating partnerships and networks to reduce the effects of disasters. An important dimension of this is to consider the poor of the world and to offer information, advice, and support to low-income countries prone to natural disasters. Other organizations, such as the World Economic Forum, have the potential to facilitate cross-border and private-public sensitivity to the problems and to foster awareness that action is both possible and necessary. They have the authority to provide leadership and to help foster schemes that encourage information sharing and the resources needed on a global basis, and thus to help mitigate the inequalities associated with natural disasters. This is especially important in a world where the interconnectedness of problems is acute. Central to anticipation and resilience are notions of recovery and learning from adverse events. This endeavor can and should be coordinated globally.

These lessons and recommendations have parallels in other arenas. The recent financial crisis has demonstrated the dangers in relying on models and data that are unreliable indicators of future risks. It underlines the need to think about the longer term and the interconnections between actions in different parts of the world. The need to increase resilience in the financial sector has been dramatically emphasized. There are now demands for greater attention to contingency planning and crisis management, for better information about the possible risks that could be encountered, and the need for the development of tools to achieve the orderly winding down of firms. As with disasters, there is also recognition of the value of strong government mandates for regulatory discipline and the importance of macro oversight and communication.

8

Hedging Against Tomorrow's Catastrophes: Sustainable Financial Solutions to Help Protect Against Extreme Events

Erwann Michel-Kerjan
The Wharton School, University of Pennsylvania (United States) and École Polytechnique (France)

Overview

Two-thirds of the 25 most costly insured catastrophes in the past 40 years have occurred since 2001. Is this a sign of what the twenty-first century has in store for us? Most likely, because of the increasing concentration of population and value in high-risk areas, as well as a change in weather patterns toward more extreme events. This poses a real challenge as to *who* will provide financial protection against future large-scale risks, if such protection is indeed available. Although governments and traditional insurers/reinsurers have a key role to play here, recent innovations in the financial markets can also help access needed capital from investors internationally. This chapter discusses some of these new financial products as they apply to both developed and developing countries. There is an opportunity here for value creation—in protecting assets and people and also in creating new markets for those who are responsible for leading major institutions (corporations, governments, NGOs), and even royal families.

Introduction

The accelerating rhythm of large-scale catastrophes worldwide has become one of our biggest economic and social challenges. Indeed, one of the hallmarks of this new century will be more and more such unthinkable and extraordinary events, previously unseen contexts, and pressure for individuals, private companies, and government authorities to react extremely quickly, even when they cannot predict the cascading impact their actions will have.

Conventional wisdom holds that major accidents and disasters remain low-probability events. In today's world, this view is clearly outdated. Catastrophes have unfolded at an unprecedented rate in the past few years: financial crises, large-scale natural disasters, intercontinental pandemics, and mega-terrorism. Think also food and water scarcity, global warming, and new types of war, nuclear proliferation, and cyber-attacks.

I predict that there will be more of these mega-crises as well as new ones in the future. Dealing with an average of one or two such catastrophes every 20 years is one thing; dealing with 5 or 10 on many different fronts almost simultaneously, as is currently occurring, is an entirely different matter. We must begin to anticipate a world in which extreme events occur more and more often as part of our daily life. And with that, we must begin to better proactively assess and manage them before they occur, and also create the foundations for a more resilient society when they do occur.[1]

To turn risk management into value creation, this new era of catastrophes demands new services, new types of protection, and innovative new financial solutions. The demand for such services and products is indeed likely to significantly increase in the next decade. Here, I want to focus on one aspect of this question: What financial solutions can be developed to provide coverage against some of the aforementioned global risks so that one does not have to pour billions of dollars in a rushed and disorganized way in the aftermath of disasters?

Answering this question has become even more pressing today because the rhythm of costly disasters is accelerating due to the growing concentration of population and assets in high-risk areas, combined with the potential consequences of a change in climate patterns. One figure is eye-opening: Of the 25 most costly insured disasters anywhere in the world between 1970 and 2008 (a 39-year period), two-thirds of them occurred since 2001. Most of these insured catastrophes occurred in rich countries where exposed assets and insurance penetration are high; a disaster occurring in a poor country where insurance coverage is very low would likely not enter into this ranking.

As a reaction to these historical losses, we are already witnessing a radical change in the loss sharing between public and private sectors in many countries, with governments taking a more important role in what were traditionally private insurance markets. Sadly, the recent financial crisis has shown us the dark side of finance, most notably the uncontrolled used of sophisticated instruments.[2] Still, I believe some of the most innovative and sustainable solutions to meet the challenge of providing adequate coverage against extreme events will come from the financial world, working in collaboration with governments and the insurance industry. Some of these instruments are already in place and provide the necessary capital to support a financial safety net that helps individuals, corporations, cities and countries, international organizations, and even royal families adequately protect exposed assets so that they are resilient when the next catastrophe strikes.

The chapter is organized as follows. We first briefly discuss the evolution of economic and insured losses due to major catastrophes over the past four decades, clearly indicating that we have entered a new era of catastrophes, which is likely to stay with us for a long time to come. The discussion then turns to some financial innovations, alternative and complementary to traditional insurance. I focus in detail on two of them that transfer exposure to catastrophes to institutional investors: industry loss warranties and catastrophe bonds, which have grown significantly in volume in the past five years. Catastrophe bonds have been used not only by numerous insurers and reinsurers but also by corporations (two examples are Disney Park in Japan and the utility giant Électricité de France) to cover against hurricanes, storms, typhoons, earthquakes, or even pandemics and terrorism risks in many parts of the developed world. Innovative financial solutions can also help individuals and businesses in developing countries. To illustrate this point, this chapter presents the case of a rain indexed-based insurance tool that was developed to help farmers in one of the poorest countries, Ethiopia. The chapter concludes by looking at how we can make these financial instruments more widespread, and thus less expensive to a broader range of stakeholders around the globe.

How Much Are You Willing to Lose When the Next Catastrophe Strikes?

The economic and insured losses from great natural catastrophes such as hurricanes, earthquakes, and floods worldwide have clearly increased significantly in recent years. A comparison of these economic losses over time (based on data from Munich Re Geo Risks research) reveals a huge increase: $53.6 billion (1950–1959), $93.3 billion (1960–1969), $161.7 billion (1970–1979), $262.9 billion (1980–1989), and $778.3 billion (1990–1999). Between 2000 and 2008, there were $620.6 billion in losses, principally a result of the 2004, 2005, and 2008 hurricane seasons, which produced historic records.

Catastrophes have had a more devastating impact on insurers since 1990 than in the entire history of insurance. Between 1970 and the mid-1980s, annual insured losses from natural disasters (including forest fires) were in the $3 billion to $4 billion range. There was a radical increase in insured losses in the early 1990s, with Hurricane Andrew in Florida ($24.6 billion in 2008 dollars) and the Northridge earthquake in California ($20.3 billion in 2008 dollars). The four hurricanes in Florida in 2004 (Charley, Frances, Ivan, and Jeanne) collectively totaled over $33 billion in insured losses. Hurricane Katrina alone cost insurers and reinsurers an estimated $48 billion. In 2005, private insurers and reinsurers paid $87 billion for losses resulting from major natural catastrophes.[3] Figure 8.1 depicts the upward trend in worldwide insured losses from major catastrophes between 1970 and 2008.[4]

Table 8.1 reveals the 25 most costly catastrophes for the insurance sector since 1970 (in 2008 dollars).

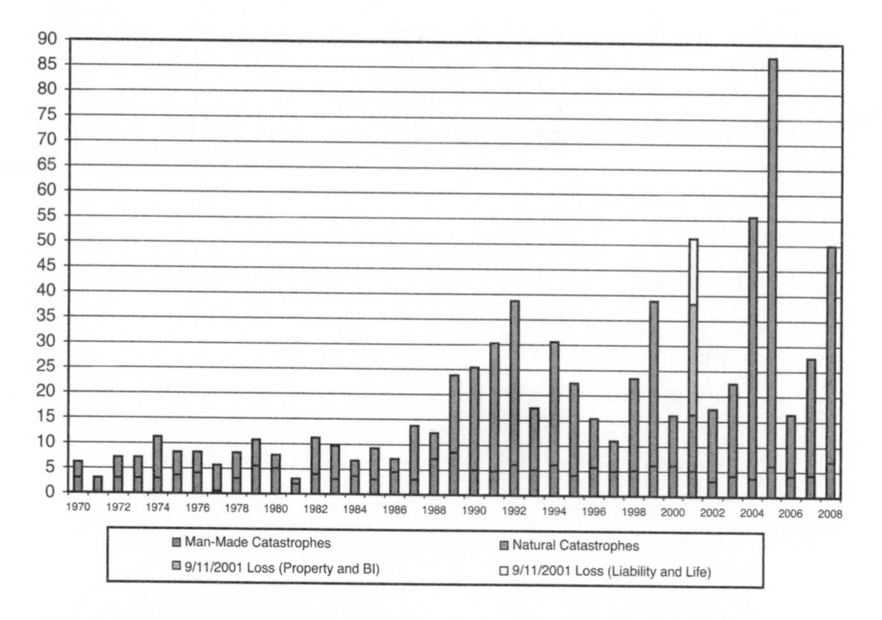

Source: Kunreuther and Michel-Kerjan (2009)[6]

Figure 8.1 Worldwide evolution of major catastrophe insured losses, 1970–2008 (9/11: All lines, including property and business interruption (BI); in U.S. $ billon indexed to 2007; except for 2008, which is current)[5]

TABLE 8.1 The 25 Most Costly Insured Catastrophes in the World, 1970–2008

U.S.$ Billion	Event	Victims (Dead or Missing)	Year	Area of Primary Damage
48.1	Hurricane Katrina	1,836	2005	United States, Gulf of Mexico, et al.
36.8	9/11 Attacks	3,025	2001	United States
24.6	Hurricane Andrew	43	1992	United States, Bahamas
20.3	Northridge Earthquake	61	1994	United States
16.0	Hurricane Ike	348	2008	United States, Caribbean, et al.
14.6	Hurricane Ivan	124	2004	United States, Caribbean, et al.
13.8	Hurricane Wilma	35	2005	United States, Gulf of Mexico, et al.

TABLE 8.1 The 25 Most Costly Insured Catastrophes in the World, 1970–2008

U.S.$ Billion	Event	Victims (Dead or Missing)	Year	Area of Primary Damage
11.1	Hurricane Rita	34	2005	United States, Gulf of Mexico, et al.
9.1	Hurricane Charley	24	2004	United States, Caribbean, et al.
8.9	Typhoon Mireille	51	1991	Japan
7.9	Hurricane Hugo	71	1989	Puerto Rico, United States, et al.
7.7	Winterstorm Daria	95	1990	France, UK, et al.
7.5	Winterstorm Lothar	110	1999	France, Switzerland, et al.
6.3	Winterstorm Kyrill	54	2007	Germany, UK, NL, France
5.9	Storms and Floods	22	1987	France, UK, et al.
5.8	Hurricane Frances	38	2004	United States, Bahamas
5.2	Winterstorm Vivian	64	1990	Western/Central Europe
5.2	Typhoon Bart	26	1999	Japan
5.0	Hurricane Gustav	153	2008	United States, Caribbean, et al.
4.7	Hurricane Georges	600	1998	United States, Caribbean
4.4	Tropical Storm Alison	41	2001	United States
4.4	Hurricane Jeanne	3,034	2004	United States, Caribbean, et al.
4.0	Typhoon Songda	45	2004	Japan, South Korea
3.7	Storms	45	2003	United States
3.6	Hurricane Floyd	70	1999	United States, Bahamas, Columbia

Note: This table includes only payments by private insurers (governments' payment excluded). In billions, indexed to 2008.

Source: Wharton Risk Management and Decision Processes Center with data from Swiss Re and Insurance Information Institute

When viewed all together—along with many other disasters and crises that occurred recently in the developing world where insurance penetration is low and which, for that reason, do not appear in a ranking of insured losses—extreme events are clearly not low-probability events anymore. No country, and no organization, can ignore the possibility of being hit by extreme events in the coming months. The question is not *whether* future catastrophes will occur but *when*—and *who* will pay for them.

How Alternative Risk-Transfer Instruments Provide Financial Protection Against Extreme Events

As one would anticipate, recent catastrophes have forced insurers and reinsurers (those companies that insure the insurers) to significantly increase the premiums they charge to provide financial coverage against such events. This is the case because catastrophes have inflicted record losses in a twofold, concentrated way: First, many people in the same region suffer from the same disaster when it occurs, and so it is more difficult to diversify the risk geographically; second, because catastrophes are occurring much more frequently, insurers have a harder time diversifying risk over time.

Even though insurers have been able to increase the premiums they charge to cover catastrophes, many consider insurance price regulation to be much too stringent. Indeed, legislators are often reluctant to let premiums increase too much (even to reflect reestimated exposure based on recent catastrophes) because people and firms might not want to move to a city or state where insurance cost is extremely high, and also because those already living or working there might decide to leave, thus impacting the local economy. As a result, insurance regulations often restrict insurers from charging premiums that adequately reflect risks and the high cost of capital associated with truly catastrophic risks.[7] Especially for potential mega-disasters that could inflict losses in the $100 billion range, the capital of property and casualty (re)insurance industry is clearly limited.[8] And although governments have typically taken on a significant part of the financial burden of the consequences of extreme events, one might wonder whether they can continue to do so in the future, as budget deficits continue to grow.

In this context, it becomes more and more important to find other complementary sources of capital to cover large-scale disasters. Because of the significant variability of financial markets, and because numerous investors are active on these markets, there was a strong motivation to develop financial instruments that can transfer part of this exposure directly to the financial markets. This has led to new financial products.

The field of alternative risk transfer (ART; "alternative" as opposed to traditional insurance and reinsurance mechanisms) grew out of a series of insurance capacity crises in the 1970s through 1990s that led purchasers of traditional reinsurance coverage to seek more robust ways to buy protection. Although ART instruments can comprise a wide range of alternative solutions (including the creation of captives or risk-retention groups), I concentrate here on instruments that transfer part of the risk exposure directly to investors in the financial markets. Most of these risk-transfer techniques permit investors to play a more direct role in providing insurance and reinsurance protection. One of the main advantages for investors (typically catastrophe funds, hedge funds, and money managers) is that these instruments constitute a different class of assets that can enhance their returns since they are not highly correlated with other financial risks (for example, fluctuations in interest rates).

Here I focus on two insurance-linked instruments—industry loss warranties and catastrophe bonds—which have significantly grown in volume as a reaction to the 7 hurricanes that hit the United States over a 15-month period in 2004 and 2005, and which are likely to continue to grow as a market as we witness more and more costly catastrophes in the coming years.[9]

Industry Loss Warranties

The first industry loss warranties (ILWs) were issued in the 1980s to cover airline industry losses. ILWs were then developed in the property and casualty insurance industry in the aftermath of major natural disasters that have occurred since the early 1990s. In the insurance world, an ILW is a financial instrument designed to protect insurers and reinsurers from severe losses due to extreme events such as natural disasters.

ILWs operate as follows. The buyer who wants to hedge risk pays the seller a premium at the inception of the contract. In return, the buyer can make a claim in the event of a major industry loss that is equal or higher of a predefined threshold. For example, the buyer of a $200 million limit hurricane ILW in New York in 2010 attached at $20 billion will pay a premium to a protection writer (for example, a hedge fund acting as an insurer) and in return will receive $200 million if total losses to the insurance industry from a single hurricane in the New York region in 2010 exceeds $20 billion.

As the name indicates, the payout of ILWs is based on the loss suffered by the entire industry, not a single company. (The amount the insurance industry has lost after a disaster is estimated by specialized third-party firms [for example, Property Claims Services in the United States, or the 2009-created Perils, AG in Europe]). For that reason, ILWs are particularly attractive to companies with a higher concentration of business in a limited number of locations, thus enabling them to take on larger books of business in their primary area of operation. In terms of volume, the ILW market has no recognized exchange or clearing source to track volume, but it is estimated its size has been between $2 billion (before the 2005 hurricane season) and $5 billion outstanding at the end of 2008.

Catastrophe Bonds

In a manner similar to ILWs, catastrophe bonds (hereafter "cat bonds") enable an insurer or reinsurer, or more generally any company or government, to access funds if a severe disaster produces large-scale damage. But cat bonds typically cover narrowly defined risks. To illustrate how cat bonds work, consider a company, SafeCompany, which would like to cover part of its exposure against catastrophes. To do so, it creates a new company, BigCat, whose only purpose is to cover SafeCompany. In that sense, BigCat is a single-purpose reinsurer (also called special-purpose vehicle, SPV). When the reinsurance contract is signed, the sponsor (SafeCompany) pays premiums to BigCat. On the other side, investors place their funds with the SPV BigCat; these funds constitute the initial principal for the bond to be issued by BigCat. Premiums collected from SafeCompany will be used to provide the investors with a high enough interest rate to compensate for a possible loss should a disaster occur. Suppose the losses from a disaster covered by the contract exceed a given trigger. (This can be a *parametric* trigger, for instance an earthquake of magnitude 7 or more on the Richter scale in a specific region or a storm with sustained wind speed higher than 150 km/93 miles per hour; this can also be an *indemnity* trigger that is directly related to the level of losses incurred by SafeCompany for a given disaster or period of time.) Then the interest on the bond or the principal, or both, is forgiven, depending on the specifications of the issued catastrophe bond. These funds are provided to SafeCompany to help cover its claims from the event.

Cat bonds have been on the market since 1997, which enables some comparisons as to the evolution of issuances and capital outstanding. Figure 8.2 illustrates this evolution and the number of bonds issued between January 1997 and December 2007.[10] The market recorded total issuance of over $4.7 billion in 2006 (20 new issuances, twice as many as in 2005), a 125 percent increase over the $2.1 billion in 2005. This was a new record high, and a 75 percent increase over the $1.14 billion issued in 2004, and a 20 percent increase over the $1.73 billion issuance in 2003 (the previous record). The risk capital issued during 2005 and 2006 was equal to the total capital issued over the preceding five years. Bonds outstanding increased significantly, too, which reflects the issuance of multiyear bonds in previous years. This trend continued in 2007, with 27 new catastrophe bonds issued for a total of $7 billion in capital and $14 billion outstanding.[11]

In the context of highly volatile reinsurance prices that often occur after large catastrophes, cat bonds offer an important element of stability for their users by guaranteeing a predefined price over several years, assuming that the entire capital of the bond is not triggered. I believe that this stability advantage has been largely undervalued so far.

Furthermore, more and more cat bonds cover against multiple events. In fact, in 2005, 2006, and 2007, over half of the capital at risk through cat bonds was for multi-event bonds rather than single-event bonds. In terms of capital outstanding, U.S. earthquakes and hurricanes represented the largest volume of cat bond at risk in both 2006 and 2007, followed by storm exposure in Europe, and then typhoons and earthquakes in Japan.

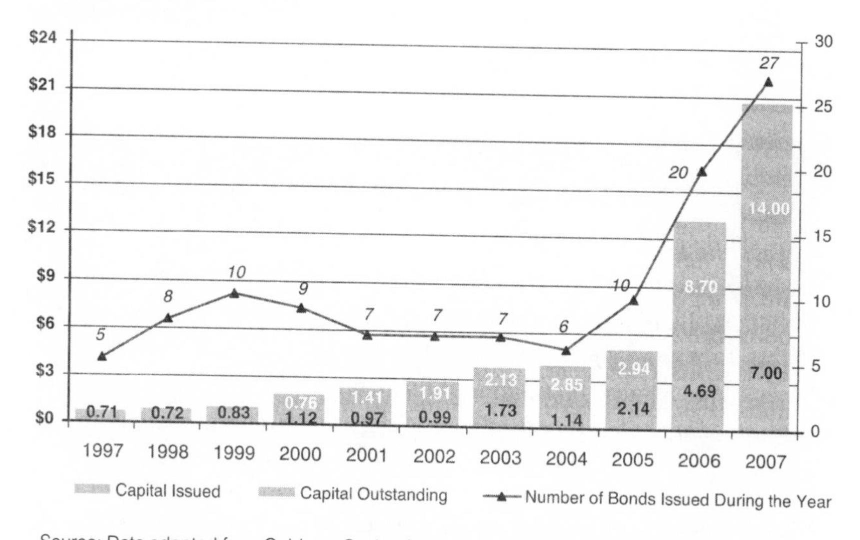

Source: Data adapted from Goldman Sachs, Swiss Re, and Guy Carpenter

Figure 8.2 Catastrophe Bonds: Capital Risk Issued and Outstanding 1997–2007 (In $ Billion)

Also, whereas most cat bonds so far have been issued by insurers and reinsurers to protect part of their portfolio against natural disasters, there have been several other transactions to cover other types of risks (pandemics, terrorism) and also several transactions issued by noninsurers (a sport federation, utility or oil companies, and even by a government). Some of these transactions are noted in the following sidebar.

As have other financial instruments, catastrophe bonds have suffered from the 2008–2009 financial crisis. After the 2007 record-setting year, catastrophe bond issuances fell 62 percent by volume ($2.7 billion in new and renewal capacity) and nearly by half in transaction account (13), with almost no transactions taking place in the second two quarters of 2008. Indeed, given the uncertainty associated with the future of financial markets, the cost of capital, and due to more favorable reinsurance rates, many transactions were postponed. Still, with $2.7 billion of new issuances, 2008 was the third busiest year since catastrophe bonds were introduced in 1997. As of June 2009, it seems that 2009 will not be a record year, but should bring enough capacity into this market to replace capacity from maturing deals.

Alternative Uses of Catastrophe Bonds

Pandemics and Terrorism

In 2003, a securitization of catastrophe mortality risk was undertaken (Vita Capital) by reinsurance giant Swiss Re, in response to the realization that terrorist attacks or large-scale pandemics could have a serious impact on its portfolio (high concentration of losses the same year). The bond protected against losses associated with an abnormal number of deaths in a selected number of countries.

Sport Federations: International Federation of Association Football (FIFA)

The world governing organization of football (soccer), the Fédération Internationale de Football Association (FIFA), which organized the 2006 World Cup in Germany, developed a $262 million catastrophe bond in August 2003 (Golden Goal Finance) to protect its investment. The bond sale was fully subscribed at a moderate cost (a spread of 150 basis points above LIBOR). Under very specific conditions, the cat bond covered losses resulting from both natural and terrorist extreme events that would have resulted in the cancellation of the World Cup final game.

Corporations: Disneyland, Universal Studios, EDF, and Dominion

The first corporate catastrophe bond was issued in 1999 by Oriental Land in Japan, owner and operator of Tokyo Disneyland, to help insure the company against the risk (to property and earnings) that an earthquake could damage its theme park. In 2002, Vivendi Universal (Universal Studios) issued a $175 million bond (Studio Re) to cover its production studios against an earthquake in Southern California. The first European corporate bond was issued in 2003 by EDF, the French utility giant; the $230 million bond (Pylon) covered the company against severe windstorms in France. In 2006, another corporate sponsor went with coverage by cat bond: Dominion Resources, an energy producer, obtained protection for oil-drilling assets located off the coasts of Louisiana and Texas by issuing a $50 million bond (Drewcat).

Governments: Mexico

The government of Mexico, which through its FONDEN facility sponsored a three-year maturity earthquake catastrophe bond for $160 million (CAT-Mex) in May 2006, was the first government to securitize natural catastrophe risk. In years of low fiscal revenues, issuing bonds was viewed by the Mexican government as a solid alternative to the risk of stopping government contribution to the national catastrophe fund (given pressure on government budget). A new bond was issued in October 2009.

An important change that resulted from the financial crisis, and specifically from the fall of Lehman Brothers, is that there are now tighter requirements to assure that the money invested in the bond is more adequately protected. This should make catastrophe bonds a more robust financial instrument moving forward. Indeed, before 2008, most cat bonds used only one company (so-called counterparty; for example, an investment bank) to guarantee the entire amount of collateral backing the bond. Lehman was this investment bank in many cat bond transactions. When Lehman fell, many cat bonds became unprotected.[12]

The new post-2008 structures have higher transparency and provide greater access to information about the risks associated with the underlying assets; they also facilitate the replacement of the counterparty or can even unwind the transaction in case of default. These improvements should serve the interests of the sellers and buyers alike.

How Financial Instruments Can Help the Developing World

Although most of the ILWs and cat bonds have been issued in the developed world, in recent years, there has been an effort to create innovative solutions to provide financial protection to inhabitants of developing and poor countries where private insurance coverage against natural disasters does not currently exists, or is not affordable.[13] Under the leadership of the United Nations, the World Bank, and other international organizations, large insurers and reinsurers working with modeling firms that assess risks have completed several transactions that augur well for the future.

A recent example was undertaken in Ethiopia in 2006 under the leadership of the U.N.'s World Food Program. Even though Ethiopia was considered the fastest growing non-oil dependent African nation in 2007, it remains with a GDP per capita at US$806 one of the poorest countries.[14] Agriculture represents an important part of the local economy, and farmers are exposed to important risks of droughts. A weather derivative—a financial asset, the value of which depends on the weather (rain or temperature)—was successfully developed and provided coverage to local farmers in the case of an extreme drought during the agricultural season. The objective of this pilot program was to develop a disaster-management system to protect the livelihoods of Ethiopians vulnerable to severe and catastrophic weather risks as a first step in a process involving governments, donors, and insurance and financial markets.[15] How did this work?

Challenge: Collecting Objective Weather Data

In 2004 and 2005, the World Food Program partnered with the French insurer AXA to develop an index-based weather derivative instrument calibrated with rainfall data from weather stations across Ethiopia. To satisfy market concerns about the quality and integrity of data for risk transfer, capacity building was needed for the National Meteorological Agency to ensure that data were reported in real time.[16] The agency monitors more than 600 weather stations across the county, but only 44 of these stations are Class 1 stations, meaning stations recording pressure temperature, relative humidity, wind speed and direction, rainfall, evaporation, and soil temperature every three hours from 06:00 to 18:00. These 44 stations had data missing, particularly because of nonweather extreme events such as civil war. Therefore, two companies that specialize in modeling, EarthSat and Risk Management Solutions, were hired to clean data and replace values missing or erroneous. The quality of the final dataset was qualified as excellent by both of these companies when compared with similar datasets from industrialised countries.

An index was then created that aggregated all livelihood losses due to drought for certain preselected districts around the weather stations. This drought index was based on 62,000 households (a total of 310,000 people) during the 2006 agricultural season from March to October 2006. Based on historical data, the average index of this population was $28 million per year, with a maximum loss of $80 million in 1984 and a theoretical worst-case potential loss of $154 million.[17] The contract between the World Food Program and AXA stipulated that if the index was higher than $55 million at the end of the contract (December 31, 2006), then the World Food Program would receive a payout from AXA up to a maximum of $7.1 million, which could then be used to provide aid to the farmers.

It turns out that 2006 was a good year for crop production in Ethiopia. The index value at the end of 2006 was well below the $55 million trigger level, and no payout came out of this innovative weather derivative contract. But the Ethiopia drought insurance project is a powerful illustration that market mechanisms can be used to provide financial coverage even in very low-income countries that are not seen as natural insurance markets. To do so, however, it is necessary to develop objective, timely, and accurate risk indicators.

Long-Term Impact

Another lesson learned from this initiative links to the principle of appreciating the long-term impact of disasters on an area's politics and culture. Indeed, the development and implementation of the risk-financing solution previously described was also an incentive for the Ethiopian government to better develop its contingency plan, resulting in better preparation and earlier response to future shocks of all types, not only droughts. According to the World Food Program, "In drafting the implementation rulebook, the (Ethiopian) Government upgraded its contingency planning; the guarantee of predictable and reliable contingency funding catalyzed institutional interest and commitment."[18]

Further Expanding Alternative Risk-Transfer Markets

Notwithstanding these very encouraging examples, it is surprising that despite the tremendous capacity offered by financial markets today, the alternative risk-transfer market has not expanded to a larger extent. Today, it represents just a small proportion of capital in the global insurance markets worldwide, mainly because these instruments are not standardized yet. Below are several recommendations that, if followed, should considerably enhance this market by overcoming some of the challenges it currently faces.[19]

First, ART instruments require good risk assessment, so it is important to promote the collection and dissemination of high-quality data on catastrophe risks and losses according to standardized criteria across the world. Second, most transactions are handled directly between companies and details of the deals are not necessarily made public—there is no transparent market yet. Moving forward, it will be important to promote transparency in the catastrophes-linked securities market so that these instruments become more standardized. Third, it is important to examine the accounting and solvency rules presiding over the catastrophes-linked securities market to remove any unnecessary impediments.[20]

Moving forward, proper risk-reduction measures *must* be put in place to reduce exposure to future disasters, but there will always be residual risks to protect against. In the new era of catastrophes we have entered, it is very important for top decision makers to think strategically in a *what if* mode, rather than simply pretend (and hope) that catastrophes will not happen.

This is a paradigm shift from the way that many used to see risk management. But one thing is sure: A new era calls for a new model. It is thus important to develop a new model of management and also new solutions adapted to times of disaster. Well-designed financial innovations can help do just that. While insurers and reinsurers are natural consumers for these innovative financial instruments, other stakeholders (corporations, governments, NGOs, royal families) should think more about how they could protect their assets by buying ART tools specifically designed for their needs.

9

A Financial Malignancy

Suzanne Nora Johnson
Former Vice Chairman of The Goldman Sachs Group, Inc.

Overview

The financial crisis of 2008–2009 was a disaster that triggered a global economic recession, the most acute since the Great Depression of the 1920s and 1930s. This chapter highlights certain elementary attributes of this financial and economic disaster and suggests ways to recover. Given that much of the financial crisis was driven by governmental, institutional, and individual actions that undervalued or misunderstood risk, the chapter focuses on the "cascade of confidence" required to restore a better balance between risk and reward and growth and stability. This chapter describes six basic conditions required for the restoration of confidence in the midst of a financial disaster: (1) coordination and cooperation, (2) clarity of communication, (3) control of toxins, (4) capital and cushion, (5) co-investment, and (6) courage.

The 2008–2009 financial crisis—arguably a disaster—was an economic cancer that metastasized. The global depression of the 1920s and 1930s (the Great Depression) demonstrated how damaging a financial malignancy could be if government failed to respond. In this financial crisis, unlike the one that triggered the Great Depression, governments around the world responded aggressively and creatively with a broad range of fiscal and monetary policies designed to stabilize their financial systems, to limit economic destruction, and to prevent wholesale political upheaval. However, it is critical to understand that the markets are fundamentally different than they were after the Great Depression. Furthermore, like many current cancer therapies, interventions on the current financial crisis have never been tried before to quite the same extent or even in the same way, and like existing cancer treatments, it is not yet known whether such interventions will have any lasting therapeutic impact and what the side effects will ultimately be.

Much has been written about the proximate causes of the current financial crisis that has had a devastating impact on economies around the world. Although there is much commentary and even greater debate as to where the failures were most egregious and where blame is most appropriately placed, it is clear that the aggregated and interconnected nature of the failures was central to the magnitude and ferocity of the disaster. Many of the primary causes of the financial crisis were known and discussed long before the crisis was upon us.[1] However, no commentator actually understood how immunocompromised the entire global financial system had become, what the ultimate carcinogen would be, and when exactly it would metastasize. Indeed, it is likely that the actual causes and triggers of the financial crisis will be analyzed and subject to historical revisions for many years to come.

The primary purpose of this chapter is to make some limited observations on the financial crisis and to suggest ways to recover, recognizing that there have been, and will continue to be, acute and chronic dimensions of this crisis. Given that so much of the financial crisis was driven by governmental and institutional actions and individual behaviors that undervalued or misunderstood risk, this chapter focuses only on the "cascade of confidence" required to restore a better balance between risk and reward and stability and growth.

Although the bursting of the U.S. housing bubble was the apparent trigger to this financial crisis, the overheated housing market was only one of the symptoms of the ill health of the economic cycle. After months of collapsing asset prices, it became clear that the financial system was gravely ill. Monetary policies, exhibited as bold and unconventional central bank liquidity measures (2008–2009), were designed to disrupt the fall in asset prices and real estate before the financial system became terminally ill (insolvent). The aggressive actions of the central banks stabilized the financial system and slowed the metastases but have not cured the underlying economic conditions. Even when the financial system becomes less leveraged and better capitalized and prepared to lend again, qualified and willing borrowers may still be in short supply. As long as there is too much debt on the household sector in the developed markets, there will be more interest in increasing savings and reducing debt than in investing and spending. The significant deterioration in household wealth and income from reduced housing prices and investment portfolios and high unemployment rates may dampen financial recovery.

The financial metastasis was exacerbated by the loss of confidence and the panic and despair that ensued. As a result, throughout the global financial system, institutional and individual investors shunned all but the safest assets, consumers stopped spending, and firms retracted accordingly. Therefore, the disaster response must be focused on creating the conditions for a cascade of confidence in which the financial system unfreezes, world trade resumes, institutions begin to invest and households spend, and firms rebuild. This chapter describes six basic conditions for the restoration of confidence in the midst of a financial disaster.

Coordination and Cooperation

Global Considerations

The financial crisis exposed serious flaws in many aspects of our financial system. Much of the severity of the crisis was due to global economic imbalances, aggregated risks, and uncoordinated policies. Increased coordination and cooperation between countries is a necessary starting point. The economic substrate in the world is one in which different nations are highly dependent on one another for their economic well-being.

Global imbalances are at the core of the financial crisis. Excess savings have accumulated in some of the world's largest economies, which are, along with their accumulated reserves, largely invested in assets denominated in U.S. dollars rather than in their own local currencies. The biggest creditors are primarily in emerging market countries pursuing export-led economic growth policies, often on the basis of undervalued currencies. It is not only the size of the imbalances that are unusual, but also which particular countries are actually the debtors and the creditors. This situation runs counter to historical economic theory, which suggests that emerging economies with relatively low capital intensity, high rates of return, and the prospect of higher income levels in the future should save less than they invest and therefore run current account deficits. Developed economies, on the other hand, with mature capital stocks and low internal rates of return would be expected to save more than they invest and therefore run surpluses. Yet from 2000 onward, emerging economies collectively began to save significantly more than they invested; while the more developed economies began to run large current account deficits.[2] Part of this effect was the result of the rise in commodities prices, particularly of oil, in resource-rich countries such as Saudi Arabia. But many non-natural resource-rich countries, notably China, also saw improvement in their positions. Indeed, China's surplus rose from 1½ percent of GDP in 2000 to 10 percent of GDP in 2008.[3]

The global economic crisis brought into sharp relief the extraordinary level of interdependence, most markedly between China and the United States.[4] A stable recovery of the U.S. economy and ongoing funding of its national debt will likely require continued support from China for many years to come. China's future growth will also depend on the health and vitality of its world trading partners and providers of natural resources, and on the redeployment of domestic savings into domestic demand. In particular, U.S. consumers helped feed the expansion of China's export-oriented economy, which allowed for massive development of the country's physical infrastructure and manufacturing base and, in turn, fueled China's demand for commodities from regions around the world in places as diverse as Africa, Australia, the Persian Gulf, Latin America, and Russia. In addition, the demand for U.S. dollar resources by much of the developing world kept U.S. interest rates low and allowed the U.S. consumer to go on an extraordinary buying binge—manifested most dangerously in the overheated and leveraged residential housing sector and driven by the financial innovations of the last decade.

As interest and inflation rates significantly contracted during this period, institutional and individual investors began an aggressive search for investments that would provide attractive returns. This extreme search for attractive returns lowered the risk premium on almost all asset classes—even those viewed to be relatively risky by historical norms (for example, stocks and bonds in emerging markets). According to a report by the McKinsey Global Institute, developing countries' financial assets grew to $38 trillion in 2007, which represented a 35 percent increase over 2006 and nearly 5 times the growth rate of developed markets.[5] Cross-border lending and deposits grew from slightly over $900 billion in 2002 to $6 trillion at the end of 2007. These investment/capital flows, particularly to the emerging markets, helped fuel an unprecedented rise in global economic growth. However, after the crisis hit, those elevated capital flows severely retracted. The World Bank has stated that net private capital flows to emerging economies in 2009 are likely to be only half the record $1 trillion in 2007; whereas global trade volumes will shrink for the first time since 1982.[6] Indeed, trade is the most serious casualty of the financial crisis with a vicious circle of decreases in exports leading to falls in production and rising job losses leading to further reductions in consumer demand and exports. It is increasingly clear that countries reliant on exports have been particularly hard hit. Neither developed nor emerging economies have been spared. Japan lost nearly half of its export market over the first quarter of 2009 versus the first quarter 2008. Germany, the largest European exporter, lost more than a fifth of its exports in the same time period. And U.S. exports declined 30 percent from the fourth quarter of 2008 to the first quarter of 2009. Recently, the World Trade Organization (WTO) forecast global trade to fall by 9 percent in 2009.[7] The need for the world to repair and restore these capital and trade flows is clear. What started as a "financial" problem quickly became an economic one.

The political realities of our world make even the nomenclature around "coordination and cooperation" challenging. At the very least, common problems must be identified and acknowledged. To get to solutions, there must be a commitment to cooperate in a multilateral way. Whether it is the G20 or a broader group of nations, there must be forums where inclusive standard setting can be established—even if the ultimate enforcement is done at a local or regional level.[8] Unilateralism or even bilateralism fails to recognize the fundamental realities of fixing a systemwide problem that requires a collective response and ongoing vigilance and preparedness. It is quite difficult to subdivide many of these problems by political jurisdiction.

Although bodies such as the Financial Stability Board, a group consisting of major finance authorities, can serve invaluable functions in the coordination and standard setting process and building global connective tissue, such bodies are unlikely to have the requisite resources to drive sustainable solutions.[9] There needs to be a new global institutional framework that provides a forum for reconciliation and disaster preparedness and response and recovery. Ultimately, what must emerge is a stable global financial system in which capital can flow safely between the more developed and the developing nations without ongoing cycles of financial crisis and increasingly polarizing economic stratification. Although economic activities and cultures are more globalized than ever, politics is still constrained by the geographic and sometimes philosophical boundaries of nations. Global engagement will need to significantly intensify. This will likely entail significant political risk at the level of nation states. However, there will be much greater risk in the future if the existing macro imbalances are not addressed.

Local Considerations

This crisis also suggests two important policy goals that must be achieved at the local level: (1) the coordination of macroeconomic policies and financial institution regulations, and (2) the rationalization of domestic regulatory architecture. As Martin Wolfe has so succinctly stated, it is "in finance that microeconomics and macroeconomics meet."[10]

The surge of financial innovation typified by the securitization of credit and the development of contingent contracts (for example, derivatives) radically transformed the financial system from a relational one (where the lender knew the borrower and underwrote and held and serviced the loan) to a transactional one (where the originator of the loan may or may not know the borrower, the underwriter would not necessarily hold the loan, and yet another third party might service it). Clearly, the financial system should have been better regulated. But the leverage and credit in the financial system is unlikely to have reached such extremes without the macroeconomic imbalances that have existed.

Given how related such macro imbalances are to global financial health and to the attendant risk taking by financial institutions, it is clear that macro-economic policies and financial institution regulations needed to be synchronized. This does not necessarily require losing independence of central bank or financial institution regulators, but it does require that some supervisory institution have primary responsibility and accountability for ensuring that areas of systemic risk are identified and mitigated.

Fundamental reform and modernization of domestic regulatory architecture is also needed. Although there have been some laudable efforts at cooperation in the past, this crisis has made obvious the conclusion that overlapping jurisdictions, gaps in regulations, uneven technological, and informatic capabilities and regulatory competition have created an environment where market excesses can thrive.[11] In addition, the fragmented, yet also in many ways redundant, regulatory structure between federal and state authorities and the myriad of federal regulatory organizations in the United States and elsewhere was not only inefficient, but it was also ineffective, particularly in the oversight of organizations or activities that could have systemic risk. For example, consider that although AIG presumably had capable state insurance regulatory oversight, the fact that many of its non-insurance activities were not adequately supervised at least partially contributed to its systemic risk.

In the United States, a firm's regulator is determined largely by its business form. As a result, two financial firms providing exactly the same products might be regulated differently. Further, even in cases where firms have identical business structures, they may opt for different regulators. Consider the choices of Goldman Sachs and Morgan Stanley following their emergency conversion to bank holding companies in September 2008. The Federal Reserve Board approved applications of Goldman Sachs and Morgan Stanley to become bank holding companies based on the conversion of their industrial loan companies to commercial banks. As bank holding companies, the consolidated supervisor of these organizations will be the Federal Reserve; the SEC will continue as the functional regulator of the broker dealers of both organizations. A number of other regulators, including, among others, the Commodities Futures Trading Commission (CFTC) and the Financial Services Authority (FSA) will regulate other parts of their businesses. However, the primary regulator of Goldman Sachs's *state* chartered bank subsidiary will be the State Banking Department of New York, and of Morgan Stanley's subsidiary *national* bank, the Office of the Comptroller of the Currency.

Markets, financial products, technology, and business models will continue to evolve. Regulatory authorities will need to do so, too, even where that means authority will need to be shared/ceded. Within a number of countries, sharing jurisdiction between regulators may be among the first practical challenges.[12]

Clarity of Communication

One of the most dangerous aspects of this financial crisis was the uncertainty as to the diagnosis of the problem and the attendant government responses. The markets generally abhor uncertainty. In an environment where information, disinformation, and inaccuracies are turbocharged and "truthiness"[13] is often the standard, it is critical that the nature of the problem be defined and the responses well communicated. It is an area that requires clear and accessible articulation of the problem because the negative feedback loop has particularly dangerous consequences in the midst of such a disaster. Indeed, transparency may make it easier to determine where problems and possible solutions actually lie. Consider the following analogy. If there is a belief that the electrical grid causes cancer, one response might be to disable every substation. Until the original theory is debunked, it will be quite a while before the power is back on.

There also must be greater consistency of the government response. Although it is recognized that the situation may be so complex and dynamic that selected interventions will need to evolve and change and at times be scrapped, defining the path forward and the appropriate metrics for judging effectiveness will be a critical government responsibility. Consider that cancer treatments are often modified as real-time determinations are made as to the balance of effectiveness, safety, and side-effect profile. However, much of the patient's decision to follow the therapeutic regimen is trust in the oncologist's explanation of the road forward—for good and for bad.

Control of Toxins

One of the most critical and often difficult actions is to identify the sources of systemic risk. Often, it will not be a single point of risk but aggregations of risk that transform generally safe activities into dangerous ones. In the first instance, this might be an institution that is large and represents a pivotal role in the financing function (for example, a Fannie Mae or Freddie Mac), or it may be an organization whose demise would trigger an avalanche of other failures (for example, Lehman Brothers), but it might also be an activity that if unsupervised and unmonitored could be fatal (for example, derivative contracts, collateralized debt obligations). When the cause of disease is identified, it is critical to ring-fence the institution (for example, conservatorship, nationalization, receivership) or to restructure the asset or activity (for example, bankruptcy, good bank/bad bank, mergers) so that it cannot continue to infect and invade the system. There is no question that systemically important financial institutions or activities should be identified and subjected to strict limits on leverage. These limits should consider potential exposure to off-balance-sheet risks, which have proven to be a major source of vulnerability in the past. In addition, a systemic risk regulator should have jurisdiction regardless of business model, financing function, or unregulated status of a firm.

As Richard Posner highlights, one must also consider that "an interrelated system of financial intermediaries, is inherently unstable. Any firm that borrows short term and lends long term is at a risk of a run, and the run and the resulting collapse of the firm may have a domino effect on the lenders to it and the borrowers from it and the financial companies with which they are entwined."[14] The response to this financial crisis has also provided a potentially important marker for future systemic risk. The recent rating agency decision by Standard & Poor's to downgrade its outlook for British sovereign debt from "stable" to "negative" has implications for the United States.

The United States has responded to the current financial crisis with unprecedented deficits. These deficits imply enormous U.S. federal debt in the future. The U.S. federal debt was approximately 40 percent of GDP at the end of 2008; the Congressional Budget Office projects it will increase to approximately 80 percent in the next decade. A scenario of debt exceeding 100 percent of GDP in another five years (particularly considering projected healthcare entitlement spending) is not implausible. Standard and Poor's has provided a red flag for the United States that a "government debt burden of...[100 percent] level would be incompatible with a triple A rating."[15] John Taylor has recently argued that the risk posed by this debt could be characterized as systemic and could be far more lethal than the current financial crisis.[16]

This challenge is not limited to the United States and the United Kingdom. The International Monetary Fund projects that the gross public debt of the ten richest countries in the G20 will reach 106 percent by 2009 and 114 percent by 2014, up from 78 percent in 2007.[17] It is imperative that governments develop a way to reign in not only private-sector risk but public, as well, particularly given the demographics of aging in much of the world.

Capital and Cushion

After the financial cancer has been attacked, restoring the financial system's capacity and resilience will require providing capital. As part of its response to the crisis, the United States government introduced "stress tests" on banks.[18] These tests were an exercise designed to show how much capital the banks needed to support their activities. The idea behind these stress tests was to make pessimistic assumptions with no more than a 15 percent chance of likelihood. The challenge is that such tests are not perfect science, and their effectiveness will be highly dependent on whether the economic assumptions underlying the requisite capital cushions are ultimately correct. Certain commentators are already skeptical that the exercise did not consider a "seriously bad case."[19] To the extent the economic assumptions are too optimistic, there may be ongoing failures and a negative feedback loop reinforced. Alternatively, the assumptions may be too pessimistic, and institutions will be relatively overcapitalized and not as efficient in the allocation of capital.

A number of recent reports have argued for "countercyclical" capital.[20] This would require banks to have significantly higher capital in boom times, while allowing for somewhat reduced capital in bust times. A related recommendation comes from Raghuram G. Rajan, who argues that to create real stability through the cycle, new regulations must be "comprehensive, contingent, and cost-effective."[21] To be comprehensive, he suggests that all leveraged firms be regulated to discourage the drift from heavily regulated activities to lightly regulated activities during the boom period. Instead of permanent capital, financial institutions would be required to have contingent capital that could be infused when the system is in trouble (for example, debt convertible upon specified conditions). Permitting financial institutions to enter into these contingent arrangements in good times when the chances of a recession are relatively remote would be more cost-effective than raising capital in the midst of a recession. Rajan argues that because the infusion is seen as an unlikely possibility, firms would not be able to raise their risk levels using future converted capital. Similarly, because the conversion would occur in bad times when capital is scarce, the system and the taxpayer would be protected.

Co-Investment

The fifth condition for building the cascade of confidence is the emergence of private and public capital in the system. Private capital provides a critical signal that the worst has passed and the current risk/reward trade-off is a reasonable one. The longer public money remains the only alternative, the greater the risk that the particular industry and overall market will be distorted (for example, government advantage or disadvantage given to noninfected competitors) or that other countries will seek some type of protectionist measures to offset such distortions on behalf of their own industries and markets. Indeed, one of the largest and most influential global fixed income investors has noted the overriding government role in the markets by suggesting that investors "position their portfolios predominantly under the umbrella of government support.... The time will come when the authorities will return to being just the referees of markets. For now, they both are referees and players."[22]

There is also a risk that confidence will be undermined where the government is the dominant economic actor and uses the markets primarily for political gain (for example, injecting populist politics into economic decision making).[23] In certain cases, governments may exercise virtual control of an investment without formal representation or rules—impacting everything from contracts to incentives to lines of business. Central banks and finance ministries will need to lay out the rules that will govern their exit from their unconventional forms of monetary policy and from the significant industrial and financial investments in which they are now deeply embedded.

An important part of restoring private participation will be the reworking of incentives. Incentives, including compensation schemes, will need to recalibrate the periods of performance (long versus short) and risk levels (less versus more) and the absolute and relative amounts of compensation.[24] For example, many executive incentive plans are based on annual targets. Note, however, that many public equity market institutional investors get measured on quarterly results. This will be a relatively challenging undertaking given that much of the discussion focuses on aligning the interests of managements with common shareholders, (for example, restricted common stock). In addition, there may be divergence between the interests of the common shareholders and those of the government as preferred shareholder, lender, and guarantor of bank obligations.[25] At the same time, incentives must not be artificially constrained or misdirected to areas of limited economic value.

The private sector, to fully participate in a responsible way, will also have to improve risk-management systems and cultures. Many institutions were focused on short-term earnings and either relegated risk management to an internal back office or compliance function or outsourced it to third parties such as credit-rating agencies or auditors. Although third parties such as rating agencies could theoretically provide an important check and balance, even sophisticated mathematical models failed to predict the magnitude of the problems—often because they were based on relatively short-term economic history or because they failed to consider qualitative issues.[26]

A real economic recovery will require government therapies being replaced by sustainable sources of private investment. The confidence cascade can also be significantly enhanced if historic trading partners have confidence that there is sufficient financing capacity to ensure the continued success of private enterprise.

Courage

The sixth condition and perhaps the most difficult to restore is courage. Many of the first five conditions require concerted government actions/forbearances, but in the final analysis, it is at the individual or household level where trust must be reestablished. This implies that governmental actions must be consistent with people's expectations as to the safety and fairness of the system.

This reengagement with the public will be done at a time of extreme uncertainty. The degree of risk taking by banks (many of which are arguably still short of capital) will be muted as the deleveraging process continues and as regulators likely move them closer to a utility model. The deleveraging process and the overall shrinkage of the finance sector will exacerbate the massive contraction in economic activity. There will be enormous ongoing political pressure to introduce new laws and regulations designed to improve stability but which may act as restraints on trade, immigration, and innovation. Perhaps, most important, the political consequences of the crisis have been considerable. Indeed, in many ways the crisis has undermined the perceived advantages of globalization and open financial and capital markets and the United States financial system as the best model for financial intermediation.[27] Furthermore, ongoing economic weakness and instability will create increasing geopolitical tensions that are manifest in discussions by Brazil, China, and Russia, among others, about the need for a super sovereign reserve currency to replace the United States dollar as a way to correct macro-imbalances over the longer term.[28]

In this scenario, informed and brave leadership will be required to restore confidence and reduce fear without restoring to protectionism and xenophobia. The ability to face up to the problems and their actual causes, to reform the system, and to change behaviors and to be crisis-prepared versus crisis-prone will be the true signs of leadership.

We know that the next financial cancer may likely be of a different origin and may manifest itself in different sites, but our ability to learn from this financial crisis can improve our ability to respond better whether the next crisis is relatively benign or even more malignant. Responsible risk taking—growth with stability—is what provides opportunity for the next generation and security for the present one.

10

Climate Change: Nature and Action

Thomas E. Lovejoy

The H. John Heinz III Center for Science, Economics, and the Environment

Overview

All over the world, ecosystems that adjusted to the stable climate of the past 10,000 years are already showing responses to the current 0.75 increase in global temperature and the acidification of the oceans (0.1 pH). Although the changes observed so far are mostly minor ripples in the fabric of nature, threshold changes have already appeared, including coral bleaching and massive coniferous tree dieback in North America and Europe. Consequently, 350 parts per million (ppm) is most probably a level beyond which dangerous change will occur. Policy implications, beyond the usual implications for a revised energy base for society, include revised conservation strategies and a global effort to remove some of the carbon from the atmosphere by restoring degraded terrestrial ecosystems.

The Earth as a Biophysical System

In 1896, Swedish scientist Svante August Arrhenius[1] addressed the question of why the earth was a habitable temperature for humans and other forms of life. His answer was the Greenhouse effect and the heat (energy) trapping properties of the greenhouse gases, without which it would be a much colder planet. Interestingly, his pencil and paper calculations of the temperature consequence of doubling preindustrial (early-nineteenth-century) levels of carbon dioxide (CO_2) (from 280ppm to 560) are quite close to the results from the fancy supercomputer models used today, namely an increase of 3 degrees Celsius.

Arrhenius would not have been aware of the temperature of the planet over the past 100,000 years.[2] In contrast to the gradual and linear change that is the way computer models work, temperature change for most of this period (the first 90,000 years) is mostly a matter of abrupt change. More important in many ways, the past 10,000 years has been a period of unusual stability. This basically means the entire human enterprise—from the origins of agriculture and the origin of human settlements down to the current day—is based on the assumption of a stable climate. The planet's ecosystems have also adjusted to the stable climate during the same period.

The planet is well on its way to that doubling. There is considerable momentum, but doubling is not inevitable.[3] Current CO_2 levels are close to 390ppm, with preindustrial levels being at 280ppm. The climate system is responding with the current average global temperature about 0.75 degrees C warmer than preindustrial. Including another 0.5 degrees built in because of lags in the system, the planet's average temperature will rise to 1.25 degrees above preindustrial temperatures. At the same time, greenhouse gas emissions are climbing more rapidly than the worst-case scenario of the Intergovernmental Panel on Climate Change (IPCC).[4] That scenario was meant to be the upper bound of possible emissions and consequent climate change. Yet more worrisome, current stated national commitments on emissions reduction mean that CO_2 concentrations would rise to the vicinity of 700ppm.

The natural world is already responding to global warming. Some of the changes are physical. Glaciers are in retreat in much of the world, and all tropical glaciers are receding at a rate at which they will be gone within 15 years, threatening certain city water supplies as well as the ecosystems that depend on them.[5] In the Arctic, the consequences are dramatic, so much so that the first summer projected for an ice-free Arctic Ocean has advanced from 2100 to 2050, to 2030 (and even perhaps sooner than that).[6]

Sea level has been rising primarily from the thermal expansion of water but more recently also from glacial melt from land. (The loss of

Arctic sea ice does not affect sea level because ice floats and behaves like an ice cube in a glass of water.) The IPCC—a conservative entity—is now projecting that sea level rise this century will be one meter. (Although this is likely to be an underestimate.) A mere 3-foot rise is enough to triple the area of San Francisco Bay.

Other physical changes include drought and heat. In the American West, snow melt is earlier, and the summers are longer and dryer, so there is a statistically significant increase in wildfires.[7] Australia is undergoing a prolonged drought. In addition, there is the possibility of greater frequency of more-intense tropical storms, a matter that is still debated in scientific circles, although computer models all point to more extreme weather events.

Associated with these physical changes are changes in the living fabric of the planet so essential to human well-being through goods, ecosystem services, and the living library from which the life sciences advance. Plants are changing their life cycles (for example, blooming earlier).[8] Animals are changing their timing, too. Tree swallows are migrating earlier, nesting earlier, laying eggs earlier.[9]

In addition, species are changing where they occur geographically.[10] For example, in the American West, Edith's Checkerspot butterfly has been moving northward and upward in altitude. In the United States, the National Arbor Day Foundation has found it necessary to publish a new hardiness zone map that guides people as to which tree species they can successfully plant where they live. In the Chesapeake Bay, the southern boundary of the eel grass communities is moving northward year after year because eel grass has a very strict upper temperature limit. Projections at double preindustrial levels of CO_2 show sugar maple will no longer be a U.S. species and will be found only in Canada.[11]

These changes are relatively tiny ripples in the natural world, but much more substantial change—ecosystem failure—is already apparent.

Tropical coral reefs—colorful, diverse, and productive biologically and important economically—are sensitive to temperature increase, which causes a breakdown in the fundamental partnership between a coral animal and an alga so that the animal ejects the alga.

The result is called "bleaching" in which the colorful world essentially becomes black and white, while diversity and productivity crash. This first happened in 1983 and happens with greater frequency almost every year.[12]

Ecosystem failure is also occurring in the coniferous forests of North America, in this case because of native bark beetles.[13] First observed in British Columbia but now widespread in the United States, too, longer summers and warmer winters tip the balance in favor of the beetles, leading to massive tree mortality of 70 percent or more of all trees. In the United States, 7 million acres of forest are already so affected, and it is estimated that the number will quadruple.[14]

In addition, there are signs that certain classes of species will be particularly vulnerable as they move to track their required climatic conditions. Among them are species living at high altitudes, such as the American pika (currently being considered for listing under the Endangered Species Act), because as they move up in altitude in response to warming temperatures, at some point there will be no farther up to go. Island species will be also be especially vulnerable, not only from climate change but also—on low-lying islands—from sea-level rise.

In the oceans, change way beyond ecosystem failure, namely system change, is already taking place. (Whereas ecosystem change involves a tide pool, a lake, or a small patch of forest, system change involves vast areas with multiple ecosystems and ecosystem types; for example, all the world's oceans.) Although the oceans absorb a huge amount of CO_2 every year, a small fraction of it converts to carbonic acid, which makes the ocean more acidic. The oceans are already 0.1 pH units more acidic as a consequence, which because of the logarithmic nature of the pH scale equates to 30 percent more acidic.[15]

This acidification is of particular consequence to all those marine species that build skeletons and shells of calcium carbonate depending on the carbonate equilibrium. The colder and more acidic the conditions, the harder it is for those species to lay down calcium carbonate. Ominous effects are already being seen at the base of food chains in the North Atlantic and off the Alaskan coast.

Additional system change was previewed in 2005 when changes in the Atlantic circulation—similar to those projected in the Hadley Center climate model[16]—produced the greatest drought in recorded history in the Amazon basin. The Hadley model initially projected Amazon dieback (dieback of the forest in the eastern half of the basin) to occur at global temperature increase of 2.5 degrees C over preindustrial,[17] but more recently projects it at 2.0 C. (The planet is currently headed to 1.25 C over preindustrial.) In addition, a new World Bank study shows that when deforestation and fire are included, the combined effect—which is, of course, how things actually work—will lead to dieback even sooner.[18]

The loss of a substantial part of the Amazon forest would mean not only horrific biodiversity loss, a huge release of biological carbon to the atmosphere, and terrible impact on local peoples and economies, but also, because of the Amazon hydrological cycle,[19] drying in Brazil south of the western Amazon (a major agro-industry area).

So rather than a low-probability, high-consequence event, climate change is a virtual certainty. In addition, adaptation to climate change becomes more difficult and more expensive the greater the climate change.

The big issue is how far should greenhouse gas concentrations be allowed to rise in the atmosphere. That is, how much climate change is too much? The United Nations Framework Convention on Climate Change specifically refers to avoiding "dangerous interference" in the climate system.

For some time, those conscious of the living planet have held the view that atmospheric CO_2 concentrations of 450ppm is the point beyond which it is not safe for ecosystems.[20] We are already beyond the point at which, in the language of the U.N. Framework Convention on Climate Change, "ecosystems can adapt naturally." Consequently, the biological view leads me to agree with James Hansen's view that 350ppm should be the limit. The problem, of course, is that the concentration is already 390ppm.[21]

This puts an even greater premium on ways to remove CO_2 from the atmosphere—something that most geo-engineering approaches ignore by focusing solely on temperature, thereby ignoring not only the fundamental forcing mechanism but also its acidifying effect on the oceans.

Currently, there is only one way to remove CO_2 from the atmosphere: biological processes, primarily photosynthesis and preferably in the form of ecosystem restoration. Life on Earth is built from carbon. In particular, green plants convert CO_2 into molecules that form plant tissue and that in turn provides food for animals, which, of course, are built of carbon, too.

Human activities and effects on terrestrial ecosystems over the past two to three centuries may have released as much as 200 billion tons of carbon into the atmosphere. This has been the net result of deforestation and other forms of land clearing, draining wetlands, degrading grasslands, and forms of agriculture that release carbon stored in the soil.

Interestingly, twice in the history of life on Earth, extremely high CO_2 levels generated by geological events have been reduced to a level approximating preindustrial.[22] The first reduction was coincident with the advent of and was caused by land plants. In similar fashion, the second reduction was driven by the advent and photosynthesis of modern flowering plants. So, the power of biology is not trivial.

All emissions come from the release of energy trapped by photosynthesis. The greatest amount is from the burning of fossil fuels—the remains of geologically ancient photosynthesis—and the rest is burning of biomass (the product of modern photosynthesis).

Today, tropical deforestation and burning releases about 20 percent of all global emissions—more than the entire transportation sector. Halting that is important and is part of the negotiations under the United Nations Framework Convention on Climate Change under the acronym REDD (reduced emissions from deforestation and forest degradation). It will be important for REDD to work in a way that doesn't weaken efforts to transform global energy use from heavy dependence on fossil fuels—by providing easy offsets in carbon trading systems. All efforts to address climate change must embrace the inequities between the industrialized and developing worlds.

Going beyond that, an effort on a planetary scale to restore terrestrial ecosystems might remove as much as 150 billion tons of carbon as CO_2 and accumulate it back into ecosystems.[23] This would involve reforestation, management of forests for carbon, restoration of grasslands and degraded grazing lands, and managing agriculture to restore carbon to the soil. For example, restoring grazing lands in Australia could accumulate half a billion tons of carbon per year for 50 years. All such activities should bear in mind the importance of biodiversity, and that valuing an ecosystem only for its carbon is analogous to valuing a computer chip only for its silicon.

The world desperately needs other ways to remove CO_2 from the atmosphere without additional impact on ecosystems. In the meantime, the CO_2 removal/ecosystem restoration program will have to contend with a single land base from which food, biofuels, biodiversity conservation, and carbon sequestration must come. Ecosystem restoration will simultaneously the ecosystems more resilient to the climate change they will inevitably experience—and, one would hope, finally awaken people to the importance of reconciling human action with the natural world.

It is a matter of highest consequence to address the climate change challenge and reduce the impact on the living planet. We can no longer afford to ignore the imperative to actively manage the earth as a biophysical system.

11

Lessons from Risk Analysis: Terrorism, Natural Disasters, and Technological Accidents

Detlof von Winterfeldt[1]
International Institute for Applied Systems Analysis

Overview

Risk is defined as a combination of three elements: scenario, probability, and consequences. A *scenario* is a sequence of events that is a subset of mutually exclusive and exhaustive sequences of events that could happen in a particular risk context. *Probabilities* reflect the relative likelihood of scenarios. *Consequences* (for example, fatalities, injuries, economic impacts) are defined at the end of the sequence of events.[2]

This general definition of risk and has withstood the test of time and applies to natural disaster risks, technological risks, and terrorism risks. In this chapter, I briefly recount the history of risk analysis related to these three types of risks and then discuss what terrorism risk analysts can learn from risk analyses of natural and technological risks. I also turn the question around and ask what risk analysts in the natural and technological disaster area can learn from terrorism risk analyses.

A Brief History of Risk Analysis

Modern risk analysis got its unknowing start in the area of reliability engineering. In the 1960s, aerospace engineers became interested in the likelihood of failure of complex missions, like the mission to the moon, and they experimented with new reliability tools like fault trees and event trees to gauge these risks. Risk analysis in the aerospace industry had a rocky history, with some notable failures (the poor estimate of the failure rate of shuttle missions) and some successes (the correct identification by risk analysts of losing heat-shielding tiles as a likely cause of shuttle failures).[3]

The breakthrough event of risk analysis was the study of nuclear power plant risks and the subsequent publication of the so called WASH 1400 report by the U.S. Nuclear Regulatory Commission in 1975.[4] Previous "worst case" analyses of nuclear power plant accidents had concluded that thousands of people would die in such an accident due to immediate high-level doses of radiation and, much later, due to low-dose induced cancer. Proponents of nuclear power and many scientists argued that one surely had to balance these catastrophic consequences against their extremely low probabilities. Thus the notion of scenarios with their associated probabilities and consequences was born and implemented in WASH 1400, the first full-fledged probabilistic risk analysis of a major industrial facility.

An innovation in WASH 1400 was the notion of *exceedance probability curves* that depict the probability of exceeding certain levels of consequences (for example, the probability of exceeding a given number of fatalities) as a function of the consequences. This was a useful tool, not only to describe the risk from one source, but also to put different types of risks—including natural and technological disasters—into perspective. The original exceedance probability curves of the WASH 1400 report are shown in Figure 11.1. In this example, the exceedance probability curves plot the annual frequency of exceeding a given number of fatalities for different types of disasters. (For example, the frequency of dam failures that result in more than 10,000 fatalities is 1 in 3,000 years.)

Since this seminal publication, risk analysis has been used routinely for assessing nuclear power plant safety[5] and risks and safety issues in other industries.[6] An important risk analysis was conducted on the Columbia Space Shuttle risks in 1995, several years before the actual shuttle disaster where the heat shielding tiles were identified as a weak element in the shuttle safety system.[7] Risk analysis also took hold in other industries, especially concerning the risks of accidents in industrial processing and storage plants (chemical, petroleum, liquefied natural gas) and with regard to the health and environmental impacts of pollutants.[8]

Meanwhile, a quite separate risk-analysis tradition had developed in the natural disaster area, starting with work by Gilbert White and

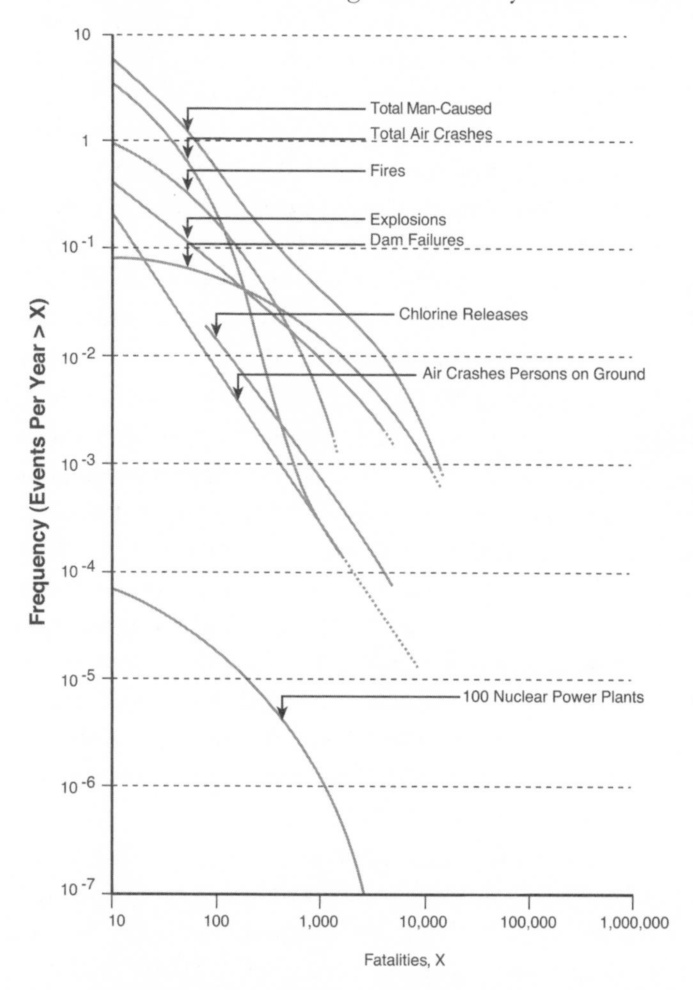

Figure 11.1 Exceedance probability curves for selected risks in WASH 1400 (Nuclear Regulatory Commission, 1975)

later Howard Kunreuther and his colleagues.[9] These researchers were primarily concerned with the risks and consequences of natural events like earthquakes, volcano eruptions, hurricanes, tornadoes, and floods. The technical tools were similar to those used in technological risk analysis: Statistical analysis of past events, development of exceedance probability curves, analysis of the costs and risk-reduction benefits of mitigation, and response and recovery options. There was also a significant emphasis on the role of insurance as an alternative to reduce the need for post-disaster relief and to encourage investments in mitigation measures.

By 2000, about 25 years after its early start with the WASH 1400 report, risk analysis was a mature discipline with its own society (Society for Risk Analysis), journal (*Risk Analysis: An International Journal*), and a broad multidisciplinary following. The medical community also had developed a strong risk-analysis component, which grew apart from the traditional risk-analysis community, with its own journal (*Journal of Medical Decision Making*) and conferences. The financial and business community also developed risk-analysis tools, for example, project risk analysis and options pricing, which were generally successful for "normal" financial and management transactions.[10]

When terrorists attacked the World Trade Center in New York on September 11, 2001, it was therefore natural to turn to risk analysis to assess the risks of terrorism and to evaluate the costs and benefits of policies to counter terrorism. Shortly after the U.S. Department of Homeland Security (DHS) was created in 2003, the first university-based center of excellence was awarded to the University of Southern California with a mandate to study the risks and economic impacts of terrorism. USC's Center for Risk and Economic Analysis of Terrorist Events (CREATE) immediately started to apply risk analysis and related tools to study terrorism risks, borrowing heavily from the models, mathematics, and tools of risk analyses of natural and technological disasters.

I was the cofounder and director of this center until 2009. Some of the experiences described here reflect the excitement and challenges of this early period of applying risk analysis to terrorism. Although terrorism risk analysis was very much informed by traditional risk analysis, there also were new challenges related to ability of terrorists to identify our vulnerabilities and to adapt to counterterrorism policies.

What Can Terrorism Risk Analysts Learn from Risk Analyses of Natural and Technological Disasters?

Former DHS Secretary Michael Chertoff embraced a risk-based approach to allocate government funds to reduce the risks of terrorism:

> "We have to identify and prioritize risks—understanding the threat, the vulnerability and the consequence. And then we have to apply our resources in a cost-effective manner...."[11]

The three elements of risk analysis mentioned in Chertoff's statement are closely related to scenarios, probabilities, and consequences previously identified as the building blocks of risk analysis. However, there are complications with translating the traditional risk-analysis paradigm to terrorism. First, the notion of "threat" is quite different from the notion of a rare but random natural event or a technological accident. Unlike nature or accidental failures of technologies, an intelligent adversary seeks out our vulnerabilities and tries to hurt us at a time and place where the damage is maximized. Furthermore, an intelligent adversary adapts to our defenses and sometimes uses them to his or her advantage. Some analysts, therefore, have concluded that traditional risk analysis is not applicable to terrorism[12] and look instead for new models and tools in game theory and related disciplines.

At the Center for Risk and Economic Analysis of Terrorist Events, researchers pursued several paths, including game theory and traditional risk analysis.[13] In line with traditional risk analysis, the team developed a framework that included threat and vulnerability as new elements in terrorism risk analysis. In this framework, which was closely linked to one proposed previously by the RAND Corporation,[14] threat is defined as a scenario of a possible terrorist attack with an attached probability. Vulnerability is defined as the probability of success, given an attack. Consequences are defined in terms of fatalities, injuries, and economic and psychological impacts that occur if an attack is successful.

Identifying and quantifying threats is the most difficult task. The CREATE team borrowed liberally from ideas developed in the military—for example, "red-teaming" (a war gaming method in which the "red" player acts out the role of the attacker and the "blue player" acts out the role of the defender) to develop credible scenarios of attack—and from intelligence agencies to identify the terrorists' intentions and capabilities, and possible paths of attack. We also used concepts and tools from project management to lay out a specific attack in the form of a complex project and analyzed its risks of failure and success.

A useful way to represent terrorism events is in an extended form of a game (a sequence of defender-attacker actions) in which the attacker chooses actions that are responsive to our defenses. We assume that the attacker's responses are probabilistic, with probabilities that change as a function of our defensive actions. A first implementation of this approach was an analysis of the costs and benefits of MANPADS (Man-Portable Air Defense Systems, or surface to air missiles) countermeasures proposed to protect commercial airplanes in the United States.[15]

Figure 11.2 shows the structure of the defender-attacker decision tree in the MANPADS analysis. At the root of the tree is the defender decision: whether to install MANPADS countermeasures on commercial airplanes. These countermeasures consist of devices that detect an incoming missile and use lasers to deflect its infrared homing system. They are expensive (about $30 billion life cycle cost for 5,000 large commercial planes in the United States alone) but also relatively effective. (The actual efficiency of deflecting missiles is classified, but anything less than 80 percent effectiveness would render the countermeasure useless for practical purposes.)

In this tree, squares represent chance nodes under the control of the decision maker. Circles represent decision nodes. Triangles represent consequences. The symbols below the branches represent probabilities or efficiencies of countermeasures. The x's represent the aggregate consequences, which are different at each end point of the tree.

The decision to install countermeasures is followed by a chance node indicating whether a terrorist group will attempt to launch a MANPADS weapon in the next ten years. The probability of this attack depends on the decision to use countermeasures. With "no countermeasures," it is denoted as p (a parameter varied over a wide range in the analysis); with countermeasures, it is denoted by $(1 - d) * p$, where d stands for the deterrence effect of the countermeasures. With 90 percent deterrence, the original attack probability would then be reduced by a factor of 10.

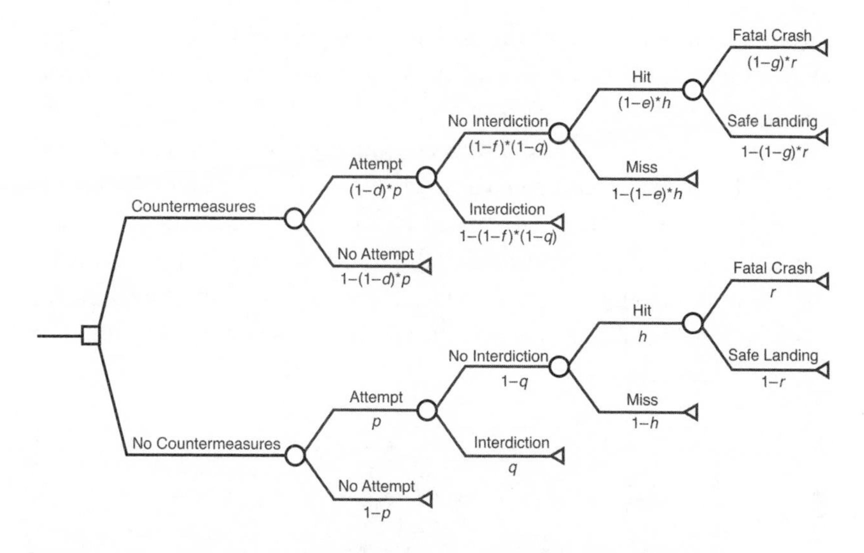

Figure 11.2 Defender-attacker tree for the MANPADS problem

The rest of the tree describes events that follow an attempt to use a MANPADS as a weapon to attack a commercial plane: The attempt could be interdicted, and if not, the launched missile could hit or miss the plane, and if it hits the plane, there could be a fatal crash or a safe landing.[16] The respective probabilities, given no countermeasures, are denoted with symbols in the lower part of the tree in Figure 11.2. With countermeasures (upper part of the tree), these probabilities are modified to account for the impact of the countermeasures. For example, the probability h of the plane being hit by the missile, is reduced to $(1 - e) * h$, where e stands for the efficiency of deflecting the missile with the countermeasure.

The MANPADS analysis illustrates one possibility for dealing with the unknown (or highly uncertain) probability of a specific threat. Instead of estimating the probability of a MANPADS attack, we parameterized this probability and conducted sensitivity analyses that varied it through its possible range from 0 to 100 percent. Even with this wide range, important lessons could be learned regarding the cost-effectiveness of MANPADS countermeasures. The analysis suggested that these countermeasures were not cost-effective at the estimated total life cycle cost of $30 billion. Figure 11.3 shows an analysis in which the national economic impacts of a MANPADS attack and the probability of an attempt were systematically varied through a large range and for each combination of the cost and probability the action (countermeasure versus no countermeasure) with the lowest expected cost was determined. In the lower-left part (low-probability, low-economic impacts), no countermeasures are preferred. To prefer countermeasures, the probability of an attack must be high (for example, above 0.50 in ten years) and the economic impacts must be high (above $200 billion). Most reasonable estimates are lower, thus suggesting that countermeasures are not cost-effective. Partly as a result of this analysis, the MANPADS program at the DHS was eventually canceled.

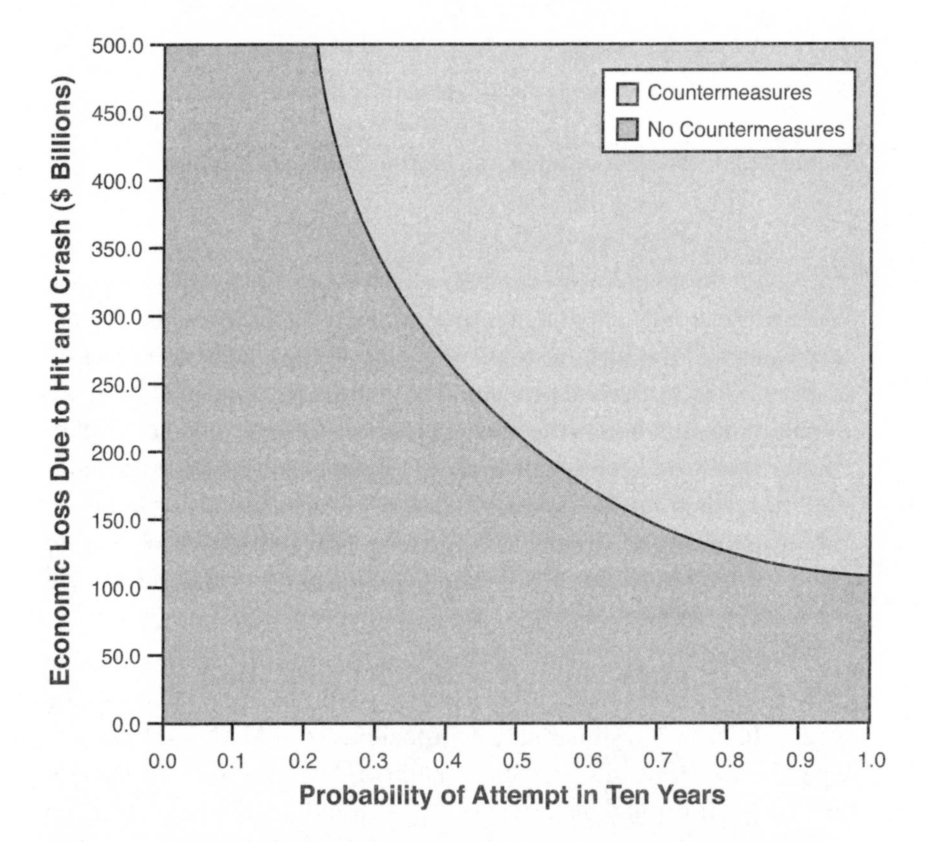

Figure 11.3 Sensitivity analysis of the probability of an attempted MANPADS attack and the economic impact, if the attack is successful (assuming $30 billion life cycle cost of countermeasures)

With natural and technological disasters, there is no concern about the motivation of the agents generating the initiating event—they are neutral and random. (A possible exception is sabotage in technological systems, which is, in fact similar in nature to terrorism.) In terrorism, the agents' motivation is important when considering their likely course of action. Therefore, a significant portion of the work at CREATE has been the study of terrorists' motivations. Using a rational decision-maker framework, we identified the values and objectives of terrorists[17] and a conceptual framework for quantifying their preferences.[18]

In line with the assumption that terrorists attempt to exploit our vulnerabilities, terrorism risk analysts are concerned with systemic risks, interlinked and interdependent systems, and ripple effects of an initiating event through the economy. Thus, several attempts were made at CREATE and elsewhere to quantify these broader risks, using both economic tools (input-output models and computable generalized equilibrium models) and behavioral studies.

The major lessons learned from less than a decade of terrorism risk analysis are as follows:

1. Threat scenarios and probabilities are still the most problematic part of terrorism risk analysis; studying terrorist motivations and capabilities and using expert judgments to assess initial relative threat likelihoods in response to our defensive policies seem to be promising.
2. Adaptive and dynamic decision trees seem to be a promising approach to study terrorism risks; in these trees, the defenders actions are optimized, but the terrorists' actions are modeled as probabilistic, but adaptive, as shown in Figure 11.2.
3. Vulnerability can be quantified as the probability of success, given an attack. This operational measure avoids many complications of defining vulnerability as a property of the attacked system, but it requires specific attack scenarios.
4. Consequence analysis seems to be similar for terrorist acts, natural and technological disasters. When the initiating event occurs, the progression of events, the spread of the agents that are being released, and the ultimate health and direct economic effects are well understood and traditional models can be used for this purpose.

5. Indirect economic effects can be large in terrorism events, primarily because of behavior changes resulting from the fear of a repeat attack. For example, after 9/11, there was a significant drop in air passenger volume, which accounted for total economic impacts exceeding those of the direct destructions of the World Trade Center and the tragic loss of life.[19]

What Can Natural and Technological Disaster Risk Analysts Learn from Terrorism Risk Analysis?

Terrorism risk analysts are using three novel techniques that may help improve risk analyses of natural and technological disasters:

- Red-teaming to enrich scenarios
- Emphasis on systems interlinkages, dependencies, and systemic failures
- Analysis of behavioral responses to disasters

Regarding the first area, it is interesting to note how many "surprises" risk analysts register after a disastrous event. For example, while the overtopping of the levees during Hurricane Katrina in New Orleans in 2005 surprised few, the levee failures had not been considered in the risk analyses by the U.S. Corps of Army Engineers, when building the flood protection system. To enhance the capability of risk analysts to "expect the unexpected" or to map out the "unknown unknowns," it may be useful to bring traditional risk analysts together with risk analysts who have been exposed to red-teaming and counterfactual argumentation, which is common in the military and intelligence communities.

Consider, for example, an elicitation of a probability function that mapped the pressure in a nuclear power plant containment (the concrete, usual dome-like structure that surrounds the reactor core and prevents escape of radioactive material) against the probability of failure.[20] When initially asked, the engineer stated that there would be a zero chance that the containment would crack at pressures below 120 pounds per square inch. When challenged, he stated that the design pressure was 100 pounds per square inch, and the additional 20 pounds per square inch provided ample protection. He was then told that there was evidence that a containment had cracked at 90 pounds per square inch, and he was asked to explain this. Even though this "evidence" was made up by the questioner, the expert's immediate response was: "That's easy to explain. It must have been faulty rebars or bad cement mix." He later lowered his assessment of the "zero risk pressure" to 90 pounds per square inch. It is this sort of counterfactual thinking that red-teams and intelligence analysts may be able to infuse into traditional risk analysis.

Terrorism risk analysts have spent a fair amount of research on systems interconnections and dynamic interactions, particularly in the infrastructure vulnerability area. In addition, terrorism risk analyses often consider multiple attacks on different parts of a system (for example, an attack on a regional electrical grid by disabling a substation, cutting a major transmission line, or conducting a cyber-attack on the electrical grid control system). Thus, there has been an accumulation of experiences of interconnected and coupled systems in terrorism risk analysis that can be beneficial for other types of risk analyses.

The systemic financial risk of 2008 and 2009 adds another dimension to studying risks in coupled dynamic systems. Neither risk analysts working in the natural or technological disaster field nor terrorism risk analysts had been prepared for this crisis. In fact, the traditional financial risk analysts had, by and large, ignored extreme events and certainly had underestimated the ripple effects throughout the worldwide financial system. Developing a better understanding of systemic risks and of the closely coupled, interlinked, and interdependent systems is an important task for future risk analysis of all kinds. Risk analysts will have to work more closely with network theorists, dynamic systems modelers, and behavioral researchers to develop appropriate models for these types of systemic risks.

Understanding and predicting human behavior is an important element in all risk analyses. Because terrorists attempt to instill fear and insecurity, behavioral changes are an important part of the analysis of the psychological and economic impacts of terrorism. Studies on the impacts of the 9/11 terrorist attack on air travel behavior[21] found $100 to $200 billion in GDP losses due to fear of flying, less air travel, and the resulting ripple effects through the economy. Similarly, a dirty bomb attack on the twin ports of Los Angeles and Long Beach could cost as much as $26 billion per month due to fear of radiation and the resulting port shutdown.[22] It is important that future impact studies in the natural and technological disaster area also include an assessment of psychological, business, and macroeconomic impacts of disasters.

Conclusion

Risk analysis is a mature discipline that consists of theories, models, and techniques to quantify a wide range of risks, from natural disasters, to technological accidents, to terrorism. Risk analysis can provide important information about the cost-effectiveness and cost-benefit information of risk reduction measures to policy makers.

When risk analysts first attempted to apply their methodology to terrorism, they borrowed heavily from traditional approaches, including event trees, fault trees, and decision trees. They also found the need to modify risk analysis because, unlike nature and technologies, the terrorists are not neutral or behave randomly, but they are purposeful and adaptive adversaries. Dynamic and adaptive decision trees methodologies proved to be a useful approach to study terrorism risks. Other methods, based on game theory and decision theory, are currently developed and tested.

Just as terrorism risk analysts can learn from traditional risk analysis, the reverse is possible, too. Red-teaming, analysis of ripple effects of risks through interlinked and interdependent systems, and analysis of behavioral responses as a key driver of consequences are now common in terrorism risk analysis and can also benefit traditional natural and technological risk analyses.

The world will remember the first decade of the twenty-first century for three extreme events: the terrorist attack on the World Trade Center in New York City, which killed 3,000 people and changed the way a nation looked at its own security environment; the tsunami in Southeast Asia, which killed 300,000 people and changed the way we look at natural disasters, especially in developing countries; and the financial meltdown of 2008 and 2009, which changed the way we are looking at systemic risks across the world. These three events also highlight the need for better and more sophisticated risk analysis that includes considerations of extreme events, interlinked systems, and behavioral responses that can magnify consequences of disasters.

12

Turning Danger (危) to Opportunities (机): Reconstructing China's National System for Emergency Management After 2003

Lan Xue, School of Public Policy and Management, Tsinghua University

Kaibin Zhong, China National School of Administration

Overview

This chapter provides an overview of the efforts in building a new national system for emergency management (NSEM) in China after the Severe Acute Respiratory Syndrome (SARS) crisis in 2003. The weaknesses in the old system hampered the response to SARS and amply demonstrated its vulnerabilities and weaknesses in dealing with unexpected and catastrophic disasters. Consequently, over the past several years since the SARS crisis, a number of measures have been put into action to radically reconstruct the NSEM. A systematic approach was taken to change the old practice of dealing with different kinds of emergencies separately by different government agencies to a new approach that is aimed at building a risk-based, all-hazards, and integrated national system for emergency management. The new NSEM is based on four key elements: the contingency plans at national and regional levels; institutional mechanisms that are dedicated to coordinate emergency management among different levels of government and agencies; operational procedures in dealing with these activities; and an Emergency Response Law dedicated to emergency management. The catastrophic disasters in 2008 in China and the responses by China's new NSEM have shown the effectiveness of the new system while at the same time posted new challenges that will provide new directions for reforms of the current NSEM.

Introduction

Since the founding of the People's Republic of China in 1949, China developed a national system for emergency management (NSEM). This system, the Chinese NSEM 1.0, was departmentalized—the governance of risks and disasters was handled by different ministries or bureaus according to the nature of the disasters. For example, the China Earthquake Administration was responsible for earthquake-related disasters, the China Meteorological Administration was responsible for meteorological-related disasters, the Ministry of Water Resources was responsible for floods and droughts, the Ministry of Health was responsible for epidemic diseases or public health-related accidents, and the Ministry of Public Security was responsible for terrorist threats and social unrest. There are also corresponding organizations in the local governments at all the levels in China. The main characteristics of this system were the strong vertical/sector line of command and the weak horizontal coordination.[1]

The traditional NSEM 1.0 was relatively effective in planning for, mitigating, and recovering from routine natural and man-made disasters with which decision makers are experienced and familiar. For example, under the leadership of the State Council, China lunched its largest national mass mobilization in more than 40 years during the flooding of the Yangzi River in 1998, a flooding that killed more than 3,000 people and affected 2.3 million people. Top national leaders were on the frontlines of disaster relief work, and more than 280,000 soldiers and 5 million army reservist were deployed for relief work across China's southern provinces.[2] However, in facing nonroutine and unpredictable catastrophic disasters like SARS in 2003, the weaknesses of the traditional emergency management system became apparent. Chinese leaders began to take decisive actions only after the tardy and ineffective response from November 2002 to February 2003, when SARS spread from Guangdong Province into Hong Kong and many other cities in mainland China.

The failure of the traditional system in dealing with the emergency at the beginning of the SARS episode and the potential devastation of the epidemic have provided strong incentives for the Chinese government to change the system radically. The Chinese word for *crisis* is made of two characters, 危 (danger) and 机 (opportunity), which shows the Chinese perspective on the dialectic nature of crises. China's effort in restructuring its national system for emergency management after SARS crisis in 2003 is a good illustration of how a danger can be turned into opportunities.

After SARS, a systematic approach was soon taken to change the old practice of dealing with different kinds of emergencies separately by different government agencies to a new one that is aimed at building an integrated national emergency management system. The first section of this chapter provides a general background for the analysis of emergencies management system in China. The chapter then provides a review of the weaknesses of the traditional NSEM and discusses how these weaknesses were hampering the response to SARS. We then cover the efforts made by the Chinese government and society in building up the national emergency management system since 2003. The discussion then analyzes new challenges to the current system and points to improvements needed for moving to NSEM 3.0.

Weaknesses in the Traditional Model: Lessons from SARS

When the first case of SARS originated in the city of Foshan, Guangdong Province, in November 2002, nobody thought that within just a matter of weeks the epidemic would quickly spread from the Guangdong Province to 24 provinces, autonomous regions, and municipalities on the Chinese mainland, and that it would eventually infect individuals in some 37 countries around the world.[3] According to the World Health Organization (WHO), the SARS virus infected 8,098 people and killed 774 worldwide—mostly in Asia—before it was brought under control in June 2003.[4] It was officially reported that in mainland China alone more than 5,300 people were sickened and 349 died of the disease, with more than half of those in the capital, Beijing, the hardest-hit city in the world.[5]

The epidemic of SARS represents a new type of threat that is faced by our global society in the twenty-first century.[6] At the early stage of the SARS crisis, the Chinese government agencies—particularly the government of Guangdong Province and the Ministry of Health—were criticized for concealing information about the SARS virus for the first 4 months after it emerged in Foshan, 95 miles northwest of Hong Kong. People were wondering why it took from November until mid-April before the Chinese leadership exercised decisive action in dealing with SARS. The tardy response of the Chinese government to the challenge of the SARS virus reflects the weaknesses of Chinese traditional NSEM 1.0, which are analyzed in this chapter.

Low Organizational Cognitive Capabilities

The Chinese NSEM 1.0 had its advantage in dealing with those familiar and routine disasters that happen with a degree of regularity, thus allowing decision makers and relevant government agencies to anticipate and prepare for them accordingly. For example, in flood and drought mitigation, earthquake mitigation, tide protection, and so on, which are common and predictable in China, the Chinese government and lead agency had prepared contingency plans in advance and used them "in the moment" with adaptation at the margin.[7] However, when faced with unfamiliar disasters, the major challenge to the government was diagnosis and assessment. The core problem of nonroutine disaster management is to recognize and react to novelty, and to develop skills in problem diagnosis, improvisation, communication, and collaborative action.[8] Predetermined actions may be inadequate and possibly counterproductive in such crisis situation. The epidemic of SARS unfortunately happened to be the first severe and easily transmissible new disease to emerge in the twenty-first century.

It is not easy to identify a new virus, and it is especially difficult in southern China where SARS originated. Scientists found that the area had been the point of origin for a number of flu outbreaks, and the close proximity of livestock with humans made it ripe for producing new strains of disease.[9] Thus, with presumably mutating strains occurring each year, it was difficult for local health officials to decide what was important and what was not. It was even more difficult for any local hospital to spot a case of this new atypical pneumonia when around 100 patients each month enter hospital intensive care wards with severe pneumonia. Being inadequate in recognizing and addressing SARS as a new and dangerous virus, the Guangdong government and health officials from Ministry of Health considered the disease to be atypical pneumonia with nonvital consequence. They were quite optimistic about their ability to control the situation. Even as late as February 9, 2003, when a total of 305 SARS cases were identified (105 of them in healthcare workers), the Chinese health officials still insisted that, according to the analysis of epidemiology and clinical characteristics, this epidemic of atypical pneumonia was preventable, controllable, and treatable.[10] Therefore, after an initial flurry of rumors in late 2002, the mysterious disease seemed to disappear until early 2003, when it resurfaced in Vietnam and Hong Kong.

Because the disease appeared to be limited to Guangdong (one administrative jurisdiction), a national response was not triggered until early April 2003. Not before April 8 was it clear that this was no longer a "local" phenomenon but a new disease with serious adverse consequence. The Chinese Ministry of Health (MOH) began to list SARS as a statutory epidemic. On April 20, when the epidemic of SARS—originally a domestic health emergency—spun out of control and threatened global health and economic stability, the Chinese government began to take prompt and decisive actions to contain the spread of the virus. At that point, however, the SARS virus had spread to many provinces in China and dozens of other countries. Therefore, the inability of the government to recognize the severity of SARS and the over confidence of its capability in controlling the disease combined to result in the failure of the Chinese system to respond to the problem earlier.

Lack of Organizational Communication and Coordination

The SARS case also evinced the lack of communication and cooperation between health authorities in Beijing and Guangdong, between different government agencies, and between civilian and military sectors. During the early stage of the fight with the SARS outbreak in 2003, interagency and interregional conflicts became a major challenge. Information about the virus and subsequent fatalities were delayed by bureaucratic infighting and protectionism, which also precluded the coordination between regional government and organizations.

The conflict between different sectors and regions is an important factor that accounted for Beijing's failure to deal with SARS at the early stage. Because of the special status as China's political and cultural capital, Beijing has to deal with different sorts of conflicts between Beijing Municipality and the central government. At the early stage of the SARS crisis, the Guangdong provincial government did not share information with Beijing or other affected areas. Guangdong provincial authorities knew of the deadly disease at least as early as the beginning January 2003. They issued guidance in January that was ambiguous enough so as to avoid disruption of the New Year holiday. By late January, Guangdong leaders officially reported the situation to Beijing, but underreported the rate of infection and recommended Beijing to impose a media blackout.[11] Nor did the army share information with Beijing openly and in a timely fashion. There is evidence that by early January 2003, at least some in the General Hospital of the People's Liberation Army (PLA) in Beijing were aware of the seriousness of the disease. However, the information was not shared with the government in Beijing in a timely fashion. According to Chinese law, the army didn't have to report the disease to local governments.

Inadequate Information Disclosure and Public Communication

In times of disaster, the Chinese government used to control the disclosure of information to the public in a very tight manner so as to "avoid confusion and panic." Relevant officials described the heightened controls as *Neijin Waisong,* meaning "tight inside while appearing lax from the outside."[12] This policy worked relatively well in the past, because the government could ostensibly avert panic in a time of disaster when the public channels of information were narrow and heavily controlled. However, times have changed. In today's globalized and information-based world, a fundamental tension is growing between a system structured to control and manage the flow of information and a society that is information savvy and "wired." Modern communication technology has revolutionized the free flow of information and rendered such an approach outdated. This has made it increasingly difficult for the Chinese government to present situations of crisis as small and local events that are fully under control when the reality was otherwise.

That failure to communicate with the public effectively was dramatically demonstrated in the early stages of the SARS episode. The SARS disease was spreading rapidly in parts of China—despite repeated government claims to the contrary. Poor public communication caused public confusion about the new disease. As one survey conducted on February 12, 2003 demonstrates, nearly half of the people in Guangzhou City, the capital of Guangdong, got information from their friends and relatives, and the overseas media also served as a very important information source for the public.[13] A comparative analysis of the number of the reports about SARS by the four most important mainstream news agencies in China (*People's Daily*, *Brightness Daily*, *CCTV*, and *China Daily*) found that the mainstream mass media had carried few reports about SARS before the end of April.[14]

At the early stages of SARS, Chinese MOH maintained the stance that there was a small problem but that basically all was under control. For example, it was officially reported by MOH on April 6, 2003, that 19 people had been infected in Beijing, with 4 deaths, and that the rate of new cases in Guangdong had more than halved in the past month. However, the figure was not accepted by the public or the WHO. A Chinese military doctor, Jiang Yanyong, took the highly unusual step of publicly contradicting the authorities, claiming that at least nine people had died in Beijing's four military hospitals.[15] The growing unease of people in China corresponded with international criticism of China's handling of SARS and the belief that hospitals and officials were covering up the real extent of the outbreak. It was not until April 20 that the Chinese health authority slowly regained its reputation and confidence, as the central government launched an investigation into the true size of the epidemic and took extensive measures to curtail its spread, including firing China's health minister and the mayor of Beijing in a bid to demonstrate accountability and transparency to the public and international community.

Restructuring a New National System for Emergency Management: Chinese NSEM 2.0 After SARS

A number of prominent policy studies have pointed out that "focusing events" may provide windows of opportunity for policy change—once a focusing event or occurrence gets on to the policy agenda, policy makers will pay a significant attention to it, which will lead to the development of new institutional arrangements to forestall the future occurrences of such problems and establish and maintain political or policy equilibrium.[16] Although being the first serious test for new Chinese leaders since completing the leadership transition in March 2003, the SARS crisis also provided the new leaders with an opportunity to push forward their own political agenda. After winning the "war on SARS," the Chinese new leadership soon urged the adoption of more vigorous measures to accelerate the improvement of China's public health system. On June 17, 2003, while presiding over an experts meeting on the subject of the public health system, Premier Wen Jiabao said that the nation will definitely recover its losses from the crisis as it continues to make progress—the most important point is to learn from past experiences and lessons.[17]

Following the SARS crisis, Chinese leaders have realized the critical need to enhance the capacity of contingency planning and emergency management, particularly at the local level. Therefore, a systematic approach was taken to build a risk-based, all-hazards, integrated national emergency management system. The Chinese NSEM 2.0 is based on four key elements: the contingency plans at national and regional levels; institutional mechanisms that are dedicated to coordinate emergency management among different government agencies; operational procedures in dealing with these activities; and an Emergency Response Law dedicated to emergency management.

Creating a New Institutional Structure Nationwide for NSEM

One major initiative to create a sound emergency management system in China since SARS has been the creation of a new institutional structure nationwide for national emergency management.

According to the Emergency Response Law of the People's Republic of China, which became effective on November 1, 2007, China began to establish an emergency response management system featuring a unified leadership, comprehensive coordination, categorized management, graded responsibility, and territorial management.

In December 2005, a national level Emergency Management Office (EMO) of the State Council was officially established. This office provides a framework for a comprehensive emergency management program that directs planning, preparation, response, and recovery. The EMO functions as an operational hinge and serves as an enabling interagency liaison at the national level for all emergency management and national security program activities through the State Council. It takes charge of the daily work of the national emergency management system, responds to public security events, collects real-time information, and coordinates the related departments in fields of manpower, finance, material resources, transportation, medical care, and communications, and so forth. Expert teams were formed, when necessary, to offer suggestions on decisions during the emergency response work. By the end of 2005, emergency response offices had been set up by health departments in 27 provinces, autonomous regions, and municipalities across China.[18]

Based on this new systematic model, various types of emergencies were divided into four categories: natural disasters, accidental disasters, public health incidents, and social safety incidents. The State Council is the top administrative institution in managing public incidents and carrying out emergency responses. Each category has a corresponding national-level government committee in charge: the National Committee for Disaster Reduction to manage natural disasters, the National Committee for Work Safety to manage industry accidents, the National Committee for Food Safety to manage public health incidents, and the National Committee for Integrated Management to manage public security. Such "one office and four committees" formed China's primary disaster management system.

In addition, permanent emergency management organizations have also been established in relevant ministries, such as the Health Emergency Management Office and the Chinese Center for Disease Control and Prevention (Ministry of Health, MOH), the National

Disaster Reduction Center of China (Ministry of Civil Affairs, MOCA), the Chinese Supervision Center for Work Safety (State Administration of Work Safety, SAWS), and so on. At the local level, there are corresponding emergency management organizations in accordance with the arrangement at the national level. In the past several years, the local emergency management center and the committees for the four categories of emergencies have been gradually established. Therefore, different agencies ranging from the central to local governments work together in a system of "unified leadership combining vertical and horizontal agencies" in which the central agency at the national level provides vertical control from above to below while the local authority provides overall daily surveillance of and response to disasters.

The new general contingency plan, which was drafted since the SARS crisis in 2003, grades emergencies into four levels, represented by the colors blue, yellow, orange, and red (with the threat level ranging from the least to the most severe), based on such factors as the character of the incident, degree of harm, controlling possibility, and scale of influence, except as otherwise provided for by a law or administrative regulation or the State Council.[19] Accordingly, a unified leadership, multilevel management, and multilevel responsibility administrative model of emergency management is designed to deal with four categories of disasters so that the power and responsibility are hierarchically shared by and graded into different levels of governments. This means that the emergencies from the most to the least severe are managed by the central, provincial, municipal, or prefecture governments in each county, respectively. China's new institutional structure nationwide for NSEM 2.0 is illustrated in Figure 12.1.

Drafting Nationwide Contingency Plans

Alongside the efforts to create a new institutional structure nationwide for NSEM 2.0, the Chinese government has also taken it as a major priority to develop a nationwide contingency plan system. This contingency plan system was envisioned to cover various emergencies at different levels of the government throughout the country. First, the State Council of China was responsible for drafting the master national contingency plan. Second, the relevant ministries in the State Council drafted the ministerial contingency plans in their respective capacities in line with the master contingency plan at the State Council level. Third, the local governments at all levels (including provinces, cities, and counties) and their relevant departments would draft the corresponding contingency plans in accordance with the relevant laws and administrative regulations. In addition, the lower level governments also had to make sure their contingency plans are in line with the contingency plans at higher level of governments.

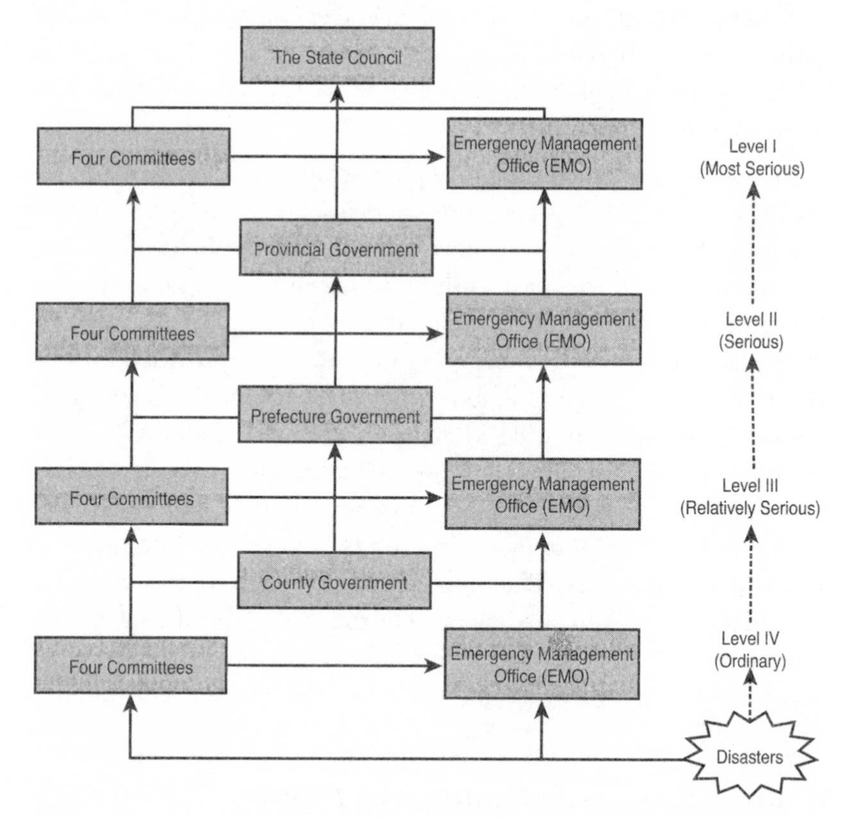

Figure 12.1 The new institutional structure nationwide for NSEM 2.0 in China

Beginning in December 2003, the State Council, China's Cabinet, created the Master State Plan for Rapid Response to Public Emergencies (the Master Plan) for emergency responses, which became a guide for the prevention of and response to various emergencies in China. After a year's effort, this general emergency response plan was endorsed in principle by the State Council. This new general contingency plan serves as the overall guideline and the criterion for the national emergency response system. If faced with new emergencies, the Chinese government will promptly initiate an effective response mechanism to ensure the safety of life and property.

The Master Plan emphasizes the establishment of an emergency mechanism based on classified management, different levels of responsibilities, and the coordination and combination of professional/technological departments and the local government at all levels, with the latter taking the lead to formulate an emergency forecast and response mechanism with unified command mandates for rapid reaction and high efficiency. It clarifies the classification and framework of the public security events and prescribes the organization system and operation mechanism for major emergency responses.

Thus, the Master Plan has become an overarching guide for a countrywide emergency response system. After completing the Master Plan, the State Council also instituted and issued 25 specific emergency response plans that cover areas such as natural disaster, flood, earthquake, geological disaster, major forest fire, work safety accident, railroad accident, civil aviation accident, salvage and rescue at sea, city subway accident and disaster, large-scale blackout, nuclear accident, environmental emergency, telecommunication emergency, public health incident, emergency mechanism for medical assistance, animal disease outbreak, critical food safety accident, food security, financial incident, and overseas incident. Major functional departments of the State Council, such as the Ministry of Health, Ministry of Agriculture, and Ministry of Public Security, have developed and implemented 80 sector-specific plans.

The Master Plan, the 25 specific emergency plans, and the 80 sector-specific plans constitute an overall system that covers those recurring major disasters in China. Moreover, all local governments, from provincial, municipal, and prefecture governments, to district and county, have already developed their own emergency plans.[20] Such initiatives prescribe action plans at the local level for municipal government or any enterprise that may get involved in large events. Communities, rural areas, and relevant enterprises and institutions are also required to draft their own contingency plans. The contingency plans increase both the capacity of and coordination among the hierarchy of first responders. It was officially reported by the Emergency Management Office of the State Council that, by the end of 2007, the total number of nationwide contingency plans had reached more than 1.3 million. All provincial governments, 98 percent of prefecture-level governments, and 93 percent of county-level governments had drafted their own general plans. By March 2009, 51 emergency plans at the national level had been developed. In addition, 138 major state-owned corporations and all mining- and chemical-related corporations had developed emergency plans, too. Figure 12.2 shows the overall system of China's nationwide contingency plans.

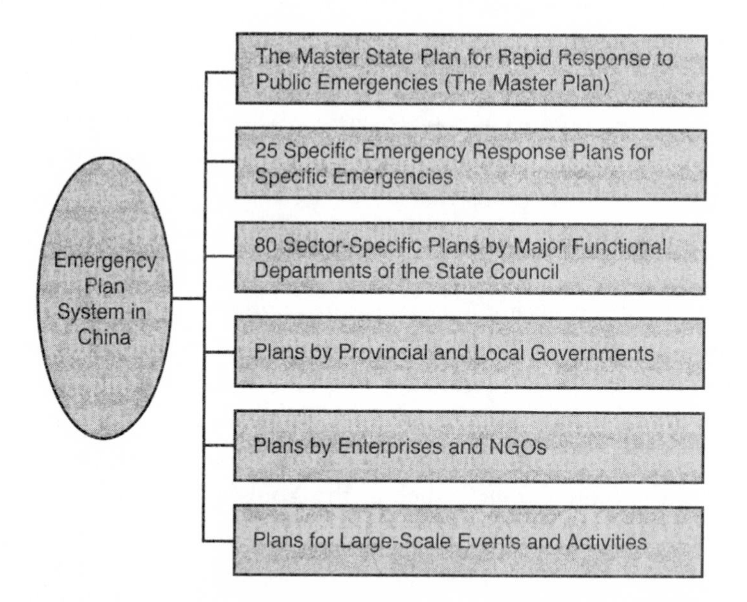

Figure 12.2 The system of nationwide contingency plans in China

Improving Mechanisms in Responding to Emergencies

Another initiative of the Chinese government to create a comprehensive emergency management system involves a number of improvements to operating mechanisms that respond to emergencies. According to the Master Plan and the Emergency Response Law, China should apply a standard operating procedure when responding to various disasters. The operation mechanisms consist of the following: prevention and emergency response preparedness, surveillance and warning, emergency response operations and rescue, and post-emergency response rehabilitation and reconstruction.

China has made great efforts to integrate activities of the sectoral and regional authorities. It is required by law that during the disaster period, the emergency management committees and their offices at all levels be in charge of the emergency response, acting as the enabling agents for the interactions among various government agencies and social organizations. They should work together with the civil affairs departments, the public security departments, the public health departments, the army, and so forth to deal with the emergencies swiftly. According to the "graded responsibility and territorial management" model, emergencies at different grades would be dealt with by government at different levels. The more severe the situation, the higher the grade, and the higher level of government that would be required to respond. In such a way, the sectoral and horizontal authorities are integrated to ensure that rescue task forces, relief supplies, funds, and information are in place to address the immediate need of the emergency response.

The information reporting and sharing system has also been reconstructed after SARS. On May 7, 2003, the State Council issued the Regulation on the Urgent Handling of Public Health Emergencies. This regulation formulated rules for the emergency report of paroxysmal accidents, and established an information report system for important and urgent diseases. Article 21 of the document stipulates that "No entity or individual may conceal, delay the report, or make a false report or hint any other person to conceal, delay the report, or make a false report of any emergency." On November 7, 2003, MOH issued "Measures for the Administration of Information Reporting on the Monitoring of Public Health Emergencies and Epidemic Situation of Infectious Diseases." According to the Master Plan, if a Class I (most serious) or Class II (serious) emergency happens, it should be reported to the State Council within 4 hours.[21] Article 39 of China's Emergency Response Law also stresses that, "The emergency incident information submitted or reported by the relevant entities and persons shall be timely, objective and true, and any act to delay the reporting, falsify the reporting, conceal the reporting or omit the reporting of such information shall be prohibited."

Accordingly, on December 30, 2007, the General Office of the State Council issued the notice on "Tentative Measures for the Administration of Information Reporting and Sharing on Public Emergency," providing the detailed requirements concerning the conditions, procedure, and time required for reporting disasters.

As an acknowledgment of the need for an effective communication channel between the government and the public, the central government required that all national and provincial departments should establish a "spokesperson and news-briefing system" for crises situations. In 2004, up to 70 ministerial organizations under the State Council and 20 provincial governments had a designated spokesperson for communicating with the public during situations of disasters.[22] On May 1, 2008, the Regulation on the Disclosure of Government Information came into effect. This regulation stipulated that governments at various levels and their departments at or above the county level shall establish and improve a government information disclosure working system and set up an office of government information disclosure of their respective administrative organ. As of August 2005, China declassified information on human fatalities from natural disaster, reversing a practice that had lasted for years.[23] Information pertinent to emergency management at the national level can now be found on the government's official website (www.gov.cn/yjgl/index.htm), which was launched on January 1, 2006.

As demonstrated by the SARS crisis, in a globalized world, disasters originating nationally can easily cross national borders. Better collaboration with the international community has also been acknowledged as imperative by the Chinese government. Article 15 of China's Emergency Response Law stipulates that the Chinese government "shall carry out cooperation and exchange with foreign governments and relevant international organizations in such respects as emergency prevention, surveillance and warning, emergency response rescue and operations and post-emergency response rehabilitation and reconstruction." Some important steps have been taken in this regard. For example, in January 2005, the Chinese government hosted the China-ASEAN Workshop on Earthquake-Generated Tsunami Warnings. In 2006, the World Health Organization Collaborating Center on Community Safety Promotion in Shandong Province instituted China's first "international safe community," which became the ninety-seventh designated safe community in the world.[24]

Drafting a New Emergency Response Law

In addition to the efforts mentioned already, the Chinese government has taken a number of measures to improve the legal framework for managing emergencies. On May 7, 2003, the Regulation on the Urgent Handling of Public Health Emergencies was passed at the seventh Executive Meeting of the State Council. This regulation put together all the government needs to combat SARS and other similar situations. It has become a fundamental regulation for future development of detail emergency plan in different tactical fields.

In March 2004, an amendment to China's constitution replaced the term *martial law* with *states of emergency*, allowing for a more inclusive legislative context that ensures action for a wider variety of emergency situations including natural, public health, and economic crises.[25] Under this amendment, the president of the People's Republic of China is entitled to declare a state of emergency. This amendment provides basic support for a law on emergency management. The constitutional amendment also stipulates that the State Council has the power to proclaim a state of emergency in sectors of provinces.[26]

In June 2003, after winning the SARS battle, the Chinese government initiated an effort to draft a new "all-hazards" emergency response law. After several years' hard work, the Emergency Response Law of the People's Republic of China was finally adopted at the twenty-ninth session of the Standing Committee of the Tenth National People's Congress in August 2007. The law came into effect on November 1, 2007. The law is a major milestone of emergency management system in China.

New Challenges and the Way Forward

As discussed previously, SARS has led the Chinese government to build a new national emergency management system, NSEM 2.0. As demonstrated by the snow crisis in southern China in early 2008 and the Sichuan earthquake on May 12, 2008, the Chinese NSEM 2.0

has both strengths and weaknesses, and to some extent it confirmed its effectiveness in dealing with both traditional and nonroutine disasters. However, as demonstrated by these natural calamities in 2008, the Chinese NSEM 2.0 is also facing a number of new challenges.

New Challenges to the System

The year 2008 witnessed a number of major emergencies in China, with the snowstorm at the beginning of the year in southern China and the Sichuan earthquake in May. Although NSEM 2.0 played a vital role in combating these two major disasters, these natural calamities also exposed the weakness China's existing national emergency management system.

First, although NSEM 2.0 has made great improvements in establishing an overall framework in addressing emergencies, the performance of such a system is still dependent on the competence and capabilities of the organizations and individuals in the system, as well as technological sophistication of the supporting infrastructure of the system. For example, Chinese weather experts admitted that they were not properly prepared for the snowstorms in early 2008, that left hundreds of thousands of people stranded at the New Year holiday. The head of the Chinese Meteorological Administration, Zheng Guoguang, conceded that "in northern China we have quite a good emergency plan to cope with unusual weather conditions; but in southern parts of China, the mechanism and emergency plan to cope with such weather needs to be improved."[27]

Second, NSEM 2.0 has put a great emphasis on the development of contingency plans and standard operating procedures, which could be useful for routine emergencies. However, for unusual major disasters such as the snowstorm in southern China and the Sichuan earthquake, these contingency plans and standard operating procedures proved much less useful (and in some cases might even hinder effective response).[28] For example, during the snowstorm in southern China, a major challenge was how to deal with the thousands of cars stranded on the highway, which were covered with thick ice. The contingency plan for highway safety management during snowstorms was to block the road so as to avoid highway traffic accidents. Most of the highway management stations followed this plan. One county in Guizhou Province, on the other hand, decided to open the road and direct the traffic to drive slowly on the highway. This not only helped reduce the pressure on the traffic network, it also, because of the continuous traffic on the road, helped alleviate the accumulation of ice.[29] Clearly, the flexible response was much more effective than following the contingency plan blindly. How to add flexibility and to allow improvisation in a more structured and standardized NSEM 2.0 is a difficult and interesting challenge that should not be ignored.

Third, China's public administration system is run under a vertical management system that suffers from bad horizontal coordination and communication. NSEM 2.0 has not solved the problem of how to coordinate among different ministries, between ministries and local governments, and among different local governments. The snowstorm evinced the conflicts between neighboring provinces of Guangdong and Hunan, between the military and local governments, between Guangdong government and the Ministry of Railway, and among different ministries. To effectively resolve some major problems in coal and oil shipments when the transportation system was paralyzed by the snowstorm, the State Council had to set up a separate Emergency Command Center for Disaster Relief and Coal, Power, Oil, and Transport Assurance at the National Development and Reform Commission.

Fourth, civil society is ostensibly inactive in China's emergency management system. To a large extent, NSEM 2.0 has not been able to incorporate the nascent nongovernment organization (NGO) sector into the existing emergency management system. The government is still at an early learning stage on how to mobilize and work with the NGOs effectively. Although NGOs played important roles in disaster relief work in the earthquake in Sichuan, the uncoordinated activities of NGOs and volunteers were also criticized for having created chaos and obstacles for professional disaster relief agencies to move in quickly. It was widely reported that in the first few days after the earthquake, the massive influx of uncoordinated and less-trained NGOs and volunteers may have caused traffic jams, which in turn delayed the transportation of essential supplies, disrupted life-saving operations, and increased the logistic burdens on the relief system. And, then, these volunteers and NGOs ran the risk of becoming victims themselves.

Moving into NSEM 3.0: Major Issues to Resolve

As demonstrated by the snow crisis and Sichuan earthquake, it is a continuing learning process to develop and maintain a risk-based, all-hazards national emergency management system that prevents, prepares for, responds to, and recovers from major threats. If SARS was the "danger" that was turned into the "opportunity" to develop NSEM 2.0, the snowstorm in southern China and the Sichuan earthquake in 2008 could be thought of as the "dangers" that could help to promote the "opportunity" to develop NSEM 3.0.

To move into Chinese NSEM 3.0, China should deepen its governance structure reform and provide a more robust and easily adaptable framework in time of disasters. The weakness of the traditional national emergency management system can be resolved comprehensively only within a national reform program dedicated to integrating social development with economic development, improving the cooperation and exchange between different levels of government and agencies, and enhancing broad participation and rule of law that will help encourage local governments to be more transparent and accept greater accountability. More specifically, both multidepartmental coordination and central-local governmental harmonization should be encouraged and institutionalized. Another key reform is to further clarify the facilitating and coordinating role of a central emergency management agency that can work effectively to enable government ministries to respond to various emergencies more effectively. Such an agency can also be set up at local government levels.

Also, the government needs to shift its approach in disaster management from one of reactive mode toward preventive mode. When facing unexpected catastrophic disasters, China responds by setting up headquarters in a reactive mode. Their first option is a reactive strategy, acting slowly and postponing any reaction until clear evidence implicating the government is made public. Therefore, the disaster management mode should change from reactive to proactive and become more vigorous. The critical elements of a reactive and preventive emergency management system should include risk identification and assessment, risk mitigation and management, and open communication about potential risks between the public and decision makers. Such a system can be implemented only with robust political support to create an environment whereby all competent authorities, institutions, and officials are willing to be accountable for their actions.

Another measure toward the promotion of a risk-based, all-hazards national emergency management system entails building greater social capital. The monitoring, prevention, and handling of various disasters require not only actions of the government, but also that of the whole society. Through the social networks and partnerships, government can mobilize civil society to help prevent and respond to crises. At the same time, the public can also better understand the rationales behind various policies related to emergency management. Overall institution building will rely heavily on the formation of such social networks and the partnership. To date, the potential value of NGOs and other nonofficial players has largely remained untapped in China.

Moreover, as China is becoming part of the global community, the governments should also develop an international network of contacts, associations and relationships in dealing with catastrophic disasters. Marshall McLuhan's thesis of an increasingly integrated and interdependent global community is ever more tangible in times of disasters.[30] As coping with emergencies is a worldwide phenomenon and disasters increasingly spill over national borders and affect regional and international orders, China should learn to become an active member of the international community in the field of disaster management.

In addition, China needs to improve the training and education in disaster prevention and relief, emergency management, and self-protection and self-rescue. It is necessary to provide a multilevel model exercise designed for progressive training of emergency management staffs, and to educate the public. China can also learn about emergency management systems from international norms and best practices through international cooperation and partnership.

As demonstrated by the progress made after SARS crisis in 2003, China has been able to take advantage of crises as a catalyst for change, turning "danger" into "opportunities."[31] We are sure that emergencies in future years could provide further impetus for institutional reforms that will contribute to the development of NSEM 3.0, which will serve as a safeguard for the economic and social development in China in the coming years.

13

Dealing with Pandemics: Global Security, Risk Analysis, and Science Policy

Jiah-Shin Teh and Harvey Rubin
Institute for Strategic Threat Analysis and Response, University of Pennsylvania

Overview

Low-probability, high-consequence biological events may result in tremendous loss of lives, livestock, and property, and often exact a serious toll on the social, economic, and political health of the communities involved. Examples of low-probability, high-consequence biological events include pandemic influenza, the Black Plague pandemic, and the smallpox epidemics early in the first millennium. One current example is the ongoing plague of HIV/AIDS.

This chapter discusses measures for enhancing preparedness against low-probability, high-consequence biological events. Earnest collaboration between governments, private corporations, academia, and ordinary citizens need to be established, and there must be incorporation of effective technologies for information sharing, biomedical research, and development, as well as policy formulations. We will also delve into how a regulatory framework or compact can enhance all these interconnected areas and allow better feedback, coordination, and guidance.

Introduction

Significant progress has been made against infectious diseases. Basic science research has contributed to a deeper understanding of the pathogenesis of many diseases. The advent of antibiotics in the last century has enabled successful treatment of diseases that were once incurable and frequently lethal. Advances in clinical practice, public health and epidemiology gave rise to accurate diagnostic tests and effective measures to curb the spread of disease.

However, critical challenges still exist: Resistance against many of the current lineup of antimicrobials is increasing across many microbial species worldwide; threats of various pandemics continue to exist as exemplified by the current H1N1 outbreak; and infectious diseases continue to devastate many developing countries and threaten developed nations no longer buffered in this interconnected world. The Global Burden of Disease Study indicates that infectious diseases account for 22 percent of all deaths and 27 percent of disability adjusted life years, with a disproportionate impact on the developing world.[1]

The HIV/AIDS pandemic, for example, claimed the lives of 2.1 million people in 2007 out of a total of 33.2 million living with HIV, while 2.5 million were newly infected.[2] *M. tuberculosis* remains the deadliest bacterial pathogen worldwide, causing an estimated 1.7 million deaths in 2004 among an infected population of approximately 2 billion people, according to the World Health Organization (WHO). In 2004, malaria is endemic in a total of 107 countries and territories, putting a total of 3.2 billion people at risk.[3] Approximately 350 to 500 million clinical disease episodes occur annually and over 80 percent of the deaths occur in sub-Saharan Africa, where most victims are children under 5 years of age. In addition to acute disease episodes and deaths, these diseases also contribute significantly to morbidity, which in turn impacts the socioeconomic future of the countries involved. For example, malaria was estimated to be responsible for an estimated average annual reduction of 1.3 percent in economic growth for those countries with the highest burden.

It is a therefore paradoxical situation in that in spite of progress in medical science, diseases are emerging and/or re-emerging, either as adaptations of existing diseases that lose their responsiveness to current treatment regimes or as new diseases caused by previously unknown pathogens. In fact, the overall situation in controlling naturally occurring infectious diseases has actually deteriorated for a number of interrelated reasons, such as:

- Increase in antibiotic-resistant bacterial infections, worsened in part by incorrect prescription practices, increased availability, and lay use of counterfeit antibiotics.
- Sparse pipeline of new molecular entities that lead to effective anti-infective agents as large pharmaceutical companies have, in many cases, abandoned anti-infective drug development and discovery.
- Although antiviral research and development is progressing, work developing antibacterial, antifungal, and especially antiparasitic agents lag far behind.
- Absence of harmonized regulatory processes, both intra- and internationally, hinders rapid development of anti-infectives.
- Woefully underdeveloped distribution of anti-infective agents to clinics and patients in many parts of the world.
- Inadequate infrastructure for rapid and accurate diagnostic testing in the developing world.
- Incomplete global infectious disease surveillance and reporting and inadequate shared, interoperable, real-time databases.
- Agencies working for increased access to anti-infective agents must coordinate goals and policies with agencies that work to limit the emergence of resistance to anti-infective agents.
- Insufficient number of well-trained medical workers that are necessary to ensure proper diagnosis, prescribing, and monitoring practices, especially in developing nations.
- Lack of consideration of zoonotic and food borne infections in the increased incidence of the spread of infectious diseases.
- Increased incidence of national insurgencies and of failed states which might resort to acquiring biochemical and biomedical weapon capabilities.
- Globalization: economic globalization, demographic globalization (urbanization and refugee movement), technological global changes, and environmental/climate global changes that

alter patterns of communicable diseases, frequently in unpredictable ways.

- New threats from the emergence of new research in synthetic biology from the synthetic creation of new infectious agents, the reintroduction of infectious agents that no longer exist in nature, or in generating infectious agents that exist in nature but are hard to isolate.

In addition, deliberate spread of infectious diseases is a major national security concern, facilitated by advances in biotechnology that has made it easier to nefariously manipulate infectious agents for enhanced pathogenicity and spread.

This appropriately leads us to consider low-probability, high-consequence biological events. We define these as natural or man-made catastrophic events involving infectious or other biological agents that result in significant loss of life, livestock and property. They include epidemics or pandemics of dangerous pathogens, as well as deliberate acts of bioterrorism. As with any serious cases of infectious disease, they exact a debilitating burden on the socioeconomic health of societies. As illustrated by Table 13.1, the financial costs of some recent infectious disease crises were staggering, which places enormous pressures on affected countries. The Congressional Budget Office predicted in 2005 that a potential H5N1 influenza pandemic would cost at least $600 billion to the United States.[4] The analysis indicated that in the near term there will be a "sharp decline in demand as people avoided shopping malls, restaurants, and other public spaces, and a shrinking of labor supply as workers became ill or stayed home out of fear or to take care of others who were sick." Depending upon the scope of the pandemic, short-term economic effects could rise to the level of the average postwar recession.

TABLE 13.1 Economic Consequences of Naturally Occurring Diseases

Disease	Costs
Avian Flu, Hong Kong 1997	$100 million dollars in lost poultry production; air travel declined by 22%
Bovine Spongiform Encephalopathy, UK 1995	$9-14 billion dollars
Cholera, Peru 1991	$775 million dollars lost in ban on seafood exports

TABLE 13.1 *Continued*

Plague, India 1994	$2 billion dollars; half a million people displaced; aviation and tourism shut down
Potential H5N1 Influenza, United States	$600 billion dollars (Congressional Budget Office Report)

However, the effects of low-probability, high-consequence events are not confined to economics—disruptions occur in practically all aspects of society. There is physical suffering, lost workdays, and unmet social responsibilities for the afflicted individuals; for the community, anxious behavior may translate into altered daily patterns, reduced interaction and assistance, and disrupted school operations; for public infrastructure, there may be strained medical services, reduced commercial productivity, and interrupted municipal work; and for the military, there may be impaired readiness and responsiveness. For example, such disruptions were apparent during the SARS epidemic, which led people in China to minimize their travel, business meetings, and other social interactions, including attendance for China's Canton Export Exhibition, which generated far fewer visitors and contract deals than previous years.[5] In Hong Kong, the epidemic also caused hospitals service disruptions, and affected a total of 386 healthcare workers out of the cumulative tally of 1,755 cases of SARS in the province.[6]

International development scholars have described the role that serious infectious disease plays in the perpetuation of poverty in the developing world: destroying family structures and limiting economic and educational opportunities.

Preparedness is paramount. Modern medicine has definitely made great strides against disease, but advancing dual-use research of concern (legitimate biological research that could be misused to threaten public health or national security)[7] and factors outlined in Table 13.1 should give anyone pause before ruling out infectious disease as a serious threat to any society. Clearly, globally integrated infectious disease surveillance and control is an essential part of national and international security with far-reaching impacts on linked, global economies, not just public health. As stated in the 2006 *National Security Strategy:* "Public health challenges like pandemics (HIV/AIDS, avian influenza)...recognize no borders. The risks to social order are so great that traditional public health approaches may be inadequate, *necessitating new strategies and responses....*" (Italics added)[8] Given the level of interconnectedness, the challenges call for new solutions that integrate basic science, technology, and social, political, legal, and economic realities (see Figure 13.1). Paradigms of solutions against infectious disease must focus on the health of the *global* population.

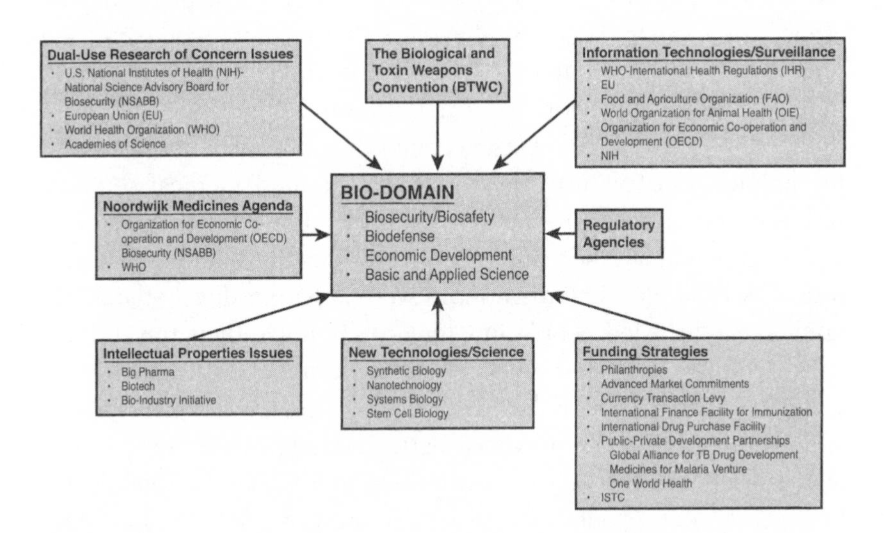

Figure 13.1 The multidisciplinary realities confronting infectious disease control

Infectious Diseases: An Enduring Threat

It is important to note that infectious agents are an enduring threat to mankind. Certain mechanisms in nature enable them to continually evolve and be recurrently pathogenic, and these mechanisms may be facilitated by some of mankind's activities. For example, antibiotic resistance would occur naturally but is accelerated by the widespread use of antibiotics in livestock farms. The main mechanisms are

- **Random genetic mutation:** Infectious diseases were never quite conquered by modern medicine. Rather, the advent of antibiotics and antivirals in the last century merely kept them at bay for a *limited* time. The pathogens responsible for infectious diseases are robust microorganisms that have the capacity to randomly mutate over time and alter their characteristics, from metabolic pathways to the structures of individual protein molecules, thereby allowing them to gradually and eventually evade the very drugs developed against them in the first place.

- **Sharing of genetic information:** Infectious disease pathogens readily share (or horizontally transfer) their genetic information, including ones that confer a growth or survival advantage. Bacteria exchange genetic elements with other strains via processes such as conjugation, transformation and transduction.[9] Some scientists have even postulated that sharing in Mycobacterium tuberculosis can occur between interkingdom strains[10] or even with eukaryotic cells.[11] Different viral strains exchange genetic segments when coinfecting a common host such as birds, a phenomenon called genetic reassortment.

Globalization has led to the near-ubiquity of modern transportation and trade routes, to the extent that it also resulted in the globalization of regional infectious diseases. Therefore, to better appreciate the risks of biological events, we need to know where threats may specifically come from. Four main categories of concern are indicated in Figure 13.2: increasing antibiotic resistance, misguided agricultural practices, emergence of new and old infectious diseases, and dual-use research of concern. Together, the categories essentially represent a definite biological arms race, both by nature and by mankind itself, against society.

Antibiotic Resistance

Microbial antibiotic resistance is facilitated by improper antibiotic use in clinical medicine and agriculture. In the clinical setting, inappropriate choice, insufficient dosing and duration, patient noncompliance, or even overuse/nonindication are attributed factors, whereas indiscreet use of antibiotics in livestock farms is also an important cause. These factors lead to sublethal selection pressure on the targeted bacterial, fungal, or protozoal microbe. This allows a hardy subset of the pleomorphic[12] microbial population to survive and replenish, and therefore opportunity for random genetic mutations over subsequent replication cycles. These mutations lead to the encoded protein targeted by the antibiotic becoming more structurally divergent from its original form, causing the antibiotic to lose its potency. The resistant microbial strain passes on their genetic advantage to subsequent progenies and even spread it to other microbes via conjugation or transduction.[13] This sequence aptly exemplifies microbial ability to rapidly evolve in response to selective pressures in their environment, if the initial instance of antibiotic application is not administered correctly.

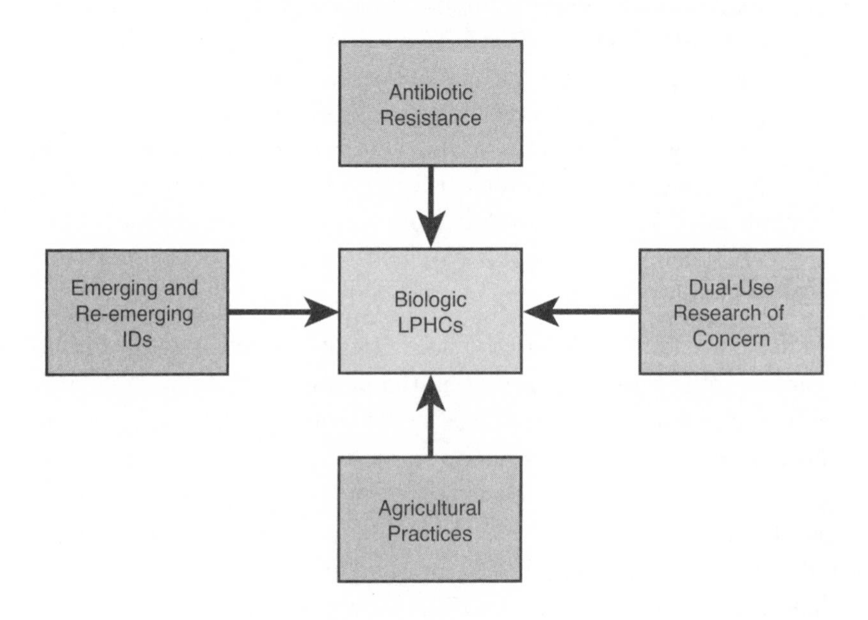

Figure 13.2 The factors contributing to risk of biological low-probability, high-consequence events

Globally, antibiotic resistance is becoming more prevalent, and the problems posed by it more serious. For example, in the United States, approximately 2 million people per year acquire healthcare-associated infections (HAIs), out of which 70 percent are resistant to at least one first-line antibiotic, according to the Center for Disease Control and Prevention.[14] Examples include *Acinetobacter baumannii* (wound infections), *Mycoplasma pneumonia* (atypical pneumonia), *Clostridium perfringens* (gas gangrene), *Staphylococcus aureus* (wound infection), *Bordetella pertussis* (whooping cough), *Pseudomonas aeruginosa* (burn wounds and pneumonia), and *Streptococcus pyogenes* (cutaneous infections and necrotizing fasciitis). Antibiotic-resistant microbes require more expensive and often more toxic second-line drugs, and the Institute of Medicine (IOM) predicted that the extra cost to the U.S. healthcare system due to antimicrobial resistance is at least $4 to $5 billion annually,[15] although another study estimated between $30.3 and $40.3 billion in extra costs for both bacterial and HIV antibiotic resistance.[16]

For many diseases, antibiotic resistance results in increasing microbial prevalence and associated morbidity and mortality. Examples include tuberculosis, where increasing resistance against first- and second-line drugs by the multidrug-resistant (MDR) and extensively drug-resistant (XDR) strains have led to increased death rates among sufferers, especially in sub-Saharan Africa where AIDS is rampant. Malaria spread across Africa is again on the rise due to drug-resistant *Plasmodium falciparum* and *Plasmodium vivax.* Methicillin-resistant strains of *Staphyloccocus aureus* and vancomycin-resistant *Enterococci faecium* are becoming more frequent and serious causes of HAIs with high morbidity and mortality.

Certain microbial resistance is even developing for all currently available antibiotics, which essentially necessitates a post-antibiotic strategy in which antibiotics unfortunately play little role in combating the disease. The problem is exacerbated by the scarcity of new compounds in the antibiotic development pipeline. As long as new drugs remain unavailable, as long as flawed prescription practices continue, and as long as misguided farming methods are not rectified, treatment failures will continue and result in an ever-growing pool of carriers harboring resistant microbes, which in turn poses significant risks of spread to the rest of the general population as exemplified by the increasing prevalence of resistant strains in the community.[17]

Experts fear that in the worst-case scenario, society may eventually face epidemics of "super-bugs" or bacteria that are resistant against every single antibiotic currently available, where healthcare professionals will not have strong antibiotic options to effectively treat patients with infections, and where hospitals will instead be hotspots for the spread of dangerous super bugs, thereby affecting all of society and its enterprises. Several major medical associations have warned that antibiotic resistance is the most serious problem facing the medical community. The Food and Drug Administration, Centers for Disease Control and Prevention (CDC), and U.S. Department of Agriculture have all increased their surveillance activities related to antibiotic resistance, an example of which is the CDC's National

Antimicrobial Resistance Monitoring System that reports on the number and type of antibiotic-resistant isolates of enteric bacteria, their associated resistance rates, and trends in resistance.

Agricultural Practices

Agricultural practices impact negatively on the risks of biological events on three principal fronts: (1) the indiscriminate use of antibiotics in livestock farming and to a lesser extent, horticulture; (2) the close confinement of animals in modern livestock husbandry, and (3) the central position of animal farms in the food chain.

Animal farms can be considered an ecologic niche in its own right, and certain diseases are endemic due to the type of animal reared and the closed system of contact networks and organic waste. They are reservoirs for microbes such as *Salmonella spp.* (predominantly in chicken), *Escherichia coli* (cow), *Campylobacter coli*, and *Yersinia enterocolitica* (pig). A microbial profile study of three diary herds in the northeastern United States found that in addition to *E. coli*, there were also a rich variety of other medically important microbes such as *Salmonella, Campylobacter, Listeria,* and *Mycobacterium avium paratuberculosis* present in the farms.[18] Spread occurs to the public through consumption or contact and causes mini-epidemics in the community that can also contaminate the local hospital and even become a permanent part of community flora. There are many examples of well-documented cases of mini-epidemics involving *E. coli,*[19,20] *Y. enterocolitica,*[21,22,23] *Salmonella,*[24] and other microbes originating from animal farms.

There is widespread use of antibiotics intended for disease prevention and growth promotion in livestock farming. A 1992 Institute of Medicine report indicated that approximately half the amount of antibiotics produced in the United States was used in livestock farming.[25] This rampant use without strict guidelines invariably leads to selection pressure and the development of antibiotic resistance in livestock-associated microbes, the mechanism of which was previously explained. The close confinement endured by animals in most modern farm facilities makes it easy for antibiotic-resistant microbial strains to spread and renders control difficult to achieve. In 1998, the

CDC reported that a strain of *Salmonella* called *typhimurium DT104* emerged in the United States in the preceding two decades, which is resistant to five different antibiotics (ampicillin, chloramphenicol, streptomycin, sulfonamides, and tetracycline).[26] The CDC attributed the emergence to the widespread use of antibiotics in livestock. The *DT104* strain was estimated to have caused between 68,000 and 340,000 cases of infection annually in the United States.

The close confinement of animals in livestock farming can also precipitate infectious disease. Having different animals in close contact may lead to significant interactions between pathogens inherent in these animals. Certain pathogens that are able to infect multiple species, such as the influenza virus, may be more likely to encounter different strains and undergo genetic segment exchange that yields a new strain. Pigs, for example, can serve as mixing vessels when infected by both human and avian influenza strains. Pandemic influenza viruses, which have historically originated in China, may have been due to the integrated pig-duck agriculture, prevalent in certain parts of China for several centuries.[27]

In addition, effort at infection control will need to be stepped up on farms. The most effective preventative measures must be researched and information shared among counties, states, and nations. Serologic and bacteriologic testing must be regimented to detect and respond to infection. Transmission routes need to be determined and livestock movement within the breeding pyramid will need infection control checks to categorize herds and establish and maintain pathogen-free segments. Establishing and maintaining specific pathogen-free breeding pyramids are indeed possible, as illustrated by a study in Norway of pig herds free of *Y. enterocolitica O:3/biovar 4* since 1996.[28] Finally, monitoring systems will need to be established to ensure quality control and innocuous microbial content of livestock feeds.

Dual-Use Research of Concern

Life sciences research has accelerated immensely in the last few decades. Technologies such as automated DNA sequencing have helped to decipher the human genome and the genomic sequences of bacteria, viruses, and protozoa, generating more questions and motivating scientists toward advanced specialties and sophisticated technologies.

The implications of such advances are just as great for constructive use and destructive potential. These advances are hence termed *dual-use research of concern*. For example, advances in systems biology can inform scientists on how bacterial pathogenicity can be attenuated, but also identify for the nefarious individual the cellular pathways which trigger toxin production. Synthetic biology provides the tools for the construction of modified micro-organisms or their derivatives for constructive as well as destructive purposes. Bionanotechnology poses unknown environmental, health, and safety impact of nanoscale constructs. The importance of occupational safety and health issues in nanotechnology has been emphasized by the interagency working group on Nanotechnology Environmental and Health, Implications under the Nanoscale Science, Engineering and Technology Subcommittee together with the National Institute for Occupational Safety and Health in 2004.[29]

There is real likelihood of a bioterrorism attack if such knowledge and technologies are in the possession of nefarious actors. The Congressional Commission on the Prevention of WMD Proliferation and Terrorism stated that "terrorists are more likely to be able to obtain and use a biological weapon."[30] Indeed, acts of bioterrorism have occurred in the past, as documented below from 1940 to 2004.[31]

1940–1941 China: Hangzhou and Nanjing

Japanese aircraft dropped packages containing fleas infected with *Yersinia pestis*. There are reports of several other such episodes later. Recent testimony was given in a Tokyo court by one of the aircraft pilots.

1957–1963 Brazil: Mato Grosso

Introduction of smallpox, influenza, tuberculosis, and measles into Indian tribal populations via contaminated gifts and mestizos was used in furtherance of large-scale land takeovers. Such instances were detailed in the Figueiredo report (1968), which led to the indictment of 134 employees of the Government Service for the Protection of Indians.

1981 United Kingdom: Chemical Defence Establishment (CDE) Porton Down, Wiltshire

"Dark Harvest Commandos" deposited outside a defense research facility a parcel of soil containing anthrax taken from a former bioweapons proving ground. The perpetrators provided their own account and CDE's soil analysis confirmed presence of *Bacillus anthracis* at less than 10 org/gram.

1984 United States: The Dalles, Oregon

Rajneeshee cultists sought to influence local elections by infecting voters with *salmonellosis* through contaminating neighborhood restaurants. This was followed by subsequent medical investigation that revealed 751 persons affected.

1989 Namibia: Near Windhoek

A covert operation was done by a South African government agency, the Civil Cooperation Bureau (CCB), to contaminate the water supply of a refugee camp with cholera bacteria. This was revealed through the perpetrator's testimony during a recent trial of Brigadier Dr. Wouter Basson.

1990–1993 Japan: Tokyo

Aum Shinrikyo cultists, prior to their 1994–1995 sarin attacks, sprayed biological agents including anthrax, against several U.S. and other facilities in and around the city, but with no discernible effect. Confessions and other information were contained in leaked police reports.

2001 United States

The U.S. Postal Service was used by perpetrators to spread anthrax spores contained in letters addressed to individuals in the media and the U.S. Senate; 22 cases of cutaneous or inhalational forms of anthrax ensued with 5 deaths; 10,286 receive post-exposure prophylaxis; and many more had their daily lives disrupted. Medical investigations were coordinated through the Centers for Disease Control and Prevention.

To complicate matters, information technology has allowed knowledge of these advances to be made available on the Internet. For example, nearly everything related to biology/life sciences, biotechnology, laboratory protocols, and operation of equipments can be retrieved. It is nearly impossible and futile to try to regulate information flow; the challenge is to determine how to organizationally and collectively prepare for the future in a dynamically changing technological environment, with a focus on preparedness and mitigation.

Emerging and Re-emerging Infectious Diseases

Our immune system serves as the main defense against infectious disease. It is an adaptive biological system that coevolves with disease pathogens. Upon encountering a particular microbial strain, specific proteins uniquely expressed by the strain act as an inducer for the immune system to develop, in a span of about a week, antibodies that bind to the proteins and specialized white blood cells that assist in the killing of the microbe. The effectiveness of our immune system therefore depends on the range of microbial pathogens to which we have been exposed. Disease is therefore more likely when the pathogen in question is novel, for example, one to which our immune system has not yet encountered. This background helps explain the concept of emerging and re-emerging infectious diseases. These are diseases in which the causative pathogens have long been known to man but have newly acquired the genetic novelty to evade our immune system and cause disease, thereby increasing in incidence and geographic range. They also include new diseases caused by pathogens never before encountered as a result of increased encroachment into untouched ecological systems such as forests and wildlife habitats. Finally, they include diseases by pathogens that are poorly immunogenic (for example, do not trigger the immune system to react to them) and pathogens so toxic that disease occurs in spite of the immune system.

Many of the emerging and re-emerging diseases are zoonotic (that is, originate at areas of interface between humans and animals at specific endemic locations throughout the world, including agricultural locations; see Figure 13.3). A review of emerging infectious

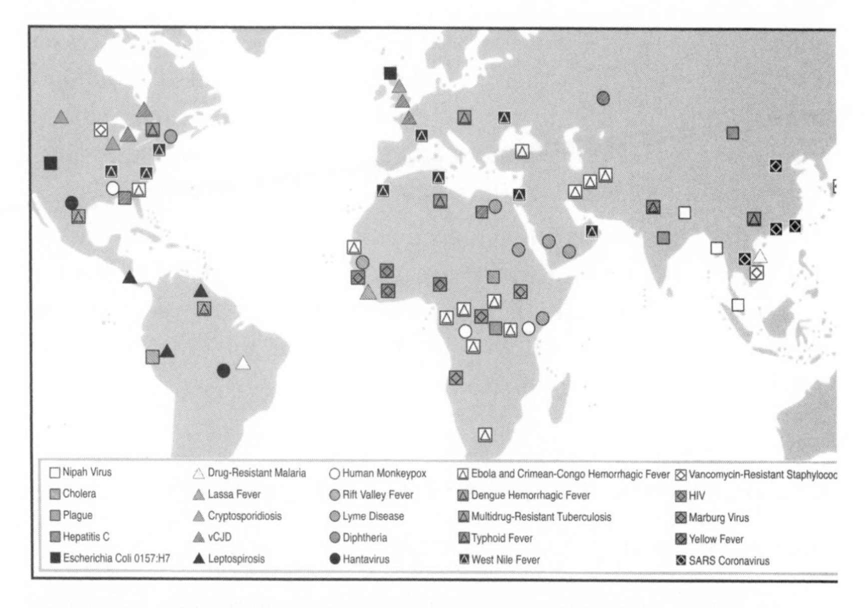

Figure 13.3 Map of emerging and re-emerging infectious diseases around the world (compiled using data from WHO and the National Institute of Allergy and Infectious Diseases)

diseases from 1940 to 2004 found that zoonoses account for approximately 60 percent of emerging infections, out of which roughly 71 percent is linked to a wildlife source.[32] In these hotspots such as Central America, tropical Africa, and south Asia, pathogens are highly prevalent in the fauna of the local ecological system.

This is evident from the list of outbreaks of emerging and re-emerging zoonotic diseases across the globe, especially in the tropical latitudes, in the past decade. These include avian influenza H5N1[33] (Asia, in particular Hong Kong), Nipah virus[34] (Malaysia, Bangladesh), Yellow fever[35] (Ivory Coast), hantavirus[36] (United States), West Nile fever[37] (United States, Canada, Middle East), ebola[38] (Gabon, Congo), monkey pox[39,40] (United States, Congo), SARS[41] (Global), rabies[42,43] (Brazil, India, China), Crimean-Congo hemorrhagic fever[44] (Afghanistan, Iran), tuleremia[45,46] (United States, Kosovo), *E. coli* 0157:H7[47,48] (United States, Canada), and BSE-vCJD[49] (U.K., United States, Canada). This list does not include the worsening epidemics of HIV/AIDS and tuberculosis, and epidemics of animal diseases such as foot and mouth disease, Exotic Newcastle disease, or swine fever that have devastated agricultural economies around the world during the same period. With worsening climate change, it is expected that more emerging and re-emerging diseases will manifest themselves as the tropical latitudes expand.

Half of the zoonotic infections that have arisen have involved the United States and there is every reason to believe that the threat of disease outbreaks from these or similar pathogens will continue. Indeed, we are as susceptible as we ever were to the diverse range of pathogens that exist in nature.

Preparedness Against Biological Events

Hallmarks of Infectious Disease

To plan appropriate preparedness and mitigation measures against biological events, the main characteristics of serious infectious diseases need to be considered.

Most infectious diseases originate at areas of interface between humans and nature/agriculture, and there are discernable hotspots of specific infectious diseases throughout the world, especially in lower-latitude developing countries.[50]

A local disease will be a global disease unless proven otherwise. Without intervention, the spread of infectious diseases can very quickly extend globally due to highly developed transportation and trade networks, as well as the rising number of refugees from lesser-developed countries and the increased movement of people from rural to urban areas. For example, the spread of the H5N1 avian influenza virus to most of Asia and to parts of Africa was facilitated by trade in infected poultry[51] and exotic birds, while the global spread of SARS from Hong Kong was greatly enhanced by air travel.[52] These factors are highlighted as point number (1) human demographics and behavior; and (4) international travel and commerce, by the IOM.[53] The most important hallmark of serious infectious diseases is the easy spread from human to human. When disease is established, spread is mainly a function of the human-human contact networks that exists in society as well as the mortality and transmission rates of the diseases. The bottom line is that disease pathogens will spread in any way they can, even through highly processed goods such as food products and medical materials such as blood and tissues.

Disease pathogens may evolve over time as they spread throughout the human population, constituting nonlinear public health threats. An excellent example is the influenza virus that causes regular annual epidemics due to antigenic drift (minor mutations) in a previously circulating strain. A slight change in a surface protein, usually the hemagglutinin (H) protein, allows the new strain to reinfect previously infected persons because the altered surface protein will no longer be recognized by the immune system. Many scientists believe that the present H1N1 influenza virus strain will be more virulent this coming winter.

Spread of disease may not just be human to human, but may also involve human to animal, adding another layer of complexity in the transmission and evolution of the pathogen. Continuing with the H1N1 example, evidence now points to the possibility that humans can pass H1N1 infection back to swine,[54] which makes curtailing spread difficult. In addition, this may impact the respective livestock industry with economic consequences.

Recommendations

Infectious disease control is a national and international security priority that demands multidisciplinary effort involving public health, epidemiology, clinical medicine, public policy, law, and many other fields. Many excellent measures against infectious disease and biological events need to be, and have been, implemented. However, the efforts are highly uneven from a global distribution perspective: Developed countries are heavily invested in infectious disease preparedness, whereas lesser-developed and Third World countries languish far behind. The international community must address this inequality especially because these countries are often the source as well as victims of devastating diseases. We highlight the broad categories of preparedness and mitigation measures that need to be funded and implemented in all countries:

1. **Public health improvements**

   Improving public health includes establishing clean water and sanitation systems, without which infectious pathogens, such as *Vibrio cholera,* can spread easily. An estimated 3.575 million people die from water-related diseases each year.[55] In addition, immunization programs must be established and funded, and vector control measures must be put in place. Emphasis must be place in developing countries and inner cities of developed nations where high population densities facilitate disease spread.

2. **Public health education on hygiene practices, health planning, sexual behavior, and handling of animal products**

   An excellent example of effective public health education is promoting public awareness of the danger of stagnant water as a breeding ground of mosquitoes, and hence a facilitator of diseases such as malaria. Sex education was shown to reduce the prevalence of HIV in Uganda and condom promotion reduced sexually transmitted diseases in India (WHO).

3. **Disease surveillance/biosurveillance**

   This includes training of health workers and educating the public to recognize signs and symptoms of infectious disease, and how to bring these to the attention of relevant authorities. It also includes using the most effective and cost-efficient diagnostic technologies for rapid and accurate disease testing.

4. **Establish public health measures and epidemiology protocols**

   Control of infectious diseases requires prompt and effective contact tracing and quarantine of contacts, and immediate prescription of the necessary antibiotics, antivirals, and vaccines. Workers who fall ill must be reminded to avoid public places and to stay at home. City- or even organization-specific contingency plans must be well communicated precrisis.

   In diseases caused by new agents whereby workable diagnostic tests and treatment are not yet available, surveillance and quarantine serve as the key tools in disease control.

5. **Information sharing**

   Includes sharing of vital information between localities, regions, and nations at the onset of any disease outbreaks, and the technological as well as the legal and political infrastructure with which information is shared. Progress in this area has not been entirely smooth sailing. For example, under the so-called viral sovereignty principle espoused by Indonesia, nations own any viruses that they discover within their boundaries and have the right to refuse sharing them with the World Health Organization or any other country. This notion was conceived following years of distrust stemming from Indonesia's claim that rich countries such as the United States took advantage of poorer nations in the interest of drug-company profits and intranational interest. Since 2005, Indonesia has not allowed access to their H5N1 strains thought to have emerged subsequently in that country.

Ultimately, early reporting of outbreaks of infectious disease to neighboring countries/regions and to the WHO is essential to prevent international spread.

6. **Evidence-based clinical practice**

   Includes adopting best practices for control of infectious diseases, including directly observed therapy, routine screening with proven diagnostic tests, and antibiotic-resistance testing.

7. **Research and development**

   Includes the vital antibiotic/antiviral discovery and development pipeline, vaccine development, basic science research, and research into best practices in public health and epidemiology. For example, it was research into best epidemiological practice that yielded the discovery that entry screening is not effective in reducing importation of SARS by air travel.[56] Antibiotic development is perennially important in the fight against the ever-evolving bacterial pathogens. In addition, advanced hybrid specialties must be encouraged to produce new technologies to combat infectious diseases. For example, network models and simulation technologies combined can help map and predict spread of disease, and identify main routes of transmission.

8. **Safe and Secure Laboratory Practices**

   The infectious disease laboratory is both the driver of novel exploratory experiments and the repository of sensitive samples and materials. As highlighted by the Bruce Ivins/Fort Detrick case, there is a critical need to ensure adequate security of laboratories against both insider and outsider threats through robust employee screening, management of security clearances, active peer monitoring, strict laboratory security, and employee training to prevent misuse of materials. The issue of personnel reliability is important especially as current laboratory security standards might not be sufficiently reviewed and updated. There needs to be initiatives, by both the federal and the nongovernmental sector, to improve security at facilities worldwide and to develop and implement universal standards of safe laboratory practice.

9. **Sharing of treatment resources**

   Treatment resources such as drugs must be directed to areas that need them the most. Effective control of infectious disease requires channeling adequate countermeasure resources to outbreak areas to promptly bring the disease under control.

10. **Ensuring adequate medical and ancillary medical personnel**

    One of the most important requirements for infectious disease control is having enough medical personnel to help diagnose and treat patients. Public health specialists and epidemiologist must be available for conducting contact tracing and providing prophylaxis.

11. **Sensible land use**

    Extent of deforestation must be tailored according to both the resource needs of the country in question as well as to sustainability requisites. On a global scale, forests are essential depots of biodiversity. Many of the antibiotics that improved public health in the last century were derived from forest organisms that have coevolved alongside dangerous zoonotic pathogens; area conservation is essential for discovering further classes of chemical compounds effective against pathogens in future. Policies surrounding deforestation must ensure that the measures to control zoonotic infections are put in place and if possible, conserve areas rich in biodiversity from development as a means to minimize encroachment and prevent the emergence of new diseases.

An International Compact for Infectious Diseases

There is much progress to be made to control infectious disease. In addition to lagging antibiotic development, preparedness suffers from the lack of adequate biosurveillance, public health improvements, resource sharing, basic science and field research, and global coordination of these efforts, among many others. In terms of strategies, one of the key aspects of disease control is availability and accessibility of vital information. Therefore, a robust and refined central information database is needed to enhance biosurveillance, research preparedness practices, and to share critical knowledge and treatment resources.

We propose a new approach, a strategy based on the creation of a unique International Compact[57] for Infectious Diseases (the Compact) distinguished by

> **Compact Core Mission I:** Establish, maintain, and monitor a shared international data and knowledge base for infectious diseases, including but not limited to biosurveillance information, basic research data, relevant pharmaceutical data, and suites of services and skills.
>
> **Compact Core Mission II:** Establish, maintain, and monitor a network of international basic science research centers that will support fundamental investigations into the pathophysiology of certain microbial threats to global health.
>
> **Compact Core Mission III:** Expand capabilities for the production of vaccines and therapeutics expressly for emerging and re-emerging infections.
>
> **Compact Core Mission IV:** Establish, maintain, and monitor international standards for best laboratory and regulatory practices.

Through the implementation of these four core missions, the Compact will minimize the impact of infectious disease on national and international health, social and economic development and international security. The key benefit of the Compact is to drive innovation and progress in these core areas: information and knowledge sharing, basic science, drug and vaccine development, and best laboratory and regulatory practices. As shown in Figure 13.4, these missions are interconnected; without a strong foundation of basic science, the drug and vaccine pipelines dry up. Similarly, in the absence of effective biosurveillance, it becomes difficult to project which strain of an emerging disease represents the most significant threat, which in turn hampers our ability to create the appropriate countermeasures. Information technology and knowledge sharing will drive new science, which in turn can modify and inform regulatory initiatives. Standardized regulatory regimes enable new drugs and vaccines that will change global epidemiological patterns and these patterns must be reintegrated into a central database, beginning the cycle again.

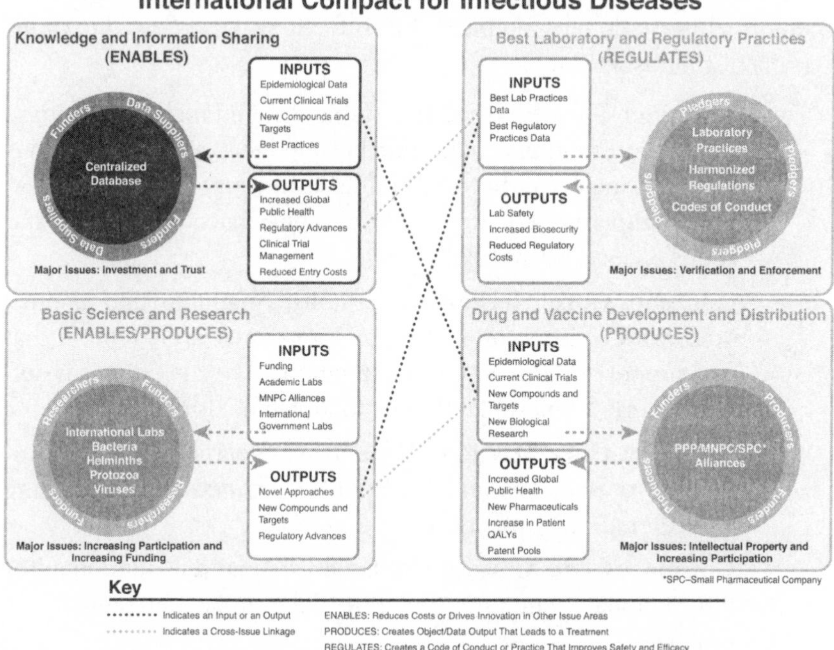

Figure 13.4 The International Compact for Infectious Diseases

Addressing the problem as a whole creates powerful incentives for stakeholders to participate. For example, to access a central database containing information on current clinical trials, epidemiological data and new compounds and targets, participants would pledge to implement best laboratory and regulatory practices. By bringing together government, the private sector, and academia, the Compact allows each group to institutionalize their relations with the others. Pharmaceutical companies and public-private development partnerships can find partners to help take promising leads through to development. With the inclusion of post-marketing/post-distribution clinical trial data in the database, philanthropic organizations and governments will be able to understand the effects their investments are having throughout the world. Academics will acquire additional funding streams for their research as well as input from their colleagues all over the world. Finally, all parties will work together to harmonize regulatory processes across the board, reducing barriers to market entry for much needed therapeutics and ensuring their wider distribution.

There already exist a large number of databases that address one or more of these issues (for example, the revised 2005 International Health Regulations). We propose developing an information technology architecture that will seamlessly integrate these databases, make them user friendly yet provide the necessary security and add new data as recommended by the wide user community. The challenges here are formidable but hardly insurmountable. The greatest obstacle is the need for trust between signatory nations and a willingness to share data. There are technical challenges, too. Any attempt to create a common architecture for information systems would require common ontologies.[58] New algorithms and models of disease spread need to be developed and validated. Lastly, the language of the Compact has to address the issue of noncompliance by establishing a robust platform for the public dissemination of compliance status.

Conclusion

We live in a world where endemic, epidemic, and pandemic diseases threaten personal, national, and international security. Efforts to control infectious diseases are exacerbated by globalization, dual-use research of concern, and other factors, such that biological high-consequence events are now concrete risks to societies. It is erroneous to think that the developed nations have conquered infectious diseases, and that they are merely a Third World problem. These diseases represent a symmetric threat that imperils the socioeconomic security of all nations. If unchecked, dangerous pathogens create human costs rivaling those of armed conflict, while simultaneously restricting the freedom of policy makers to address other pressing concerns. A study of U.S. national security issues conducted by the Woodrow Wilson School of Public and International Affairs at Princeton University unequivocally states that "American national security in the twenty-first century...is likely to be threatened by pathogens as much as people. New diseases and antibiotic-resistant strains of old ones are on the rise...."[59] Clearly, the problem of infectious disease is global and demands a globally integrated and coordinated response. We all need to act now.

14

Long-Term Contracts for Reducing Losses from Future Catastrophes

Howard Kunreuther
The Wharton School, University of Pennsylvania

Overview

Many individuals and firms do not invest in protection until after a disaster has occurred because they tend to ignore risks and are highly myopic. People tend to focus on the expected benefits of these investments over a short time-horizon in relation to the upfront costs. If the costs of reduction are high, the measure is often not viewed as economically feasible and/or financially attractive. Another reason for individuals' reluctance to invest in mitigation measures is that the likelihood of the event is perceived to be below a threshold level of concern: Those at risk might feel that the event will not happen to them.

This chapter explores how long-term contracts such as multiyear loans and insurance, coupled with well-enforced regulations, can encourage property owners and division managers in firms to invest in protection against low-probability events. Such long-term contracts can encourage decision-makers to undertake cost-effective risk reducing measures while providing stability to their planning process. Two illustrative examples highlight the tradeoffs that decision makers face when making this choice. One example involves a family's dilemma as to whether or not to elevate its house to reduce future flood losses.

The second illustrates a division in a firm determining whether to invest in protective measures. The analysis reveals that the costs of protection measures can be justified on benefit-cost grounds.

The chapter then highlights the need for property owners to invest in loss-reduction measures. I propose multiyear long-term insurance policies tied to the property and long-term loans coupled with well-enforced building codes so homeowners in hazard-prone areas will undertake cost-effective protective actions and reap short-term financial returns in the process. The chapter also shows how insurance and loans coupled with third-party inspections and regulations can lead divisions in firms to protect themselves against possible catastrophic losses so they and the firm reap financial benefits in the short term and reduce the likelihood of bankruptcy. The chapter concludes by outlining the role that the public and private sectors can jointly play by creating economic incentives and addressing interdependency issues that highlight the importance of investing in mitigation measures.

Two Illustrative Examples

Example 1: Lack of Interest by Property Owners in Protecting Against Natural Disasters

Homeowners who reside in hazard-prone areas are generally aware that they can take steps to reduce the damage from future natural disasters by investing in loss-protection measures. For example, property owners in hurricane-prone areas can install shutters and strengthen the roofs of their homes. Property owners in flood-prone regions can elevate their houses, and those in earthquake-prone regions can strap their water heater and bolt their structure to its foundation. Many of these measures are cost-effective, meaning that the expected investment expenditure is less than the expected benefits over the length of the life of the property, discounted by an interest rate reflecting the opportunity cost of money.

The Lowland family is considering whether to elevate its house so as to prevent future flood damage. The principal reason that the Lowlands decide not to undertake this measure is its high up-front cost. In addition, like many property owners, the Lowlands evaluate the expected benefits from investing in these measures by utilizing a short-time horizon (for example, two or three years). Moreover, they are likely to underestimate the risk of experiencing future floods. As do many other property owners, they believe that the disaster *"will not happen to me"* while they are residing in the region. Those who plan on relocating in several years have a hard time justifying this investment because they believe (often correctly) that it will not be reflected in increased property values.[1]

Example 2: Reluctance by Firms to Reduce Risk of Catastrophic Accidents

The economic incentive for managers in one division of an organization to invest in risk-reduction measures depends on how these managers expect the other divisions to behave. In large corporations, a failure in one unit can lead to disruption or bankruptcy of the entire firm nationwide or even worldwide. Interdependencies with respect to risks can create situations where either everyone invests in protection or no one does.

To illustrate this point, consider the BeSafe Chemical Company, a hypothetical firm that has a number of independently operating divisions, each maximizing its own expected returns and having a choice of whether to invest in a protective measure that would reduce the probability of a catastrophic chemical accident in one of its plants. Suppose Division 1 has invested in protection. There is still a risk that BeSafe will go bankrupt if its other divisions have not taken this precautionary measure. In other words, the employees in Division 1 may lose their jobs because these other divisions have not protected their operations against a catastrophic accident. If none of the other divisions in BeSafe invests in protection, Division 1 will not want to take this action; if the others do, Division 1 will want to follow suit.[2]

In the context of real-world examples, an accident at a chemical plant can lead to losses so large they cause bankruptcy of the entire operation, as evidenced by Union Carbide's demise in 1999.[3] Similarly, a failure in just one office of a large company can lead to disruption or bankruptcy of the entire firm. In 1995, Britain's Barings Bank was destroyed by the actions of a single trader in its

Singapore unit. In 2002, the accounting firm of Arthur Andersen was sent into bankruptcy by the actions of its Houston partner responsible for its Enron account. In 2008, the world's largest insurer, American International Group, was forced into public receivership when a small London office, employing less than 1 percent of the firm's workforce, bet on subprime mortgages. Despite well-performing units elsewhere and a strong risk-management system in place, reckless decisions by a single undersupervised operation killed the entire company.[4]

Behavioral Biases

Two behavioral biases discourage investment in protective measures:

- **Ignoring risks whose likelihood of occurrence is below a threshold level of concern:** Prior to the Bhopal chemical accident in 1984, firms in the chemical industry estimated the chances of such an accident as sufficiently low that it was not something they planned for.[5] Many homeowners residing in communities that are potential sites for nuclear-waste facilities have a tendency to dismiss the risk as negligible.[6] Even experts in risk disregard some hazards. For instance, even after the first terrorist attack against the World Trade Center in 1993, terrorism risk continued to be included as an unnamed peril in commercial insurance policies, so insurers were liable for losses from a terrorist attack without their ever receiving a penny for this coverage.[7]
- **Need to justify decisions using short-time horizons:** Most decision makers, be they homeowners, managers, or legislators, tend to avoid thinking about low-probability catastrophes until after they occur. They fall into a trap of believing such events will not take place, at least, not on their watch. The implicit principle is *NIMTOF* (not in my term of office). In the context of the previous examples, the Lowland family and the BeSafe Chemical Company divisions are being asked to invest a tangible fixed sum now to achieve a benefit later that they instinctively undervalue—and one that they paradoxically hope never to see at all.

The financial meltdown of 2008 illustrates these behavioral biases. Most investment managers treated the likelihood of significant losses on financial derivatives, such as credit default swaps, as being sufficiently small that they did not consider the consequences should these instruments turn into financial liabilities. Their lack of concern with these worst-case scenarios was exacerbated by the annual bonus system that rewards managers for short-term gains. Key decision makers were reluctant to undertake measures that would reduce their profits for the year. In addition, many in the financial sector believed that if theirs was the only bank to not take advantage of potentially highly profitable yet risky investments, they would not fare well because their clients would leave them for supposedly greener pastures.

Reducing Losses and Fatalities from Natural Disasters

A New Era of Catastrophes

Recent natural disasters in developing countries have killed many thousands of people and have caused severe economic disruption.[8] The economic impact of disasters can be estimated by determining the losses in relation to the country's annual gross domestic product (GDP). A major flood in the United States or a large European country will have much less of an impact on GDP than if a similar event occurred in a developing country. At one extreme, natural disasters have had a long-enduring impact on small islands, with economic losses from major natural disasters representing several times the annual GDP compared to losses in developed countries, where damage is a small percentage of annual GDP, as shown in Table 14.1.

Even in a developed country such as the United States, which has extensive experience with natural catastrophes and resources to adequately prepare, there is a lack of adequate loss-reduction measures and emergency-preparedness capacity to deal with large-scale natural disasters, as evidenced by Hurricane Katrina in 2005.

TABLE 14.1 Examples of the Impact of Disasters on Economies of Different Sizes

Year	Natural Disaster	Country	Region	Damage (U.S. $ Million)	Damage (% of GDP)
Large Economies					
2005	Hurricane Katrina	United States	North America	125,000	1.1%
1995	Earthquake	Japan	East Asia	100,000	3.2%
1998	Flood	China	East Asia	30,000	0.7%
2004	Earthquake	Japan	East Asia	28,000	0.8%
1992	Hurricane Andrew	United States	North America	26,500	0.4%
Small Island Economies					
1988	Hurricane Gilbert	St. Lucia	Caribbean	1,000	365%
1991	Cyclones Val and Wasa	Samoa	Oceania	278	248%
2004	Hurricane Ivan	Grenada	Caribbean	889	203%
1990	Cyclone Ofa	Samoa	Oceania	200	178%
1985	Cyclones Eric and Nigel	Vanuatu	Oceania	173	143%

Sources: Cummins and Mahul (2008)[9]

To Invest or Not to Invest in Loss-Reduction Measures?[10]

Suppose the Lowland family lives in central East Jakarta, Indonesia, and is considering whether to elevate their masonry house to significantly reduce the damage should there be severe flooding from the Ciliwung River. Major flooding from this river occurred in February 1996, February 2002, and February 2007. Based on this historical data, it is estimated that there is a 20 percent annual chance that there will be severe flooding.

A typical residential structure located near the Ciliwung River is valued at approximately $19,300, and the cost to elevate the house by 1 meter is $9,200. If the home is not elevated, the damage to the structure and contents is estimated to be $10,000. For ease of exposition, assume that elevating the house will eliminate the damage to the house. (In reality, a severe flood of the Ciliwung River could still cause damage to an elevated house.) If the chance of a severe flood is 1 in 5, the reduction in average annual damage from adopting this loss-reduction measure will be $2,000 (that is, 1/5 x $10,000).

The Lowland family and other households residing in these hazard-prone areas are relatively poor, so they cannot afford the relatively high costs of this risk-reducing measure. Even if they had the financial resources, they might be reluctant to elevate their home if they are myopic and focus only on the expected benefits over the next two or three years. The $2,000 expected reduction in annual flood losses pales relative to the $9,200 investment.

However, if one focuses on the expected life of the structure which could be greater than 20 years, elevating the house by 1 meter is highly cost-effective. Even if the annual interest rate used to convert future returns to the present is as high as 15 percent, the expected discounted benefit for a family adopting this measure is $12,520. In fact, after 8.5 years, the measure would be viewed as financially attractive. With an annual interest rate of 10 percent, the discounted expected benefit of elevating a masonry house on the Ciliwung River based on a 20-year time horizon would be greater than $17,000, and the measure would be deemed cost-effective after 6 years, as shown in Figure 14.1.

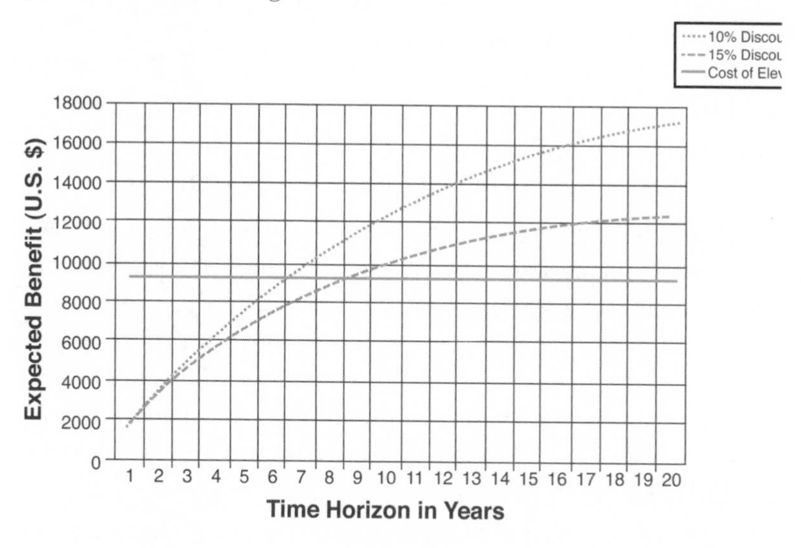

Figure 14.1 Discounted expected benefit of elevating a masonry house on the Ciliwung River

Long-Term Loans Coupled with Long-Term Insurance

Consider the challenges in persuading homeowners such as the Lowland family to adopt cost-effective measures to reduce losses from future hazardous events. One way to make investments in protection more palatable is for financial institutions or the government to provide long-term mitigation loans. To illustrate, if the Lowland family were given a 20-year loan for $9,200 at a 10 percent interest rate to elevate its structure, the annual payments would be $890. Suppose insurance were available to cover damage to the structure from flooding and the premiums reflected risk. Then if the Lowland's house were elevated, the insurer would be willing to reduce annual premiums by at least $2,000 to reflect the absence of future flood losses. The Lowland family would now have a sound financial basis for investing in the mitigation measure: The annual net savings from taking out the bank loan would be at least $1,110 (that is, $2,000 insurance savings minus $890 annual loan payments).

Property owners may not want to take out such a loan—even if they obtain a premium reduction on their insurance policy that exceeds the annual loan payments—if they are unsure how long they will reside in the house. In addition, they might believe that their insurance company is unlikely to provide them with premium discounts should they invest in these measures. One way to address this issue is to couple the long-term loans with a long-term insurance policy. Today, property insurance is marketed only on an annual basis. By offering multiyear policies tied to the property with rates that reflect risk, homeowners are much more likely to view mitigation measures as attractive.[11]

In many emerging economies that are now considering insurance as a way of reducing risks, there is an opportunity to provide long-term contracts using the public sector to assist in this process. One country that would benefit from such a strategy is Turkey. Indeed, immediately after the two extremely destructive earthquakes in 1999, the government of Turkey decided to enforce earthquake insurance on a nationwide basis through the Turkish Catastrophe Insurance Pool (TCIP) at affordable premiums.[12]

Initially funded by the World Bank, TCIP was founded on August 2000, and the TCIP program began marketing annual policies. With its 2.7 million policy count as of April 2008, the TCIP has the potential to become the largest earthquake insurance company in the world. Due to inadequate enforcement, only 21 percent of residential structures in Turkey have coverage, even though this insurance is required. There is also no system to link insurance premiums with efforts by residents to reduce losses from future earthquakes by retrofitting their structures or investing in other mitigation measures. The rates are based only on construction type and seismic zone in which the structure is located. The TCIP could offer long-term loans to encourage residents to adopt cost-effective loss-reduction measures and consider offering long-term insurance policies with reduced premiums. The long-term insurance program should increase the percentage of homeowners who are financially protected against the next earthquake.

A Proposal for Long-Term Flood Insurance

Many homeowners purchase flood insurance only after suffering damage in a flood, then cancel their annual policies when several years pass without their suffering any damage from flooding.[13] This finding is particularly striking in the United States, especially considering that flood-insurance premiums on existing homes are highly subsidized by the National Flood Insurance Program, and residences located in special flood hazard areas are required to purchase insurance as a condition for federally backed mortgages. As an example, consider the flood that damaged property in northern Vermont in August 1998. Of the 1,549 victims of this disaster, the Federal Emergency Management Agency (FEMA) found that 84 percent of the homeowners in special flood hazard areas did not have insurance, even though 45 percent of these individuals were required to purchase this coverage.[14]

Long-term flood insurance would prevent individuals from canceling their policies if the hazard falls below their threshold level of concern. Banks and financial institutions have often not enforced the flood insurance requirement because few of them have been fined and/or because the mortgages are transferred to banks in nonflood-prone regions of the country that have not focused on either the flood hazard risk nor on the requirement that homeowners may have to purchase this coverage. Homeowners would be more likely to want this coverage if they are given information on the chances of a flood over the lifetime of the insurance policy, rather than just the next year.

For a long-term flood-insurance program to be viable, premiums on any new structures built in flood-prone areas need to reflect risk so that those considering residing in these areas are apprised of the dangers. They also could then be rewarded with premium reductions for adopting loss-reduction measures. Those currently residing in flood-prone areas and deemed to be deserving of special treatment (for example, low-income homeowners) will still be charged a premium that reflects risk, but they should be given a grant (in this case from the federal government) in the form of an insurance voucher to defray portions of the costs of a policy. The most notable example of this type of arrangement in the United States is the food stamp program, where low-income families are charged the market price for items they purchase and use food stamps to cover a portion of the full costs. In the case of flood insurance, if a low-income family invested in mitigation measures, its premium would still be reduced to reflect their lower expected claims following the next flood.[15]

This proposed long-term policy differs from the current flood insurance program in the United States, where homeowners are given subsidized premiums rather than insurance vouchers and no premium reductions are offered to encourage investment in mitigation measures. Long-term flood insurance and long-term loans should be a winning proposition for all the interested parties: The property owner incurs lower premiums as a result of investing in mitigation measures while still maintaining insurance protection to cover the financial costs should a disaster occur. The financial institution's mortgages are more secure. The insurer will have lower claims costs following the next flood, and the general taxpayer will have lower costs of disaster relief.

For this system to work, however, these regulations must be strictly enforced. One way to do this is to require the property owner to show that she has an insurance policy when paying property taxes each year. This process is currently followed with respect to automobile insurance: Car owners need to provide proof of insurance when submitting their annual registration renewal form.

To complement the long-term loan contracts for encouraging mitigation, there is a need for well-enforced building codes. Building codes require property owners to meet standards on new structures but normally do not require them to retrofit existing structures. Such codes on existing property are often necessary, particularly when property owners are not inclined to adopt mitigation measures on their own because they perceive the disaster will not happen to them. Moreover, when a structure collapses, it may create negative externalities in the form of economic dislocations and other social costs that are beyond the financial loss suffered by the owners. For example, if a poorly designed structure collapses in a flood or hurricane, it may cause damage to other buildings that are well designed. This type of interdependency between structures provides another rational for regulation.[16]

Dealing with Interdependencies in Organizations

The reluctance of divisions in firms to invest in risk-reduction measures illustrates another type of interdependency as shown by the BeSafe Chemical Company example. Each division in a firm is concerned not only about its own expected return at the end of the year but also how well it performs relative to other units in the organization. Thus, managers may choose not to invest in risk-reducing measures simply because none of the other divisions in the firm have taken this action. Should no severe accident occur, the up-front costs of these protective measures would adversely affect the division's bottom line relative to other parts of the company and hence reduce the annual bonuses of its employees. If the possibility of a catastrophic accident is perceived to be below the key decision makers' threshold levels of concern, this is an additional reason for them not to want to incur these investments. Failure to invest in protection may thus appear to be an optimal strategy for each division, but from the perspective of the firm, it is likely to be suboptimal.

Risk-management strategies that involve multiyear worst-case scenarios may be one way to force managers to pay attention to the consequences of a catastrophic accident rather than assuming that such an event will not happen on their watch. By extending the time period, managers may consider the likelihood of such events occurring during the extended time interval as sufficiently high to trigger their concern. However, even when these events are on the radar screen of key decision makers, there is still likely to be a need for economic incentives to reward those who invest in risk-reducing measures.

Internal Organizational Rules and Other Coordinating Mechanisms

A large decentralized firm with many divisions will likely need some type of coordinating mechanism from top management to encourage protective investments if each division's objective is to maximize the expected returns of its own employees. Larger firms in the chemical industry have formed functional units that play this role across the organization. For example, DuPont has a process safety management (PSM) unit that is responsible for making sure that all the different divisions in the firm follow appropriate procedures.

Returning to the BeSafe example, BeSafe could set up such a cross-cutting process safety unit and institute a specific rule that would require its divisions to invest in protective measures when the expected discounted benefits to the firm over a multiyear period exceeds the up-front costs of the measure. One way to determine what type of rule to enforce is to focus on catastrophic accidents that could cause losses so large that it would threaten the solvency of the firm, but where the division would not want to incur the costs of investing in protective measures.

Private-Public Sector Partnerships

The public sector can also play an important role in encouraging protection and has an interest in doing so in areas such as chemical safety where a firm's actions can affect people off-site. A company such as BeSafe may not be held fully liable for the consequences of a chemical accident. For example, the firm causing an accident may not be legally responsible for losses from related decreases in property values of surrounding homes or disruptions in community life. For these reasons, government can create regulations to deal with these negative externalities. But such regulations must be enforced. With limited staffing in many public-sector agencies, this is easier said than done.

A salient example in this regard is the lack of enforcement of Section 112(r) of the Clean Air Act Amendments (CAAA) of 1990, which required firms to submit a summary report to the U.S. Environmental Protection Agency (EPA) showing how they were reducing the risks of major chemical accidents. Firms have little financial incentive to follow centralized regulatory procedures if there is a small likelihood they will be inspected by a regulatory agency and/or they face only a low fine if caught.[17] In such cases, they may be willing to take their chances and incur the fine should they be found violating the regulation. This is like putting money into a parking meter. If you know that the chances of a meter being checked are low and the fine is relatively small, then you might think twice before parting with your quarters.

One way for the government to enforce its regulations is to turn to the private sector for assistance. More specifically, third-party inspections coupled with insurance protection can encourage divisions in firms to take steps to reduce their risk from accidents and disasters. Such a management-based regulatory strategy shifts the locus of decision making from the regulator to firms, which are now required to do their own planning to meet a set of standards or regulations.[18]

The intuition behind using third parties and insurance to support regulations when the public sector agency has limited personnel to enforce its own rules is as follows: Low-risk divisions cannot credibly distinguish themselves from the high-risk ones without some type of inspection. By delegating part of the inspection process to the private sector through insurance companies and third parties, the regulatory agency can provide a channel through which the low-risk divisions in firms can speak for themselves. If a division chooses not to be inspected by third parties, it is more likely to be a high-risk rather than a low-risk one. If it does get inspected and shows that it is protecting itself and the rest of the organization against catastrophic accidents, it will pay a lower insurance premium than a high-risk division that is not undertaking these actions. In this way, the proposed mechanism not only substantially reduces the number of inspections the agency has to undertake, but it also makes their audits more efficient.[19]

The PSM unit of a firm has reasons to support this program for two reasons. It provides a rationale for the firm to hire third-party inspectors to make sure its divisions are operating safely. The PSM unit could also provide long-term loans to the divisions that it oversees to encourage them to invest in risk-reducing measures so that the division is not forced to incur large up-front costs. If insurance rates reflect risk, the reduction in premiums from undertaking these safety measures should justify the investment.

Future Research Needs

The problem of managing risks presents new challenges for risk assessment and risk perception. As indicated by the guiding principles in Chapter 1, "Principles and Challenges for Reducing Risks from Disasters," we need to collect better data to estimate the risks and consequences of large-scale natural disasters, catastrophic accidents, and other extreme events so that one can develop meaningful long-term contracts. And we need to do more to increase our knowledge of how individuals make decisions with respect to extreme events, particularly when there are interdependencies associated with the risk.

Research in these areas can improve our understanding of extreme events and the types of strategies that are likely to be effective in managing these risks. Solutions for decreasing individual and collective risk will require coordinating efforts across individuals, firms, and public-sector agencies. The need for these parties and others to work together has become even more vital in the global world in which we live. Given our myopic behavior, we need to construct long-term strategies that provide sufficient short-term benefits to the concerned parties so that property owners, managers in firms, and government policy makers find them financially attractive and are therefore willing to promote them. Should they be implemented, both individual and social welfare are likely to be improved over the status quo.

15

Developing Leadership to Avert and Mitigate Disasters

Michael Useem
The Wharton School, University of Pennsylvania

Overview

Drawing on the experience of two major companies and two fire-fighting groups that faced catastrophes, this chapter emphasizes the importance of leadership development for averting and mitigating disasters. Leadership development for managers is essential, and many well-established methods for doing so have emerged in recent years. For those responsible for managing risk and leading organizations that face severe tests, the best time to prepare their understanding of leadership precepts is well before their leadership must be exercised. And because many leadership precepts are essential but unmemorable, anchoring those precepts in tangible experience can be invaluable. The chapter also argues that to avert disasters, it is important to ensure that leaders work to prevent overconfidence about the risks they face, and that they think strategically and long-term about how to prepare for unlikely but catastrophic events before they happen.

The art of leadership includes preparing for the unexpected, and the value of leadership thus becomes more important when the world becomes more unpredictable. Because low-risk but high-consequence events are particularly unpredictable and overcoming them equally so, preparing leadership to face catastrophes is an essential step for anticipating and prevailing over them.

Of special concern are the suboptimal ways in which most of us foresee and respond to calamities. We tend to underanticipate their likelihood and overreact to their occurrence. This chapter focuses on what leaders have done and can do to constructively anticipate and guide the predictably suboptimal behavior among those facing or recovering from disasters.

We know that employees and citizens are not well wired for disaster preparation or response. As previous chapters in this volume have amply demonstrated, we tend to think myopically, to focus on a disaster when it occurs but not long afterward, avoiding preparation for preventing or responding to future disasters. One of the first obligations of leadership is to recognize these and other behavioral shortcomings and then to create instruments and cultures that reduce or mitigate the most common flaws of human intelligence.

Training in the art of leadership will help. In normal times, our natural shortcomings are worrisome and grating but usually not perilous; in catastrophic times, such flaws can become magnified and dangerous if not lethal, as evident in the avoidable loses in the 2005 landfall of Hurricane Katrina and the preventable failure of American International Group in the 2008 financial crisis. Taking steps to anticipate and transcend human shortcomings is one of the responsibilities of anybody in a leadership position, and preparing leaders is essential for most of those who carry responsibilities for the security and well being of others.

To appreciate the potential role for leadership for forestalling and overcoming disasters, we build inductively by examining two leadership moments in business, one calamitous, the other felicitous. Comparison of these two moments provides experience-anchored practical insights into the leadership precepts for averting disasters. We then turn to moments of leadership in the face of two additional disasters from which we draw pragmatic lessons on preparing leaders to face and surmount them.

Experience-Anchored Leadership Precepts

We place special emphasis on *experience-anchored* leadership precepts. By experience-anchored leadership precepts we mean that the precepts are of generic value for facing disasters *and* they are rooted in tangible specific experiences that are salient and enduringly attached to the precepts. We believe that those in leadership positions are most able to keep leadership precepts well in mind when needed if the associated experiences from which they are drawn are also kept actively in mind. To ensure that leadership precepts for averting and responding to disasters are active in our random-access memory, not just hard-disc storage, anchoring them in tangible experiences is one of the more powerful ways for doing so.[1]

By way of illustration, consider the following leadership precept: Those in positions of responsibility should actively listen to the ideas and suggestions of their subordinates. By virtue of being closer to a geographic field or financial market, subordinates often detect and appreciate early warning signs or ambiguous signals—such as landfall forecasts in the case of Hurricane Katrina or mortgage defaults in the case of Lehman Brothers—of impending disasters before more senior managers come to appreciate them. Although well substantiated by academic research, this precept by itself may not sit at the top of mind among many city managers or company executives as they face their day-to-day leadership challenges.[2]

If a leadership precept is anchored in a personal leadership moment—or, second best, a powerfully informative account of another leader's experience—the precept is more likely to become salient in a leader's mind at a moment when it had become important to apply it. An example of this—and of the leadership precept of *active listening to subordinates*—is the failure of the Challenger Space Shuttle in January, 1986. On the eve of the launch, NASA called the leaders of the booster-rocket maker, Morton Thiokol, for guidance. As is now known, the Thiokol leaders had not listened to one of their own engineers—Roger Boisjoly—who had been warning that the O-rings in the booster rockets built by Morton Thiokol for NASA would fail under the kind of cold weather conditions that would prevail at the launch site on that fateful day. By keeping this instance of leaders' failure to listen to their subordinates and the catastrophic consequence actively in mind, the leadership precept of active listening to subordinates is likely to be more vividly remembered and acted upon when another disaster is potentially pending.[3]

American International Group

We now focus on the leadership failings at American International Group (AIG) that resulted in its collapse and U.S. bailout in September 2008. Indelibly appreciating those leadership shortcomings requires brief description of AIG's history and what went disastrously wrong in 2008.[4]

Founded in Shanghai in 1919, AIG employed 116,000 by 2008, drew annual revenue of $110 billion, and held assets of $860 billion. On the eve of its sudden collapse in the autumn of 2008, it ranked among the 20 largest publicly traded companies in the world. Its scale at the time was hard to overemphasize. AIG operated in 130 countries and serviced 74 million customers, including 180,000 small businesses along with thousands of municipalities, pension funds, and 401k retirement-investment plans.

AIG had been led by just two chief executives for its first 86 years. Founder Cornelius Vander Starr passed management of the firm to Maurice R. (Hank) Greenberg in 1968, who shifted the company's focus from personal insurance to corporate coverage. By contrast, during the three years running up to AIG's insolvency, it was led by three CEOs in rapid succession. An accounting scandal forced the exit of Greenberg in 2005, his successor Martin J. Sullivan was forced out in June 2008, and his successor, Robert B. Willumstad, was pushed out in September 2008.

Amid the financial crisis of 2008, the United States effectively nationalized AIG to prevent its otherwise certain bankruptcy and significant disruption of world financial markets. Ultimately placing a total of $170 billion in the firm, the United States acquired control of 79.9 percent of the company's voting shares. AIG's shares fell from a 52-week high of $70 to just $1.25 on September 16, 2008.

Many, though not all of AIG's business lines—it owned more than 240 insurance and financial-service entities—had remained profitable in 2008. Just one AIG line, the Financial Products Division (AIGFP), had become a fatal cancer within an otherwise largely healthy bundle of assets. Under CEO Hank Greenberg's leadership, AIG had launched this division in 1987 as an insurer or large-scale debt obligations. If you were a financial institution acquiring large portfolios of corporate bonds or home mortgages and wanted to insure them against default, AIGFP had become a leading provider.

At its peak, the London-based AIGFP held a portfolio of $1.6 trillion—one estimate even placed it at $2.7 trillion, equivalent to the GNP of France—in a range of insured products, including credit default obligations on subprime mortgages, and policies against interest-rate swings, currency gyrations, auto loan defaults, and credit card receivables. At the outset, its fees were very low—just 0.02 cent (two basis points) per year for each dollar of risk insured—and even later they remained modest—0.11 cent in 1999. But across many billions of dollars in insured risk, the flow of customer fees into AIGFP coffers became very substantial.[5]

AIGFP employed just 377 people in 2008, less than 0.4 percent of AIG's total employment worldwide, but it had become an earnings juggernaut for the company. It produced 4.2 percent of AIG's total operating income by 1999 and 17.5 percent by 2005. Its profit margins had also become enormous: By 2005, operating income had reached 83 percent of revenue, well above industry norms. Division president Joseph J. Cassano told investors in 2007 that his unit was making as much as $250 million in income from insurance premiums. Those working in the unit had much to be proud of but also much to protect: the average employee earned more than $1 million annually, and collectively their compensation totaled more than $3.5 billion over the seven years up to 2008.[6]

Leaders of both AIG and AIGFP were optimistic about the absence of any low-risk, high-consequence threat from the operation. On December 5, 2007, AIG chief executive Martin Sullivan told a group of AIG investors that the risk-analysis models of AIGFP were "very reliable" and that they provided the company with "a very high level of comfort." AIGFP president Cassano similarly reported, "We believe this is a money-good portfolio" and that "the models we use are simple, they're specific and they're highly conservative." At another point in 2007, Cassano had been even more sanguine. "It is hard for us, without being flippant, to even see a scenario within any kind of realm of reason that would see us losing one dollar in any of those transactions." In an August 2007 conference call with analysts, Cassano characterized the credit default swaps in his portfolio as secure. "It is hard to get this message across," he assured the analysts, "but these are very much handpicked."[7]

What likely contributed to CEO Sullivan's and president Cassano's outward confidence was the triple-A-rated umbrella under which AIGFP operated. The credit-rating agencies, witnessing AIG's strong annual performance in its many insurance lines, ascribed it the highest possible mark, AAA. That helped AIGFP to issue credit default swaps to insure more than $440 billion in securities, including $58 billion in structured debt backed by subprime mortgage loans, and to do so cheaply. Because of the triple-A rating, under the prevailing industry practice, AIGFP did not need to set aside any collateral of its own to back-stop the insurance obligations to its customers. After all, the AAA-rating implied that the company was extremely unlikely to default on its obligations to its customers.

Yet beneath the company's robust results, AAA rating, and leaders' confidence lay a fragile fault line. First and most obvious, if any of the debt securities that AIGFP insured defaulted, the company would of course have to pay. It could readily do so for a relatively small default rate that its historical statistics had forecast, but it could not do so if the default rate soared, which its risk models did not forecast. Second and less evident, the buyers of the AIGFP swaps had the right to require collateral from AIGFP if AIG's own corporate-debt rating declined below AAA. Such a downgrade was wholly unexpected—unless the rating agencies perceived a significant drop in the market value of AIGFP's contracts, a development that AIG would be obligated to report. But neither a significant value decline nor a credit downgrade was anticipated by the company's leaders.

Available evidence suggests that in pricing its products, AIGFP had taken into account a host of anticipated risks based on historical data—the essence of how insurance firms value products whose losses are normally independent of one another, as in the case of life and auto insurance. But it did not take into account the likelihood that systemic—that is, massive and unprecedented—losses or declines would emerge, as in the case of catastrophic events for which there was little historical data.[8]

After Lehman Brothers failed on September 15, 2008, the credit-rating agencies downgraded AIG from AAA to AA on September 16, which had the effect of forcing AIGFP, as required by industry convention, to post large amounts of collateral on its contracts, some $18 billion according to one estimate. Customer collateral calls and default payouts wreaked havoc: Goldman Sachs demanded and received more than $8 billion, and other banks made their own massive collateral calls.[9]

With alarm bells sounding, investors stampeded out of AIG stock, dropping its value on a single day by 60 percent. Moody's, Fitch, and Standard and Poor's further downgraded AIG's credit rating, and that forced AIG to post another $15 billion in collateral. On September 22, AIG was removed from the Dow Jones Industrial Average. By the end of September, AIGFP was forced to find $32 billion as a result of the rating actions and declining market value of its products. By October 24, AIG had borrowed $90 billion from the United States to meet its obligations. At fourth quarter's end, it losses reached $61 billion, the largest in corporate history. For the year its deficit totaled $99 billion, and it remained solvent only because of federal life support.

Contrast AIG's performance with that of the Travelers Companies, another of America's largest insurers. In 2007, both companies offered a broad range of insurance products, including personal auto, homeowners, and commercial property. Travelers is one of nine insurance companies with which AIG compares its business and operations. Both were very large: Travelers earned $4.6 billion that year, while AIG earned $6.2 billion. But since then, their fortunes radically diverged. Travelers stock outperformed the S&P 500 in 2007 and 2008, whereas the stock of AIG lost nearly all of its value. Eight months after Dow Jones removed AIG from its industrial stock index, it added Travelers to the bellwether index.

A critical difference between AIG and Travelers: The latter had not created a unit comparable to AIGFP, and it stopped ensuring residential mortgage-backed securities in 2004, topping off at only $200 million in holdings. And that decision to exit from mortgage-backed securities came from the top. "The reason that we stopped buying it was because the risk-adjusted return," explained Travelers chief executive Jay Fishman, "in these structures simply were inconsistent from our standpoint with the newness of them." He had long been concerned about the "tails of the distributions"—unlikely but costly events such as a hurricane sweeping up the northeast coast of the United States—and thus had eschewed insuring the tails of the distribution despite their lucrative near-term value.[10]

Similar markets, similar products, but wholly dissimilar results. And much of the difference, we believe, can be traced to leadership shortcomings at AIG. According to AIG employees, for example, AIGFP president Joseph Cassano led the financial-products division with scant oversight from the company chief executive, and with an autocratic hand and little tolerance for challenge on the inside.[11] The company CEO in turn received less than effective oversight from his directors, as least as implied by the grades accorded AIG's board by a governance rating agency. With major publicly listed companies averaging a C rating on an A to F scale, AIG received a D grade in the year before its demise. One sign of the company's subpar governance practices was the board's decision to compensate CEO Martin Sullivan more than 20 percent above the median for comparable firms. This despite the fact that, as AIGFP employees later reported, the chief executive had evinced scant understanding of the risks that their operation was taking and thus exercised little oversight of a unit that should have been at the top of his concerns.[12]

AIG's governing board had been repeatedly warned about the extraordinary risk that the company was taking through its AIGFP subsidiary. The U.S. Office of Thrift Supervision (OTS), which served as the primary regulator for AIGFP, began in 2005 reporting to the AIG board what it had found to be "weaknesses in AIGFP's documentation of complex structures transactions, in policies and procedures regarding accounting, in stress testing, in communication of risk tolerances, and in the company's lines of authority, credit risk management and measurement." In the summer of 2007, on the eve of the deluge, OTS warned AIG of the risks associated with subprime mortgages and demanded that the board improve AIGFP's organizational controls and risk management. In mid-2008, AIG's outside auditor, PricewaterhouseCoopers warned the company of accounting weaknesses in the same.[13]

Even as financial storm clouds were gathering in late 2007 and early 2008, the credit-rating agencies continued to accord AIG their AAA imprimatur, and that may help explain why neither the governing board nor the chief executive tightened their scrutiny of the financial products division despite the regulatory and accounting warnings. Given the lax oversight from AIG's board and CEO, it is not entirely surprising that the president of AIGFP had, in turn, ignored or looked past warnings from the markets and the regulators. Joseph Cassano had enjoyed a period of extraordinary business growth and personal financial success over nearly two decades, and he viewed much of his division's success as a product of his own making. And we know from research that positive organizational and personal moods can lead to suboptimal decision making as over-confidence and even hubris crowds out realistic appraisals of risk, especially long-term and low-probability events whose ultimate price might not be felt until the deciding executive had long passed from office.[14]

Because this is a predictable behavioral pattern, it was up to the AIGFP president's superior—AIG's CEO—to put devices in place to guard against overoptimism. But AIG's several CEOs had themselves experienced extraordinary success as the company emerged as the world's largest insurer and had basked in its inclusion in the Dow Jones Industrial Average and other blue-chip rosters of the nation's most prominent and successful companies. Controlling the CEO's likely overconfidence bred of steady success in turn was a leadership obligation of AIG's governing board. But as indicated by the governance rater's D grade, the board itself was evidently poorly constituted and organized to prevent suboptimal decisions from naturally emerging in the top management team.

It was thus a collective leadership failure at the division, executive, and board levels. Arguably, more effective leadership at any one of the three might have better prepared the president of AIGFP to properly appreciate the massive risks that his operation was taking, to better prepare for those risks by stockpiling the collateral that would be required in case of systemic declines in the value of the insured products, to heed the regulator's and auditor's warnings, and to more properly price the insurance policies for the higher than appreciated levels of risk.

Leadership Precepts and Guiding Principles from the AIG Experience

An important leadership precept, then, for averting disaster is to ensure that the governing directors, chief executive, and operating managers are prepared and organized to *guard against overconfidence about low-probability, high-consequence events,* both in themselves and among those who work for them. More generally, creating a culture that plays down success and ratchets-up attention on unsolved problems and potential threats can be a vital principle for the leadership of any company, agency, or country. One good way to keep that precept much in mind is to remind oneself, when creating company culture or reaching leadership decisions, of what went wrong at AIG.

The AIG disaster helps underscore the importance of four of the seven guiding principles for extreme risk management identified in this book's first chapter. The world's largest insurance company's descent into government receivership thus also furnishes an experience-based anchoring of four of our guiding principles.

The first guiding principle of *Learning from Catastrophes* stresses the value of reliably estimating risks and their uncertainties if disasters are to be avoided. Partly as a result of leadership and governance lapses at American International Group, the peril of building a trillion-dollar portfolio of credit-default swaps without collateral in a AAA-rated company was completely underestimated by company executives and directors.

Our second guiding principle emphasizes the importance of appreciating that a single unit in a complex entity can potentially place all units at risk. Moreover, interdependencies that appear safe at one moment may develop into unsafe interconnections later. For two decades, AIG Financial Products had not only not threatened the enterprise as a whole, but had in fact served as a significant driver of its success. But that virtuous interdependency gave way in 2008 to a lethal mutual reliance when AIGFP's well-performing assets became toxic and dragged down the company's other 240-plus units.

Our third guiding principle calls for an abiding appreciation of the behavioral biases that people bring to the workplace. It is not surprising that both AIG's and AIGFP's unprecedented success may have contributed to a hubris in their executive suites that permitted radical underestimation of the risks that they were amassing. In the wake of success, it becomes all the more imperative for organizational directors and executives to guard against one of success's more ruinous corollaries, over-confidence about the risks ahead.

Our seventh guiding principle places a primacy on building leadership for averting disasters before it is needed. If the AIG board and CEO had invested more in explicitly developing their operating executives over the years, that training may have helped create a bulwark against the pernicious behavioral biases in AIGFP that insidiously came to ruin the entire enterprise.

Merck & Co., Inc.

We now turn to another company whose experience in developing one product tangibly illustrates—and thus anchors in experience—a second leadership precept for averting disasters: *long-term strategic thinking.* The company is Merck, a large U.S. pharmaceutical firm, and the product is Mectizan, a drug that combats a disease widespread in West Africa.[15]

As Merck's director of research and development in 1978, Roy Vagelos presided over a tightly managed scientific discovery division at a time when one of his scientists proposed developing a drug to combat a scourge of West Africa called river blindness. The scientist urged adapting and then testing an antiparasitical product named Ivermectin that had already proven effective in killing parasites in a host of animals ranging from cats and dogs to cattle and sheep. Nearly 20 million people were at risk of contracting the disease, and hundreds of thousands had already gone blind from its ravages. Vagelos appreciated that adapting, testing, and manufacturing the drug would take years and require an investment of millions of dollars, a common outlay for creating commercially successful products in the pharmaceutical industry.

The R&D director also appreciated one compelling counterpoint: Those who carried or were exposed to river blindness resided in rural

Nigeria and remote regions of other West African countries, and they had nearly no disposable income. Investing in a product with millions of prospective customers in the *developed* world was the essence of commercial drug development, but bankrolling a product whose customers in the *developing* world could never afford to purchase it was hardly the lifeblood of a profitable enterprise. Even worse, if Merck developed the product, it might also have to pay for its manufacturing and administration in the remotest regions of Africa because there was no existing infrastructure for doing so.

From the calculus of short-term return on investment, paying to develop and then distribute a product based on Ivermectin would constitute a nonstarter. But from the calculus of long-term strategic thinking, it made sense to Vagelos. Vagelos was looking not to bolster quarterly or annual sales, but to enhance income streams years and even decades in the futures. By strategic thinking, he could see that although Merck would have to give the drug away if it developed the product, the company would one day reap at least three commercial benefits from the drug.

First, if Merck's investment in a product that would save twenty million people from blindness became widely known, it could add to the company's public reputation, an important facet for a company operating in a regulated industry whose sales are dependent on physician referrals. Second, Merck's decision to go ahead could serve as a powerful recruitment story for attracting the best scientists to work for the company. And third, the creation and distribution of a free drug could one day make the brand of Merck stand out in countries like Nigeria where river blindness was so widespread.

Roy Vagelos decided to launch development of the product in 1978, and by 1987 it was tested and approved for human use under the name of Mectizan. At a press conference to announce the drug's availability, he declared that Merck would make and give Mectizan away forever. It was a costly set of leadership decisions in both 1978 and 1987, at least in the short term. Merck had invested millions to develop the product and would now have to spend some $60 million per year to manufacture it. Because River Blindness victims required annual treatment of the drug for 17 years, the ultimate investment could surpass a billion dollars.

Yet in the longer run, the strategic benefits to Merck proved substantial. When the company sought scientists for its R&D operation, the Mectizan account proved a powerful recruitment tool. When *Fortune* magazine identified America's most admired companies in the 1990s, Merck consistently stood at the top of the list. And some of Nigeria's 140-million people may one day give preference to Merck products over those of rivals because of Mectizan's free annual distribution to some 10 million Nigerians exposed to river blindness.

In Roy Vagelos's own retrospective assessment: "Some argue that corporations should not be in the business of making donations, contending that their first obligation is to reward the stockholders with higher dividends and not squander company resources on gifts. But I disagree." Mectizan and other giving programs had made Merck, he said, "a place where people were proud and excited to work because they wanted to make lives better around the world. It helped us recruit the best people and build company morale."[16]

Years later, Merck faced a financial and reputational disaster when critics questioned the safety of one of its best-selling drugs, Vioxx, a product for arthritis with two million active users and 84 million customers at one point or another worldwide. Emerging research evidence pointed to elevated rates of heart attacks among Vioxx users, and the Merck withdrew the product from the market in 2004. Expensive litigation followed, as did widespread criticism of the company for not earlier disclosing evidence that had suggested heightened cardiovascular risks.

It is not clear if the socially responsible reputation that Mectizan had earlier helped create for Merck provided some buffer against the attacks, but media coverage of the Vioxx withdrawal and litigation sometimes favorably referenced Merck's earlier commitment to Mectizan. One of Merck's own websites made the same point in announcing that the company was withdrawing Vioxx from the market. The decision, the company said, stemmed from its "commitment to maintaining the highest ethics and values," and that commitment could be seen in "the Mectizan Donation Program," an example of "our far-reaching commitment to corporate social responsibility."[17]

Leadership Precepts and Guiding Principles from the Merck Experience

An important leadership precept, then, for mitigating disaster is to think long term and strategically. Thinking long term implies that those in leadership positions actively consider the implications of decisions not just for the fiscal quarter or year but fully 5, 10, or even 20 years ahead. Thinking strategically implies that those with leadership responsibilities actively consider how their decisions will affect not just their own operations or enhance narrowly defined goals such as near-term profitability. Rather, leaders would do well to rise above their own provincial and near-term welfare to focus on the overarching betterment of the entire organization and well beyond.

The leadership precept of long-term strategic thinking can serve as an invaluable platform for better weathering unexpected disasters later on. And a device for keeping that precept much in mind is to keep salient what went right at Merck.

Like the AIG disaster, the Merck success also provides an experience-based anchoring for several of the general principles guiding this book that we believe can help prevent and mitigate disasters. Long-term and strategic thinking can be vital for appreciating prospective threats. Mectizan's enhancement of Merck's public standing eventually proved of benefit in reducing its uncertainties in recruiting research talent.

Long-term and strategic thinking can also be essential for appreciating interdependencies. The company's decision to develop a profitless but powerful drug served to cushion the company against an outcry against a controversial drug it had later placed in the market.

Finally, long-term and strategic thinking can also be invaluable for overcoming inevitable behavioral biases. Managerial myopia is always a threat, and by focusing on what the company should have in the market a decade ahead, Roy Vagelos helped ensure that his company would indeed stay on sound footing.[18]

Preparing Leadership for a Firefighting Crisis

Leading people is not a natural skill set for most managers. Yet organizations often implicitly treat leadership as inborn when they promote people into positions of responsibility because of their technical skills, not their leadership prowess, and then provide no training in the precepts of leadership. The deadly result of such underselection and undertraining can be seen in the behavior of team leaders in two well-documented disasters in wildland fire fighting. We briefly characterize each disaster and then turn to the steps taken by U.S. agencies to better prepare its firefighters in the art of leadership for fire combat. Significant errors of judgment in both episodes were likely preventable if those responsible for the firefighting groups had received adequate instruction in the precepts of team leadership under stress.[19] This section provides an experience-anchored underpinning of the guiding principle of building leadership for preventing disasters before it is needed.

At 4 p.m. on August 5, 1949, an incident commander and a crew of fourteen parachuted into the remote Montana wilderness at Mann Gulch to combat what seemed to be a routine forest fire. By 5:56 p.m., 13 of the firefighters were fatally burned—at that time, the greatest disaster in the history of the U.S. wildland firefighting. Another disaster occurred on July 6, 1994, when a group of 49 firefighters had spread out on Storm King Mountain near Glenwood Spring, Colorado. Shortly after 4 o'clock in the afternoon, 14 firefighters on Storm King Mountain were overwhelmed by a fiery blowup.[20]

In both cases, bad luck and a fatal confluence of environmental factors contributed to the flaming ambush of the firefighters, but leadership decisions were critical in each, too. Those most directly responsible on site faced a sequence of decision points during their fateful hours in the fire zone, and their decisions at those moments helped take their teams to the brink of calamity.

In the Mann Gulch disaster, the incident commander reached several good leadership actions, including a last-minute decision to burn out a safe zone to save his crew. But his firefighters refused to enter the safe zone in part because by that point they had lost faith in his leadership. He had said very little to the crew since they entered the fire zone at 4 p.m., he explained none of his actions in the gulch, nor did he share any appraisals of the situation, and he had allowed one of the least experienced firefighters to occupy the second most important position as they moved through the fire zone. Also, he had never trained with his crew members before they parachuted into Mann Gulch. As a result, the incident commander's authority had become undermined when he most critically needed to exercise it.

Though the incident commander in Mann Gulch carried responsibility for his leadership lapses, he had received no leadership training for overcoming his own natural limitations before they proved deadly. Moreover, the U.S. policy at the time was for teams of firefighters to be assembled at the moment of a fire rather than forming together well before being called into fire combat. Had the incident commander been well trained and had his team been well formed before dropping into Mann Gulch, it is likely that this disaster would never have happened.

A series of leadership lapses in the Storm King Mountain fire some 45 years later contributed to that disaster as well. Again, one of the firefighters in charge—not officially designated the incident commander but in effect operating as such—had made several good decisions on the fateful day of July 6, 1994. He had secured additional backup when the fire expanded, conducted aerial surveillance to appraise the fire conditions, and sent a number of firefighters to safety when the fire threatened to blow-up. Yet at the same time, he had taken several suboptimal actions, including decisions to build a risky defensive line in an effort to stop the fire, leave ambiguous who precisely was in charge of the fire crew, and not seek updated forecasts of the local weather that would have warned of blustery conditions.

Some of the nation's most elite wildland firefighters were on Storm King Mountain, but qualified observers have generally concluded that they were drawn into what was in fact a preventable disaster. If even those most technically adept at fire suppression were caught by a blowup, a lack of formal firefighting skills was not the primary cause. As in the case of Mann Gulch, the firefighter in charge had never received training in how to lead in fire combat. In fact, the custom at the time was for one of the first firefighters to land on the site by helicopter to take charge, regardless of prior leadership preparation or experience. This disaster and that in Mann Gulch derived from an underdeveloped leadership capacity for making sound and rapid leadership decisions under demanding conditions. To understand everything about fire behavior but little about human behavior is to possess only half the equipment that a fire leader requires. Yet government practices at the time placed much emphasis on the former but little on the latter. Simply put, good people were left on their own to exercise what leadership they could muster without prior training in it.

In the wake of the 1994 disaster, the National Wildfire Coordinating Group, a consortium of federal and state wildland firefighting agencies, established the Wildland Fire Leadership Development Program in 2001 to enhance leadership skills so that responsible firefighters could "make sound and timely decisions." Federal agencies created an array of courses with depth training in leadership decisions in the kinds of fast-changing, unfamiliar, and complex environments that often define firefighting.

These leadership courses emphasize building leadership decision-making skills for safety, speed, and suppression in a fire zone. They also emphasize learning to cope with ambiguous authority and personal stress. While sources of suboptimal decision making can never be entirely eliminated, the federal coursework is intended to mitigate one important cause of firefighting disasters: underpreparation of incident commanders for taking leadership decisions and other actions, especially when stress is intense and untrained leadership is more likely to falter.

To reinforce the classroom lessons, the Wildland Fire Leadership Development Program also created a set of learning experiences that draw on the concept of the battlefield "staff ride." Long used by the armed forces to teach military strategy, staff rides reconstruct key leadership decisions on the ground at sites such as the battlefields of Gettysburg and Normandy. The essence of these exercises helps anchor leadership principles through the indelible experience of standing where others had stood when they were in a leadership position.[21]

Leadership Precepts and Guiding Principles from Firefighting Experience

The experience of firecombat teams in Mann Gulch and on Storm King Mountain underscores the seventh guiding principle of *Learning from Catastrophes*, which stresses the importance of building leadership for averting and surviving disasters. In both firefighting incidents, an individual willingly stepped forward to lead, but neither had been trained in how to lead. Had their leadership been developed then as it is now among their contemporary successors, the incidents in Mann Gulch and Storm King might never have devolved into the human disasters that they became.

Leadership precepts such as *clear-minded judgment under stress* and *clear communication of survival strategies* are essential for leading in high-risk environments. They can be strengthened through leadership development programs, and the Mann Gulch and Storm King events point to the value of doing so before those in responsible positions are called to exercise their leadership. Taken together, the AIG, Merck, and firefighting events suggest the following experience-anchored leadership precepts and principles for averting and mitigating extreme risk.

Leadership Precepts for Averting and Mitigating Disasters

Ensure that company, community, and government leaders are prepared and organized to guard against overconfidence about low-probability, high-consequence events, both in themselves and among those who work for them.

Create a culture that plays down success and rivets attention on unsolved problems and potential threats.

Build a capacity for long-term and strategic thinking, with active consideration of the implications of leadership decisions both for decades ahead and for their impact not only on narrowly defined goals but also the over-arching interests of all stakeholders.

Guiding Principles for Leaders in Managing Extreme Risks

Develop reliable estimates of the risks and uncertainties of low-probability high-consequence events.

Appreciate that a single unit in a complex entity can potentially place all units at risk, and interdependencies that appear safe at one moment may develop into unsafe interconnections later.

Understand behavioral biases that people bring to the workplace and build ways of guarding against them.

Develop leadership throughout the organization for averting and overcoming disasters before that leadership is called upon.

The Enduring Importance of Leadership in the Face of Extreme Risk

The AIG, Merck, and firefighting events underscore the importance of two tenets of leadership development for averting and mitigating disasters. The first tenet is that because leadership for many managers is unnatural, training is essential. For those responsible for managing risk and leading organizations that face a severe test from either naturally caused or person-made disasters, the best time to prepare for their leadership is well before it must be exercised.[22]

The second leadership development tenet is that because many leadership precepts are unmemorable in abstract form, anchoring the precepts in tangible experience is invaluable. Among the more effective methods for doing so is through exposure of prospective or active leaders to incidents and experiences where leadership helped avert—or its shortcomings contributed to—avoidable disasters.

Classroom programs can serve as a good vehicle for conveying leadership precepts, and tangible venues can serve as indelible vehicles for remembering how to apply them. Personal engagement in the latter can help cut through the fog of abstraction and connect theory with practice more powerfully than most other learning methods. In the summary language of researcher Max Bazerman, an "event that evokes emotions and is vivid, easily imagined, and specific" will have greater hold on an individual's memory than unemotional and bland events and thus be more able to inform one's future leadership.[23]

From the AIG, Merck, and firefighting events we also better appreciate the importance of trained and experienced leadership in the face of extreme risk. For averting disasters, it is important, first, to ensure that directors, executives, and frontline managers are prepared and organized to prevent the emergence of over-confidence in their organization about the likelihood and impact of low-probability and high-consequent events. And second, it is valuable to prepare directors, executives, and frontline managers in long-term strategic thinking to better appreciate how best to prepare for unlikely but catastrophic events before they happen.

Endnotes

Chapter 1, "Principles and Challenges for Reducing Risks from Disasters"

[1] Ronald T. Kozlowski and Stuart B. Mathewson, "Measuring and Managing Catastrophe Risk." *Journal of Actuarial Practice* 3(2) (1995), 211–241.

[2] Paul Slovic, *The Perception of Risk* (Earthscan 2000).

[3] Oswald Huber, Roman Wider, and Odilo Huber, "Active Information Search and Complete Information Presentation in Naturalistic Risky Decision Tasks," *Acta Psychologica* 95(5) (1997): 29.

[4] Daniel Kahneman, Paul Slovic, and Amos Tversky (eds.), *Judgment under Uncertainty: Heuristics and Biases* (Cambridge University Press, 1982).

[5] Amos Tversky and Daniel Kahneman, "Availability: A Heuristic for Judging Frequency and Probability." *Cognitive Psychology* 5 (1973): 207–232.

[6] Howard Kunreuther, "Risk Analysis and Risk Management in an Uncertain World," *Risk Analysis* 22 (2002): 655–64.

[7] A 1-in-100-year probability of a flood occurring is equivalent to a .22 chance of at least one such flood occurring during a 25-year period.

[8] "Cat Bonds Persevere in a Tumultuous Market," GCCapitalIdeas.com (Marsh & McLennan), February 4 (2009) www.gccapitalideas.com/2009/02/04/cat-bonds-perseverein-tumultuous-market.

[9] Kathleen Tierney, "Impacts of Recent Disaster on Businesses: The 1993 Midwest Floods and the 1994 Northridge Earthquake," in B. Jones (ed.). *Economic Consequences of Earthquakes: Preparing for the Unexpected* (National Center for Earthquake Engineering Research, 1997).

[10] Scott S. Cowen, "Be Prepared," *Chronicle of Higher Education*, April 21, 2006; Theresa Williams, "Restoring Tulane University after Hurricane Katrina," *Catastrophe Risk Management*, April 2006, 32–33.

[11] Reuters, "Honda, Nissan to Halt Output After Earthquake," July 19, 2007.

[12] For more detail on this point, see Dennis Mileti, *Disaster by Design* (Joseph Henry Press, 1999).

[13] Howard Kunreuther, "The Weakest Link: Risk Management Strategies for Dealing with Interdependencies," in *The Network Challenge: Strategy, Profit and Risk in the Interlinked World*, Paul Kleindorfer and Yoram Wind (eds.) (Wharton School Publishing/Pearson Education, 2009).

Chapter 2, "Acting in Time Against Disasters: A Comprehensive Risk-Management Framework"

[1] The authors are faculty members of the John F. Kennedy School of Government at Harvard University, where they are affiliated with the Taubman Center for State and Local Government and the Ash Institute for Democratic Governance and Innovation. They serve as the faculty co-directors of the Kennedy School's Program on Crisis Leadership and of Leadership in Crises, an executive education program focused on crisis management. We are grateful to Arrietta Chakos and David Giles for excellent support and research assistance, comments, and suggestions, and to Doug Ahlers for comments, suggestions, and extensive discussions about the issues addressed here.

[2] Herman B. Leonard and Arnold M. Howitt, "Against Desperate Peril: High Performance in Emergency Preparation and Response," in Deborah E. Gibbons (ed.), *Communicable Crises: Prevention, Response, and Recovery in the Global Arena* (Information Age Publishing, 2007) 1–25.

[3] By *social hazard*, we mean any uncertain prospective event with negative consequences that societies face—like droughts, hurricanes, floods, earthquakes, industrial accidents, and terrorist attacks. As the examples illustrate, social hazards can be either naturally occurring or man-made, and, in the latter case, can be either accidental or intentional.

[4] *Present value* means the value of future events, adjusted for the fact that they are in the future. Because we have the capacity to invest in the present and receive positive returns in the future, in general when the same event occurs at a later time it looms as less important in our thinking; it is, in the language of economics, "discounted." Taking account of present value means examining future consequences "discounted" to their equivalent current value (so as to make all the costs and benefits, which may

appear in different time periods, directly comparable to one another). *Expected* present value makes a further adjustment for those consequences that are probabilistic—it discounts them on the basis of the probability that they will happen. *Net* means that we take account of the costs of avoidance as well as the (probabilistic) value of damage from risky events. Thus, *expected net present value* refers to the time- and probability-adjusted future damage from a hazard, together with any investments made to reduce the anticipated damage.

[5] Economists use the term *social welfare* to refer to a very general understanding of the economic and social conditions and quality of life or well-being in a community. Generally, social welfare is correlated with income, but income is not by itself a complete measure of quality of life. Social welfare would include income and consumption, health status, and sense of security in the community.

[6] To the extent to which there is consideration in most existing literature given to actions that can be taken in advance that will accelerate recovery after the fact, they are generally in this category—the suggestion is that if the event can be made less severe, the recovery period will then be faster. Thus, nearly all existing discussions of what we would call advance recovery strategies are in the domain we would call advance *mitigation*, and not truly in the domain we refer to as advance *recovery*.

[7] Whether one regards the levee system as a form of prevention or a form of mitigation depends on how one defines the "event." If the event is defined as the arrival of a hurricane (which cannot be prevented), the levees constitute mitigation. If the event is defined as floodwaters throughout 80 percent of the City of New Orleans, a robust and intact levee system constitutes prevention. Because this difference is semantic, and depends on an arbitrary choice in the way the event is described, we generally treat prevention and mitigation as synonymous, and refer to them together.

[8] The terms *prevention* and *mitigation* are, confusingly, used differently by research communities focusing on different hazards. In general (applying the standard that ordinary English usage should be preferred), by our definition, prevention refers to keeping an event from happening, whereas mitigation refers to acting so as to modify the consequences of an event if it does occur. Unfortunately, this convention is not universal. For example, climate change commentators refer to CO_2 reduction—which can reasonably be expected to prevent climate change—as mitigation. Under our usage, mitigation in climate change would involve adaptive responses that reduce social damage that would be caused by shifts in climate—but this is referred to in that arena not as mitigation, but as "adaptation." By our definition, aerial cloud seeding would constitute prevention of a drought; building a levee would constitute mitigation of the consequences of flooding. But (see note 7) the distinction between prevention and mitigation depends on the how the "event" is defined. If the event is excessive rainfall, a flood levee is a form of mitigation. If the event is defined as the flood within the city limits, the levee is a form of prevention. Because this is largely a matter of terminology, we generally find it unhelpful and unnecessary to distinguish prevention from mitigation—in the end, both change the flow of consequences, which is all that matters, and we will generally treat them as two parts of the same thing. In examining particular hazards, however, we should be careful to seek a wide

range of different possible interventions, ranging from making the event disappear (prevention) to managing its impacts (mitigation). Where the terminological difference helps in the creation of a more robust search, it should be retained.

[9] Dennis Mileti (ed.), *Disasters by Design* (Joseph Henry Press, 1999). Mileti discusses the issue of sustainable development that encompasses disaster risk reduction.

[10] Max H. Bazerman and Don A. Moore, *Judgment in Managerial Decision Making, 7th Edition* (John Wiley and Sons, 2009); and Herman B. Leonard and Arnold M. Howitt, "Improving Performance: Dealing with Novelty and Cognitive Bias," in Arnold M. Howitt and Herman B. Leonard (eds.), *Managing Crises: Responses to Large-Scale Emergencies* (CQ Press, 2009) 407–412.

[11] Brenda D. Phillips and David M. Neal, "Recovery," in William L. Waugh and Kathleen Tierney (eds.), *Emergency Management: Principles and Practice for Local Government, 2nd Edition* (ICMA Press, 2007) 207–234; see, also, Kenneth C. Topping, "Toward a National Disaster Recovery Act of 2009," *Natural Hazards Observer*, 33(3) (2009): 1–9, for a recent discussion on the need for a national approach on disaster recovery.

[12] Craig E. Colten, Robert W. Kates, and Shirley B. Laska, "Three Years after Katrina: Lessons for Community Resilience," *Environment*, 50(5) (2007): 36–47. See, also, Esther Scott, *"Broadmoor Lives:" A New Orleans Neighborhood's Battle to Recover from Hurricane Katrina (A, B, Epilogue),* John F. Kennedy School of Government, Harvard University (2008) for a detailed examination of how local residents organized themselves to spearhead recovery efforts in the New Orleans neighborhood of Broadmoor following Hurricane Katrina.

[13] Of course, the extent of resources made available for recovery varies greatly. For example, four years after the terrible events of Hurricane Katrina, some areas of New Orleans still lie in ruins. Nonetheless, as a society, we have now spent many billions of dollars recovering only partially from an event that could have been prevented by the judicious expenditure of at most only a small number of billions of dollars. Thus, while Katrina gives us an example where even the relatively advantaged form of spending—recovery, after the fact—has probably been underinvested in, it still also illustrates that the *relative* balance of spending seems to favor recovery over prevention.

[14] This phenomenon is sufficiently common that it has a name in disaster management circles—it is commonly referred to as the "big red truck syndrome." In deliberately gender-laden terms, some refer to it as "boys and their toys."

[15] Multihazard Mitigation Council, *Hazard Mitigation Saves: An Independent Study to Assess the Future Savings from Mitigation Activities* (National Institute of Building Sciences, 2005). This study quantified the benefits of predisaster mitigation by examining the efficacy of federal risk reduction grant programs.

[16] Professor Gilbert White and his fellow hazards geographers generated the field of predisaster hazard mitigation and its notion of sustainable development. Their work contributed to the establishment of the U.S. National Flood Insurance Program, America's first systemic approach to disaster risk reduction.

[17] Claire B. Rubin (ed.), *Emergency Management: The American Experience, 1900–2005* (Public Entity Risk Institute, 2007); and William L. Waugh and Kathleen Tierney (eds.), *Emergency Management: Principles and Practice for Local Government, 2nd Edition* (ICMA Press, 2007). Taken together, Rubin's and Waugh and Tierney's works provide a comprehensive overview of how emergency management is organized, administered, and structured across multiple levels of government and agencies in the United States.

[18] Other approaches that share some similarities to PPBS in this respect include zero-base budgeting (ZBB) and, in a system with broader purposes than budgeting alone, the balanced scorecard approach initially developed for business organizations and later extended to not-for-profit and public-sector applications.

[19] There is an extensive literature on the development and use of "balanced scorecards" and other mechanisms for focusing attention on outcomes in a performance management system. See, for example, Robert Kaplan and David Norton, *The Strategy-Focused Organization* (Harvard Business School Press, 2001).

[20] The American experience with disaster risk reduction has been uneven, at best. But promising practices were developed with the enactment of the Disaster Mitigation Act 2000 and the Federal Emergency Management Agency's Project Impact effort that seeded safety projects in 250 disaster-prone cities.

[21] The language of "Acting in Time" is drawn from a multidisciplinary research project by that name, developed by David Ellwood, dean of Harvard's Kennedy School of Government. Generally, this project focuses on the challenges of mobilizing public action in the face of more- or less-obvious harms with more- or less-obvious solutions—but where getting people to act is nonetheless difficult. A considerable portion of our work on crisis leadership in the last several years has been conducted under this general rubric; in our work, the harms are not always so obvious, nor their solution so straightforward, so we use a broader interpretation of the Acting in Time framework, as presented here. For an overview of the Harvard Kennedy School's Acting in Time initiative, see www.hks.harvard.edu/about/admin/offices/dean/ait.

[22] *Positive deviance* is a term and approach to social learning developed by Jerry and Monique Sternin. See, for example, J. Sternin and R. Choo, "The Power of Positive Deviance," *Harvard Business Review*, January–February 2000: 14–15.

Chapter 3, "Forecasting and Communicating the Risk of Extreme Weather Events"

[1] 7 bis, Avenue de la Paix, Geneva, Switzerland.

[2] The draft standard ISO 13000 contains a definition of risk consistent with the conceptual explanation. See also the Australian/New Zealand Standard AS/NZS4360 1999: *Risk Management*. Homebush NSW 2140, Australia, Wellington 6001,

New Zealand. 44 pp., and also and the ISDR definitions of terms such as *risk* and *risk assessment* at www.unisdr.org/eng/library/lib-terminology-eng.htm.

[3] *Probability* is a statistical term meaning the measure of relative frequency of an event. Where the likelihood of occurrence of an event is determined through analysis of a sample of data, use of the term probability can be used interchangeably with *likelihood of occurrence,* where likelihood is obtained through more subjective means (for example, through averaging the assessments of a range of experts) it is more appropriate to use the term likelihood of occurrence.

[4] In some countries, the authority responsible for weather and climate services also provides hydrological services such as flood forecasting and water resources assessment. In many countries, these functional responsibilities are managed in separate agencies. However, the term *NMHS* accommodates both circumstances, making no assumption as to whether one or more agency is responsible for the functions.

[5] See Figure 8.2 (b) IPCC, 2007: Climate Change 2007: Impacts, Adaptation and Vulnerability. Contributions of Working Group II to the Fourth Assessment Report of the Intergovernmental Panel on Climate Change (M. L. Parry, O. F. Canziani, J. P. Palutikof, P. J. van der Linden and C. E. Hanson [eds.]) (Cambridge University Press) 976.

[6] UNEP 2004: Impacts of Summer 2003 Heat Wave in Europe. Environment Alert Bulletin 2:4.

[7] Sourced from Figure 8.2(b), IPCC, 2007: Climate Change 2007: Impacts, Adaptation and Vulnerability. Contributions of Working Group II to the Fourth Assessment Report of the Intergovernmental Panel on Climate Change (M. L. Parry, O. F. Canziani, J. P. Palutikof, P. J. van der Linden, and C. E. Hanson (eds.) (Cambridge University Press) 976.

[8] Schär, C., P. L. Vidale, D. Lüthi, C. Frei, C. Häberli, M. A. Liniger and C. Appenzeller, "The Role of Increasing Temperature Variability for European Summer Heat Waves," *Nature* 427 (2004): 332–336.

[9] See page 4, IPCC, 2007: Climate Change 2007: Impacts, Adaptation and Vulnerability. Contributions of Working Group II to the Fourth Assessment Report of the Intergovernmental Panel on Climate Change (M. L. Parry, O. F. Canziani, J. P. Palutikof, P. J. van der Linden, and C. E. Hanson (eds.) (Cambridge University Press) 976.

[10] See front matter, page vii, IPCC, 2007: Climate Change 2007: The Physical Science Basis. Contributions of Working Group I to the Fourth Assessment Report of the Intergovernmental Panel on Climate Change (S. Solomon, D. Qin, M. Manning, Z. Chen, M. Marquis, K. B. Averyt, M. Tignor, and H. L. Miller (eds.) (Cambridge University Press) 996.

[11] One of the key aspects in determining what a future Earth might look like given global warming due to increased greenhouse gas releases is to estimate future rates of release. The IPCC assessed the literature on the topic in 2000 and released a

report recommending the use of four families of scenarios based upon four different storylines. The report was the IPCC Special Report on Emission Scenarios (SRES Report) and its recommendations led to a widespread use of the recommended scenarios, often called the SRES scenarios.

[12] IPCC, 2007: Climate Change 2007: The Physical Science Basis. Contributions of Working Group I to the Fourth Assessment Report of the Intergovernmental Panel on Climate Change (S. Solomon, D. Qin, M. Manning, Z. Chen, M. Marquis, K. B. Averyt, M. Tignor, and H. L. Miller (eds.) (Cambridge University Press) 996.

[13] See page 2, IPCC, 2007: Climate Change 2007: Impacts, Adaptation and Vulnerability. Contributions of Working Group II to the Fourth Assessment Report of the Intergovernmental Panel on Climate Change (M. L .Parry, O. F. Canziani, J. P. Palutikof, P. J. van der Linden, and C. E. Hanson (eds.) (Cambridge University Press) 976.

[14] See, for example, Table SPM 1, IPCC, 2007: Climate Change 2007: Impacts, Adaptation and Vulnerability. Contributions of Working Group II to the Fourth Assessment Report of the Intergovernmental Panel on Climate Change (M. L. Parry, O. F. Canziani, J. P. Palutikof, P. J. van der Linden, and C. E. Hanson (eds.) (Cambridge University Press) 976.

[15] WMO, 2008: Guidelines on Communicating Forecast Uncertainty. (J. Gill, lead author, H. Kootval, editor) TD No. 4122:21.

[16] Three examples of such literature: S. Liu, L. E. Quenemoen, J. Malilay, E. Noji, T. Sinks, J. Mendlein, "Assessment of a Severe Weather Warning System and Disaster Preparedness, Calhoun County, Alabama. 1994," *American Journal of Public Health* (1996): 86–89 J. D. Papastavrou and M. R. Lehto, "Improving the Effectiveness of Warnings by Increasing the Appropriateness of their Information Content: Some Hypotheses about Human Compliance," *Safety Science* 3 (1996): 175–189. T. F. Wong and Y. Y. Yan, "Perceptions of Severe Weather Warnings in Hong Kong," *Meteorological Applications*, 9(3) (2002): 377–382.

[17] J. Whitehead, "One Million Dollars per Mile? The Opportunity Costs of Hurricane Evacuation," *Ocean & Coastal Management* 46(11–12) (2003): 1,069–1,083.

[18] Oxfam (2008), www.oxfamamerica.org/articles/some-people-dread-evacuations-almost-as-much-as-hurricanes.

[19] National Oceanic and Atmospheric Administration (NOAA) (2008) www.nhc.noaa.gov/verification/verify5.shtml.

[20] Subtropical climates are sometimes referred to as Mediterranean climates and occur around 25 to 40 degree latitude in both northern and southern hemispheres. The geographical extent of these areas is influenced by both topography and season.

[21] Different communities use different terminology for the hazard presented by uncontrolled forest fires, including brush fires, wildfires, or bush fires; these are considered here to be essentially the same, and it is this hazard that is under consideration.

Chapter 4, "Cognitive Constraints and Behavioral Biases"

[1] Howard Kunreuther, "Protective Decisions: Fear or Prudence," in *Wharton on Making Decisions*, Stephen J. Hoch, and Howard C. Kunreuther (eds.) (Wiley, 2001).

[2] Howard C. Kunreuther and Erwann O. Michel-Kerjan, (2007) "Climate Change, Insurability Of Large-Scale Disasters, and the Emerging Liability Challenge," *University of Pennsylvania Law Review* 155. No. 6, pp.1795-1842.

[3] John D. Sterman, "Learning from Evidence in a Complex World," *American Journal of Public Health* 96(3) (March 2006): 505–514; Sterman continues: "Complexity hinders our ability to discover the delayed and distal impacts of interventions, generating unintended 'side effects.' Yet learning often fails even when strong evidence is available: common mental models lead to erroneous but self-confirming inferences, allowing harmful beliefs and behaviors to persist and undermining implementation of beneficial policies."

[4] See, for example, Howard C. Kunreuther and Erwann O. Michel-Kerjan, *At War with the Weather* (MIT Press, 2009).

[5] Thought patterns in mathematical reasoning would include harmonic oscillator dynamics, matrix theory, and solution space analysis; while those in theoretical physics would include phase transitions, structure formation dynamics, self-organized criticality, and attractor classifications. Some of these are relevant in considering the complex, adaptive systems associated with weather patterns, climate change, and ecosystemic balance.

[6] Daniel Kahneman and Amos Tversky, "Prospect Theory: An Analysis of Decision under Risk," *Econometrica* XLVII (1979): 263–291.

[7] H. A. Simon, *Administrative Behavior: A Study of Decision-Making Processes in Administrative Organizations, 2nd ed.* (Macmillan, 1957).

[8] George A. Miller, "The Magical Number Seven, Plus or Minus Two: Some Limits on our Capacity for Processing Information," *Psychological Review* (1956); A. D. Baddeley and G. Hitch, "Working Memory" in G.H. Bower (ed.), *The Psychology of Learning and Motivation: Advances in Research and Theory* 8 (Academic Press, 1974) 47–89.

[9] N. Cowan, "The Magical Number 4 in Short-Term Memory: A Reconsideration of Mental Storage Capacity," *Behavioral and Brain Sciences* 24 (2001): 87–185

[10] Libya, South Yemen, and Syria were the other three on the list of December 29, 1979.

[11] The Mujahedin-e-Khalq, the Kurdistan Workers Party, the Palestine Liberation Front, and the Abu Nidal Organization.

[12] http://en.wikipedia.org/wiki/State_Sponsors_of_Terrorism.

[13] See D. Kahneman, J. L. Knetsch, R. H. Thaler, "Anomalies: The endowment effect, loss aversion, and status quo bias," *Journal of Economic Perspectives* 5(1) (Winter 1991): 193–206; Amos Tversky and Daniel Kahneman, *Loss Aversion in Riskless Choice: A Reference-Dependent Model* (MIT Press, 1991).

[14] S. Benartzi and R. H. Thaler, "Myopic Loss Aversion and the Equity Premium Puzzle," *Quarterly Journal of Economics* 110, No. 1 (Feb. 1995). pp. 73–92.

[15] Wikipedia lists 74 cognitive biases: http://en.wikipedia.org/wiki/List_of_cognitive_biases.

[16] The emotive-cognitive interactions that characterize our interactions with the external environment are discussed under neuroeconomics, (note 31).

[17] Language always comes with "frames." Every word is defined relative to a conceptual framework. See Luca Celati, *The Dark Side of Risk Management* (FT Prentice Hall, 2004).

[18] Celati (2004) cites Janis (1972, 1982, 1983, 1985, 1989), Janis and Mann (1977), Longley and Pruitt (1980), Wheeler and Janis (1980), 89.

[19] Ron Suskind, *The Price of Loyalty: George W. Bush, the White House, and the Education of Paul O'Neill* (Simon and Schuster, 2004); Bob Woodward, *Bush at War* (Simon and Schuster, 2002); Christopher Meyer, *DC Confidential* (Phoenix, 2005); Alastair Campbell and Richard Stott (eds.), *The Blair Years: Extracts from the Alastair Campbell Diaries* (Hutchinson, 2007).

[20] www.nytimes.com/2007/08/02/business/worldbusiness/02iht-citi.4.6962026.html; c.f. Lisa Endlich, *Goldman Sachs: The Culture of Success* (Warner Books, 1999); John Rolfe and Peter Troob, *Monkey Business: Swinging through The Wall Street Jungle* (Warner Books, 2000).

[21] Greenspan admits 'mistake' that helped crisis, Associated Press, October 23, 2008.

[22] In a smaller, more recent occurrence, the Loma Prieta earthquake struck the Bay Area on October 17, 1989. In 15 seconds, it killed 63 people in Northern California, injured 3,757, and left 8,000 to 12,000 homeless.

[23] BBC News, History of deadly earthquakes, May 12, 2008.

[24] BBC News, Iran earthquake kills thousands, Friday, December 26, 2003.

[25] Individuals may report motivations varying from any putative mean response.

[26] Work on risk homeostasis was pioneered by Gerald Wilde; see *Target Risk 2—A New Psychology of Safety and Health, 2nd ed.* (PDE, 1994).

[27] Gerald Wilde, op. cit. ch. 12; cf Thomas W. Hoyes, Neville A. Stanton, R. G. Taylor, "Risk Homeostasis Theory: A study of intrinsic compensation," *Safety Science* 22(1) (1996): 1–3.

[28] Thomas W. Hoyes, "Risk homeostasis theory—Beyond transportational research," *Safety Science* 22(1–3) (February–April 1996): 15–25.

[29] Mizue Ohe and Saburo Ikeda, "Global Warming: Risk Perception and Risk-Mitigating Behavior in Japan," in, *Mitigation and Adaptation Strategies for Global Change*. Springer (2005) 10: 221–236.

[30] Colin Camerer, George Loewenstein, and Drazen Prelec, "Neuroeconomics: Why economics needs. brains," Scandinavian Journal of Economics 106(3) (September 2004): 555–579.

[31] Brain imaging uses different techniques to provide clues into which regions control which neural functions and to enable understanding of how the brain solves different problems.

[32] The constrained utility maximization theory assumes that decisions are made in a state of deliberative equilibrium, where preferences, information, and constraints would shape the decision if time and computational ability were unlimited. cf. Camerer et al. (2004).

[33] Camerer and Loewenstein quoted in *Newsweek Technology*, www.msnbc.com/id/5304846/site/newsweek.

[34] In the occipital, parietal, and temporal lobes of the brain.

[35] Observable in the orbital and prefrontal parts of the cortex.

[36] Scott C. Hammond and Lowell M. Glenn, "The Ancient Practice of Chinese Social Networking: Guanxi and social network theory," *School of Business, Utah Valley State College E:CO* 6(1–2) (2004): 24–31.

[37] For example, offers in laboratory games that are seen as unfair or insulting.

[38] In the insula cortex.

[39] Recorded by the dorsolateral prefrontal cortex, see Camerer et al. (2004).

[40] Maurice E. Schweitzer and John C. Hershey, *Promises and Lies: Restoring Violated Trust* (Wharton School, University of Pennsylvania, 2006).

[41] Camerer et al. (2004)

[42] The waste (packaging materials, magazines, and food discarded as garbage) in Western middle-class life—and elsewhere in communities copying Western standards of display—is greatly inefficient.

[43] J. D. Sterman and Sweeney L. Booth, "Understanding Public Complacency about Climate Change: Adults' Mental Models of Climate Change Violate Conservation of Matter," *Climatic Change*, http://web.mit.edu/jsterman/www/Understandingpublic.html.

[44] Sterman (2006), op. cit.

[45] Camerer et al. (2004).

[46] Zajonc (1980), (1984), (1998), LeDoux et al. (1996), cited in Camerer et al. (2004).

[47] A stochastic system is nondeterministic as its subsequent state is determined both by the process's predictable actions, and by a random element.

[48] Richard Monastersky, "Climate Crunch: A burden beyond bearing, *Nature News*, April 29, 2009.

[49] Actions to reduce carbon emissions below 450ppm involve short-term personal sacrifices and lower global economic trajectories; relocation of populations from earthquake zones or floodplains involves significant costs and social and economic dislocation.

[50] Those who have argued against the IPCC reports often refer back to the Club of Rome report, The Limits of Growth, and argue that higher agricultural productivity eliminated the threat of exhausted food supplies and led to supply outpacing demand, with secular price declines in the two decades thereafter.

[51] See also Kunreuther and Michel-Kerjan (2009).

[52] Fear, greed, and lust are highly effective stimuli in sustaining species survival. Fear enables prudent behavior to avoid threat; greed encourages consolidation of resources needed to survive later scarcity; and lust underpins procreation. Greed has become problematical, however, as we have increased our stock of economic and technological capital through urbanization, industrialization, and financial sophistication, while depleting the natural capital available to us in the earth and atmosphere. Obesity, conspicuous consumption, waste, and pollution serve no purpose; they threaten our survival and that of other species.

[53] The "earmarks" added to the 2009 fiscal stimulus bill are an illustrative example.

Chapter 5, "The Five Neglects: Risks Gone Amiss"

[1] Herbert A. Simon, *Models of Man* (John Wiley & Sons, 1957).

[2] Daniel Kahneman, Paul Slovic, and Amos Tversky (eds.), *Judgment under Uncertainty: Heuristics and Biases* (Cambridge University Press, 1982).

[3] Cass R. Sunstein, "Probability Neglect: Emotions, Worst Cases, and Law" *Yale Law Journal*, 112(1) (2002): 61–107.

[4] Cass R. Sunstein and Richard J. Zeckhauser, "Dreadful Possibilities, Neglected Probabilities," *The Irrational Economist: Making Decisions in a Dangerous World*, E. Michel-Kerjan and P. Slovic (eds.) (Public Affairs Books, forthcoming in 2010).

[5] Timur Kuran and Cass R. Sunstein, "Availability Cascades and Risk Regulation," *Stanford Law Review* 51(4) (1999): 683–768.

[6] Richard J. Zeckhauser and W. Kip Viscusi, "Risk within Reason," *Science* 248(4955) (1990): 559–564.

[7] Carolyn Kousky, John Pratt, and Richard Zeckhauser, "Virgin Versus Experienced Risks," *The Irrational Economist: Making Decisions in a Dangerous World*, E. Michel-Kerjan and P. Slovic (eds.) (Public Affairs Books, forthcoming in 2010).

[8] Richard A. Posner, "Efficient Responses to Catastrophic Risk," *Chicago Journal of International Law* 6(2) (2006): 511–525.

[9] Amos Tversky and Daniel Kahneman, "Availability: A Heuristic for Judging Frequency and Probability," *Cognitive Psychology* 5 (1973): 207–232.

[10] Some risks lose their salience quickly. For instance, individuals have been found to drop catastrophe insurance after a few years without an event. See H. Kunreuther, "Has the Time Come for Comprehensive Natural Disaster Insurance?" *On Risk and Disaster*, R. J. Daniels, D. F. Kettl, and H. Kunreuther (University of Pennsylvania Press, 2006).

[11] Carolyn Kousky, John Pratt, and Richard Zeckhauser, "Virgin Versus Experienced Risks," *The Irrational Economist: Making Decisions in a Dangerous World*, E. Michel-Kerjan and P. Slovic (eds.) (Public Affairs Books, forthcoming in 2010).

[12] Amos Tversky and Daniel Kahneman, "Belief in the Law of Small Numbers," *Judgment under Uncertainty: Heuristics and Biases*, D. Kahneman, P. Slovic, and A. Tversky (eds.) (Cambridge University Press, 1982) 23–31.

[13] Matthew Rabin, "Inferences by Believers in the Law of Small Numbers," *Quarterly Journal of Economics*, 117(3) (2002): 775–816.

[14] H. J. McPherson and T. F. Saarinen, "Floodplain Dwellers' Perception of the Flood Hazard in Tucson, Arizona," *Annals of Regional Science* 11(2) (1977). pp. 25-40.

[15] William Samuelson and Richard Zeckhauser, "Status Quo Bias in Decision Making," *Journal of Risk and Uncertainty* 1 (1988): 7–59.

[16] For more on the Napa project, see K. Ellison and G. C. Daily, *The New Economy of Nature* (Island Press, 2002).

[17] Carolyn Kousky and Richard Zeckhauser, "JARring Actions That Fuel the Floods," *On Risk and Disaster: Lessons from Hurricane Katrina*, R. J. Daniels, D. F. Kettl, and H. Kunreuther (eds.) (University of Pennsylvania Press, 2006) 59–73.

[18] Alan Berger and Case Brown, "VIA: DIRT," *University of Pennsylvania School of Design Journal*, M. Born and L. Jencks (eds.), (2009) pp 27-36.

[19] A. Linoli, "Twenty-six Centuries of Reclamation & Agricultural Improvement on the Pontine Marshes," ICID 21st European Regional Conference, Tansl. Ken Hurry, Frankfurt, Germany, and Slubice, Poland (2005).

[20] Alan Berger and Case Brown, "Waste to Place: Joint Integrative Reclamation Series," United States Environmental Protection Agency Special Publication Series, Government Printing Office (2009).

[21] R. Topper, "History of Summitville Mine Reclamation," *Rock Talk (Colorado Geological Survey)* 4(2) (2001): 8–13.

[22] S. Fields, "The Earth's Open Wounds: Abandoned and Orphaned Mines," *Environmental Health Perspectives* 111(3) (2003): A154–A161.

[23] Alan Berger and Case Brown, "Waste to Place: Joint Integrative Reclamation Series," United States Environmental Protection Agency Special Publication Series, Government Printing Office (2009).

[24] U.S. EPA. "Superfund Program: Silver Bow Creek/Butte Area," Retrieved May 18 (2009) from www.epa.gov/region8/superfund/mt/sbcbutte/index.html.

[25] D. K. Higgins and S. N. Wiemeyer, "Environmental Contaminants Program Interim Report: NV-Assessment of Wildlife Hazards Associated with Mine Pit Lakes," U.S. Department of the Interior, Fish and Wildlife Service, Region 1, Nevada Fish and Wildlife Office (2009).

[26] U.S. Department of the Interior, "Audit Report: Abandoned Mine Lands in the Department of the Interior, C-IN-MOA-004-2007," U.S. Department of the Interior, Office of Inspector General (2008).

[27] J. Brinkley "Death Toll Rises but Money In Mine Fund Goes Unspent," *New York Times*, September 26, 2002.

Chapter 6, "Can Poor Countries Afford to Prepare for Low-Probability Risks?"

[1] http://obamaspeeches.com/E10-Barack-Obama-The-American-Promise-Acceptance-Speech-at-the-Democratic-Convention-Mile-High-Stadium—Denver-Colorado-August-28-2008.htm.

[2] Anthony Mwangi, "Cyclone Nargis and talk of climate change," IFRC, Geneva (November 2008).

[3] Jeff Masters, director of Weather Underground, quoted by the Associated Press, May 9, 2008.

[4] http://www.cseindia.org/AboutUs/press_releases/press_20080507.htm.

[5] The Intergovernmental Panel on Climate Change (IPCC) in Asia has established that climate change will intensify tropical cyclones. The IPCC notes: "Based on a range of models, it is likely that future tropical cyclones (typhoons and hurricanes) will become more intense, with larger peak wind speeds. and more heavy precipitation associated with ongoing increases of tropical sea surface temperatures."

[6] Cyclone, hurricane, and typhoon describe the same phenomenon, but different terms are used depending on the ocean basin in which they form.

[7] "Bangladesh: Working to improve disaster preparedness," IRIN news, October 8, 2008.

[8] The 1991 Bangladesh cyclone that sparked modern efforts to build early-warning systems killed 138,000 people, while the 1970 Bhoha cyclone killed between 300,000 and 500,000 people.

[9] I. Burton, R. W. Kates, and G. White, *The Environment as Hazard* (Guilford Press, 1993).

[10] UNISDR and German Committee for Disaster Reduction. *Early Warning—From concept to action: The Conclusions of the Third International Conference on Early Warning* (Bonn: UNISDR, 2006(c)).

[11] UNESCO. Intergovernmental Coordination Group for the Tsunami Early Warning and Mitigation System in the North Eastern Atlantic, the Mediterranean and Connected Seas (ICG/NEAMTWS) Report on the 4th Session, Lisbon, 21–23 November 2007 (Paris: UNESCO, 2008).

[12] *Tsunami Early Warning System for the Mediterranean, a German Proposal*. 2008. Available at www.aidfunding.mfa.gr/bpufm/pdf/germaniki_protasi.pdf.

[13] "Atlas for Disaster Preparedness and Response in the Limpopo Basin," INGC, UEM-Department of Geography and FEWS NET MIND (2003).

[14] UNISDR. "Hyogo Framework for Action: Building the Resilience of Nations and Communities to disasters" (Geneva: UNISDR, 2005).

[15] "Beating the Hurricane: How are Cubans prepared to face hurricanes?" The Inter-Agency secretariat of the International Strategy for Disaster Reduction (UN/ISDR), 2006 and UNTV Geneva, available at www.unisdr.org/eng/media-room/mr-videos.htm.

[16] F. Christie, F. and J. Hanlon, *Mozambique and the Great Flood of 2000*. Bloomington: Indiana University Press. (2001).

[17] C. Howell, *Indigenous Early Warning Indicators of Cyclones: Potential Applications in Coastal Bangladesh* (Benfield Hazard Research Centre, 2003).

[18] T. Xu, "Managing Disaster Risk In A Mega-City," *WMO Bulletin* 55(4) (October 2006).

[19] "Lessons Save life: Story of Tilly Smith," video produced by the Inter-Agency Secretariat of the International Strategy for Disaster Reduction (UN/ISDR) (2005), available at www.unisdr.org/eng/media-room/mr-videos.htm.

[20] "After the Tsunami: Part 2," The Earth Report, Television Trust for the Environment, available at www.tve.org/earthreport/archive/doc.cfm?aid=1661.

[21] LIRNEasia, *Evaluating Last-Mile Hazard Information Dissemination: A Research Proposal* (LIRNEasia, 2008).

[22] See www.ranetproject.net.

Chapter 7, "The Role of Risk Regulation in Mitigating Natural Disasters"

[1] United Nations International Strategy for Disaster Reduction Secretariat (UNISDR) (2009), "Global assessment report on disaster risk reduction: risk and poverty in a changing climate," www.preventionweb.net/english/hyogo/gar/?unisdr, accessed May 21, 2009.

[2] Parliamentary Office of Science and Technology, "Postnote: Early Warnings for Natural Disasters" (2005).

[3] A. Giddens, "Risk and Responsibility," *Modern Law Review* 62(1): 1–10.

[4] U. Beck, "Living in the World Risk Society," *Economy and Society* 35(3) (2006): 329–345.

[5] Beck, 2006 op cit.

[6] See generally B. Hutter, "Risk Regulation and Management, *Risk in Social Science*, P. Taylor-Gooby and J. Zinn (eds.) (Oxford University Press, 2006b).

[7] See note 1.

[8] U.N. op. cit.

[9] *Lancet* 373(9676) (May 16, 2009): 1659.

[10] This is true of all disaster situations; with respect to the financial situation see N. N. Taleb, *The Black Swan: The Impact of the Highly Improbable* (Penguin, 2007).

[11] P. Showalter and M. Myers, "Natural Disasters in the United States as Release Agents of Oil, Chemicals, or Radiological Materials Between 1980–1989: Analysis and Recommendations," *Risk Analysis* 14(2) (2006): 169–182.

[12] C. Perrow, *The Next Catastrophe: Reducing Our Vulnerabilities to Natural, Industrial, and Terrorist Disasters* (Princeton University Press, 2007).

[13] M. Balamir, "Painful Steps of Progress from Crisis Planning to Contingency Planning: Changes for Disaster Preparedness in Turkey," *Journal of Contingencies and Crisis Management* 10(1) (2002): 39.

[14] Balamir, op. cit.

[15] Balamir, op. cit.

[16] R. Palm, "Educating Business and Industry about Disasters: Legislative Problems in the Adoption of Modified Lending Terms by Home Mortgage Lenders," *Review of Policy Research* 4(4) (2005): 655—661.

[17] M. Comerio, "Public Policy for Reducing Earthquake Risks: A US Perspective," *Building Research and Information: The International Journal of Research, Development and Demonstration* 32(5) (2004): 403.

[18] R. Spence, "Risk and Regulation: Can Improved Government Action Reduce the Impacts of Natural Disasters? *Building Research and Information: The International Journal of Research, Development and Demonstration* 32(5) (2004): 391.

[19] H. Kunreuther and E. Michel-Kerjan, *At War with the Weather: Managing Large-Scale Risks in a New Era of Catastrophes* (MIT Press, 2009).

[20] R. J. Burby, "Flood Insurance and Floodplain Management: The US experience," *Environmental Hazards* 3 (2001): 111–122.

[21] Balamir, op. cit.

[22] OECD Recommendation Concerning Guidelines On Earthquake Safety in Schools, www.oecd.org/dataoecd/11/45/31968539.pdf, accessed June 1, 2009.

[23] Spence op. cit.

[24] Spence op. cit.

[25] R. J. Burby and L. C. Dalton, "Plans Can Matter! The Role of Land Use Plans and State Planning Mandates in Limiting the Development of Hazardous Areas," *Public Administration Review* 54(3) (1994): 229–238.

[26] A. Wildavsky, *Searching for Safety* (Oxford Transaction Books, 1988).

[27] J. Linnerooth-Bayer and R. Melcher, "Insurance against Losses from Natural Disaster in Developing Countries," Background paper for United Nations World Economic and Social Survey (2007).

[28] See H. Kunreuther and Michel-Kerjan op. cit.

[29] Comerio op. cit.

[30] Spence op. cit.

[31] See J. Linnerooth-Bayer and R. Melcher (2007) op. cit. and Spence (2004) op. cit. The United States also operates a Federal Crop Insurance Program to offer insurance against crop loses caused by natural disasters. See Barry J. Barnett, "US Government Natural Disaster Assistance: Historical Analysis and a Proposal for the Future," *Disasters* (0361-3666), 23(2) (1999): 139.

[32] Spence op. cit.

[33] See E. Michel-Kerjan, "Insurance against Natural Disasters: Do the French Have the Answer? Strengths and Limitations" *Working Paper, Ecole Polytechnique* (2001): 1–28; J. Linnerooth-Bayer and R. Melcher op. cit. and Spence op. cit.

[34] See Spence op. cit.

[35] See S. E. Harrington, (1999). "Rethinking Disaster Policy." *Regulation* 23(1): 40; H. Kunreuther, "Mitigating Disaster Losses through Insurance," *Journal of Risk and Uncertainty* 12 (1996): 2–3; and J. Linnerooth-Bayer and R. Melcher (2007) op. cit.

[36] Comerio op. cit.

[37] Balamir op. cit.

[38] P. Berke, "Reducing Natural Hazard Risks through State Growth Management," *Journal of the American Planning Association* 64(1) (1988): 76.

[39] J. McClure, M. W. Allen, and F. Walkey, "Countering Fatalism: Causal Information in News Reports Affects Judgments about Earthquake Damage," *Basic and Applied Social Psychology* 23(2) (2001): 109–121.

[40] Spence op. cit.

[41] R. Wolensky and W. Wolensky, "Local Government's Problem with Disaster Management: A literature review and structural analysis," *Review of Policy Research* 9(4) (2005): 703–725.

[42] Berke op. cit.

[43] Wolensky and Wolensky op. cit.

[44] Comerio op. cit.

[45] E. Chamlee-Wright, "Disastrous Uncertainty: How Government Disaster Policy Undermines Community Rebound," *Mercatus Policy Series* 9 (2007): 1–24.

[46] S. Ikeda, "Toward an Integrated Management Framework for Emerging Disaster Risks in Japan," *Natural Hazards* (Dordrecht) 44(2) (2007): 267.

[47] M. Erdik and E. Durukal, "Earthquake Risk and Its Mitigation in Istanbul," cited in A. Amendola, J. Linnerooth-Bayer, N. Okada, and Shi Peijun, "Toward Integrated

Disaster Risk Management: Case studies and trends from Asia," *Natural Hazards* 44 (2008): 163–168.

[48] Balamir op. cit.

[49] Chamlee-Wright op. cit.

[50] P Green, "Disaster by Design: Corruption, Construction and Catastrophe," *British Journal of Criminology* 45(4) (2005): 528.

[51] Wildavsky op. cit.

Chapter 8, "Hedging Against Tomorrow's Catastrophes: Sustainable Financial Solutions to Help Protect Against Extreme Events"

[1] For a discussion of the necessity to profoundly rethink risk management in this new environment, see E. Michel-Kerjan, "Haven't You Switched to Risk Management 2.0 Yet? Moving Toward a New Risk Architecture," in E. Michel-Kerjan and P. Slovic (eds.), *The Irrational Economist* (Public Affairs, 2010).

[2] For an analysis of the factors influencing these changes, see H. Kunreuther and E. Michel-Kerjan, *At War with the Weather: Managing Large-Scale Risks in a New Era of Catastrophes* (MIT Press, 2009). See also the contribution by Suzanne Nora Johnson in this book.

[3] This figure excludes payment by the U.S. National Flood Insurance Program (NFIP) for damage due to 2005 flooding (over $20 billion in claims).

[4] Only catastrophes inflicting insured losses above $38.7 million or total losses above $77.5 million are considered "major catastrophes" by Swiss Re and are reported here. The true total losses are thus higher.

[5] Man-made catastrophes include major fires and explosions (in a chemical plant or oil refinery for instance), aviation/rail/shipping-related losses (fires, crashes, collisions) and mining accidents and collapse of infrastructure.

[6] H. Kunreuther and E. Michel-Kerjan, *At War with the Weather: Managing Large-Scale Risks in a New Era of Catastrophes* (MIT Press, 2009).

[7] H. Kunreuther and E. Michel-Kerjan (2009) op. cit.

[8] For instance, as of December 2008, the policyholders' surplus of the private U.S. P&C insurers was $455 billion. As an element of comparison, it is estimated that

insured values located on the U.S. coasts from Texas to Maine are more than $8 trillion (even though probability needs. to be factored in of course).

[9] Other types of ART instruments have been developed, such as collateral debt obligations (CDOs) and sidecars, which was a phenomenon of the post–Hurricane Katrina market environment. A sidecar is a special-purpose company that provides reinsurance coverage exclusively to its sponsor (a reinsurer or a large insurer) by issuing securities to investors. Unlike ILWs or cat bonds, which generally provide excess-of-loss reinsurance, sidecars are often based on quota-share reinsurance. The sidecar company shares the risks of certain insurance or reinsurance policies with the underwriter in exchange for a portion of the premiums (generally up to 50 percent) and dividends in shares. In 2005, the total volume was $2.2 billion, in 2006 it was $4.2 billion, and in 2007 it was $1.7 billion.

Other instruments include exchange-traded catastrophe/weather derivatives such as contracts on the Insurance Futures Exchange (IFEX) and Chicago Mercantile Exchange (CME).

[10] The figure combines bonds for natural disasters in the United States and abroad, as well as the first liability cat bond (Avalon Re), issued by Oil Casualty Company in 2005 for $405 million.

[11] I thank the Goldman Sachs team for providing me with the most recent data on the cat bond market.

[12] In addition, there was a clear duration mismatch between short-term placements of cat bonds (maturity is typically a few years) and long-term investments for the assets used as collateral. When the market collapsed, the value of the swaps increased significantly and the investors lost value on the collateral (without Lehman's guarantee anymore).

[13] For an analysis of the main reasons of this lack of insurance development and other innovations currently under study, see J. D. Cummins and O. Mahul, *Catastrophe Risk Financing in Developing Countries* (The World Bank, 2008).

[14] Source: International Monetary Fund, www.imf.org.

[15] World Food Program (2005), Projects for Executive Board Approval. Agenda item 8. Pilot Development Project. Ethiopia Drought Insurance, Executive Board, Second Regular Session, Rome, 7–11 November 2005.

[16] The challenge of collecting weather data—very much aligned with the importance of a good knowledge of the underlying risks—can be a real limitation because poor countries often do not have high quality weather data collection tools.

[17] World Food Program (2007), Operational report. Agenda item 10. Final Report on the Ethiopia Drought Insurance Pilot Project, Executive Board, First Regular Session, Rome, 19–21 February 2007.

[18] World Food Program (2007), op. cit.

[19] These recommendations are based on E. Michel-Kerjan and F. Morlaye, "Extreme Events, Global Warming, and Insurance-Linked Securities: How to Trigger the 'Tipping Point,'" *The Geneva Papers on Risk and Insurance* 33 (2008): 153–176; Milken Institute *Financial Innovations for Catastrophe Risk: Cat Bonds and Beyond* (2008); Organization for Economic Cooperation and Development (OECD), *Catastrophe-Linked Securities and Capital Markets*, Directorate for Financial and Enterprise Affairs, Paris (2009); World Economic Forum *Convergence of Insurance and Capital Markets*, Geneva, (2008).

[20] Organization for Economic Cooperation and Development (OECD), *Catastrophe-Linked Securities and Capital Markets*, Directorate for Financial and Enterprise Affairs, Paris (2009).

Chapter 9, "A Financial Malignancy"

[1] Nouriel Roubini, an economist at New York University, is widely credited with forecasting the financial and economic crises of 2008. A number of other commentators also forecast dangers of the financial system. Noted below, by topic area are some leading examples.

Housing: Thomas Helbling and Marco Terrones, "When Bubbles Burst," The International Monetary Fund, *World Economic Outlook* (April 2003), Chapter 2, pp. 61-94. http://www.imf.org/external/pubs/ft/weo/2003/01/pdf/chapter2.pdf; Dean Baker, "The Run-Up in House Prices: Is It Real or Is It Another Bubble?", *Center for Economic and Policy Research* (Washington, DC), 2002; Dean Baker, "The Menace of an Unchecked Housing Bubble," The Economists Voice, *Center for Economic and Policy Research*, (Washington, DC), March 30, 2006; Paul Krugman, "Bursting Bubbles Blues", *The New York Times*, October 30, 2006, http://select.nytimes.com/2006/10/30/opinion/30krugman.html?_r=1.

Robert J. Schiller; *Irrational Exuberance (2nd Edition)*, Princeton University Press, (2005); CNBC, "How to Profit from the Real Estate Boom" program, appearance by Robert J. Schiller (2005); Jan Hatzius, "Housing Holds the Key to Federal Policy," *Goldman Sachs Economics Analyst, Paper, No. 137* (February 3, 2006).

Financial Engineering and Innovation: Raghuram G. Rajan, "Has Financial Development Made the World Riskier," Proceedings, Federal Reserve Bank of Kansas City (August 2005), pp. 313-369, http://www.kansascityfed.org/publicat/sympos/2005/pdf/rajan2005.pdf; Richard Bookstaber, *A Demon of Our Own Design: Markets, Hedge Funds: and the Perils of Financial Innovation*, John Wiley & Sons, Inc. Hoboken, New Jersey (2007); Nassim Nicholas Taleb, *The Black Swan: The Impact of the Highly Improbable*, The Random House Publishing Group, a division of Random House, Inc., (2007).

Derivatives: Warren Buffett, *Berkshire Hathaway, Inc., 2002 Annual Report* (February 21, 2003); Brooksley Born, "A Regulatory Reform: Looking, Back, Looking

Ahead, Remarks of Brooksley Born, Chairperson, Commodity Futures Trading Commission Before the Futures Industry Association, 2^{3rd} Annual International Futures Industry Conference, Boca Raton, Florida," (March 19, 1998).

Macro imbalances: Benjamin Bernanke, "The Global Saving Glut and the U.S., Current Account Deficit," *Sandridge Lecture*, Virginia Association of Economics, Richmond, Virginia, Federal Reserve Board, (March 10, 2005); Martin Wolf, *Fixing Global Finance*, The Johns Hopkins University Press, (2008).

Monetary Policy: Alan Greenspan, "Remarks by Alan Greenspan, chairman, Board of Governors of the Federal Reserve System, before the World Bank, Conference on Recent Trends in Reserve Management," Washington, DC, (April 29, 1999).

[2] Germany and Japan were the notable exceptions.

[3] Kevin Daly and Ben Broadbent, "The Savings Glut, the Return on Capital, and the Rise in Risk Aversion," Goldman Sachs Economics Paper, No. 185, (May 27, 2009). Note, however, that the economic literature on the merits of financial globalization is evolving rapidly. A very comprehensive review of the literature presents newer approaches that depart from the neoclassical framework. See M. Ayhan Kose, Eswar Prasad, Kenneth Rogoff, Shang-Hin Wei, "Financial Globalization and Economic Policies," *Institute for the Study of Labor Discussion Paper No. 4037* (February 2009).

[4] Elizabeth C. Economy and Adam Segal, "The G-2 Mirage: Why the United States and China Are Not Ready to Upgrade Ties," *Foreign Affairs* (May/June 2009) 14–23; Niall Ferguson and Moritz Schularick, "Chimerica and Global Asset Markets," 13–21 (http://jfki.fu-berlin.de/faculty/economics/team/persons/schularick/chimerica.pdf) (2007).

[5] McKinsey Global Institute, *Mapping Global Capital Markets: Fifth Annual Report,* (October 1, 2008) 14.

[6] *The Economist* (April 25, 2009) 1.

[7] Gordon Brown, "Don't Go Wobbly on Trade," *The Wall Street Journal* (May 28, 2009) A15.

[8] The Group of 20 (G20) Finance Ministers and Central Bank Governors was established in 1999 to bring together systemically important developed and developing economies to discuss key issues in the global economy. The G20 was created as a response both to the financial crises of the late 1990s and to a growing recognition that key developing countries were not adequately included in the core of global economic discussion and governance. The G20 is made up of the European Union and 19 countries (Argentina, Australia, Brazil, Canada, China, France, Germany, India, Indonesia, Italy, Japan, Mexico, Russia, Saudi Arabia, South Africa, South Korea, Turkey, the United Kingdom, and the United States).

[9] The Financial Stability Forum (the FSF) was founded in 1999 to promote financial stability. The FSF facilitates discussion and cooperation in supervision and surveillance of financial institutions. Its founding resulted from discussions among G7

Finance Ministers and Central Bank Governors. At the 2009 G20 Summit in London it was decided that a successor to the FSF, the Financial Stability Board, would be established. All members of the G20 who are not currently part of the FSF will be invited to be members.

[10] Martin Wolfe, *Fixing Global Finance* (Johns Hopkins University Press, 2008) 2.

[11] Henry Paulson, "Reform the Architecture of Regulation," *FT.com* (March 19, 2009).

[12] "The Regulatory Rumble Begins," *The Economist* (May 30, 2009) 75–76.

[13] *Truthiness* is a term first used in its recent satirical sense by American television comedian Stephen Colbert in 2005, to describe things that a person claims to know intuitively or "from the gut" without regard to evidence, logic, intellectual examination, or facts. Colbert introduced this definition of the word during the pilot episode of his political satire program *The Colbert Report* on October 17, 2005, as the subject of a segment called "The Wørd." *Truthiness* was named Word of the Year for 2005 by the American Dialect Society and for 2006 by Merriam-Webster. See Wikipedia.com.

[14] Richard A. Posner, *A Failure of Capitalism*, Harvard University Press (2009), p. 128.

[15] Note that the other major U.S. credit rating agency, Moody's, said it had no plans to reduce the U.S.'s AAA rating. Buttonwood, "Not So Risk Free," *The Economist* (May 30, 2009) 76.

[16] John Taylor, "Exploding Debt Threatens America," *Financial Times* (May 27, 2009) 9.

[17] International Monetary Fund, "Fiscal Implications of the Global Economic and Financial Crisis," International Monetary Fund Staff Positions Note, www.imf.org/external/pubs/ft/spn/2009/spn0913.pdf (June 9, 2009).

[18] U.S. Department of Treasury, "White Paper on the Capital Assistance Program," www.financialstability.gov (February 25, 2009).

[19] Clive Crook, "We're on Course for the Next Crisis," *National Journal* (May 16, 2009), 15–16; see also: Nouriel Roubini, "The 'Stress Tests' are Really 'Fudge Tests,'" *Forbes.com* (April 16, 2009); "Hospital Pass: America's Stress Tests Were Too Easy," *The Economist* (May 16, 2009) 81; Congressional Oversight Panel, "Panel Finds That Stress Test Models Were Reasonable, but Serious Concerns Remain," http://cop.senate.gov/press/releases/release-060909-report.cfm (June 8, 2009). However, note that the IMF has developed similar loss estimates. See *The Economist* (May 16, 2009) 81.

[20] Group of Thirty, *Reform: A Framework for Financial Stability*, Consultative Group on International Economic and Monetary Affairs, Inc. (January 15, 2009); Benn Steil, "Lessons of the Financial Crisis," *Council on Foreign Relations Special Report, No. 45*, (March 2009); Financial Services Authority, The Turner Review: A Regulatory Response to the Global Banking Crisis, (March 2009); The Committee on

Capital Markets Regulation, *The Global Financial Crisis: A Plan for Regulatory Reform* (May 2009).

[21] Raghuram G. Rajan, "Economics Focus: Cycle-proof Regulation," *The Economist* (April 11, 2009) 79.

[22] Mohamed El-Erian, "Every Official Action Must Trigger Market Reaction," *Financial Times* (January 8, 2009) 26.

[23] Ian Bremmer, "The End of the Free Market," *Foreign Affairs* (May/June 2009) 40–55.

[24] Alan S. Blinder, "Crazy Compensation and the Crisis," *Wall Street Journal* (May 28, 2009) A15.

[25] Lucien A. Bebchuk and Holger Spamann, "Regulating Bankers Pay," *The Harvard John M. Olin Discussion Paper Series: Discussion Paper No. 641*, www.law.harvard.edu/programs/olin_center/ (June 2009).

[26] Jane Croft, "An Examination of Weaknesses in the System," *Financial Times* (April 20, 2009) 2; "Rebuilding the Banks," *The Economist* (May 16, 2009) 14–17; Roger. Lowenstein, "Triple-A Failure", *New York Times Magazine, April 27, 2008.*

[27] Joseph E. Stiglitz, "Wall Street's Toxic Message," *Vanity Fair* (July 2009).

[28] Zhou Xiaocchuan, "Reform the International Monetary System," March 2009. See also, Michael Hudson, "Washington Is Unable to Call All the Shots," *Financial Times* (June 15, 2009) A9.

Chapter 10, "Climate Change: Nature and Action"

[1] Arrhenius, S., On the influence of carbonic acid in the air upon the temperature on the ground. *Philos. Mag.* (1896) 41:237-276.

[2] T. E. Lovejoy and Lee Hannah (eds.) *Climate Change and Biodiversity* (Yale University Press, 2005) 7.

[3] Although estimated to occur between 2040 and 2050, this is likely to happen earlier as the rate of greenhouse gas emissions is increasing. Obviously, the date is a function of emission rates and rates at which emissions are absorbed, but also the consequence of a changing mix of technologies, and possible positive feedbacks (for example, release of methane from thawing tundra).

[4] The Fourth Report of the Intergovernmental Panel on Climate Change (2007) included emissions scenarios. That emissions have exceeded the worst of those cases obviously makes addressing climate change even more challenging.

[5] L. G. Thompson, E. Moseley-Thompson, M. E. Davis, K. A. Henderson, H. H. Brecher, V. S. Zagorodnov, T. A. Mashiotta, P. N. Lin, V. N. Mikhalenko, D. R. Hardy, and J. Beer, "Kilimanjaro Ice Core Records: Evidence of Holocene climate change in tropical Africa," *Science* 18 October 2002, 298: 8,589–593.

[6] X. Zhang and J. E. Walsh, "Toward a Seasonally Ice-Covered Arctic Ocean: Scenarios from the IPCC AR4 model simulations," *Journal of Climate* 19 (2005): 1730–1747.

[7] A. L. Westerling, H. G. Hidalgo, D. R. Cayan, and T. W. Swetham, "Warming and Earlier Spring Increases in Western U.S. Forest Wildfire Activity," *Science* 313 (2006): 940–943.

[8] A. H. Fitter, S. R. Fitter, I. T. B. Harris, and M. H. Williamson. "Relationships between first flowering date and temperature in the flora of a locality in central England," *Functional Ecology* 9 (1995): 55–60.

[9] P. O Dunn and D. W. Winkler, "Climate change has affected the breeding date of tree swallows throughout North America," *Proc. Roy Soc. Lond., B, Biol. Sci.*, 266 (1999): 2,487–2,490.

[10] C. Parmesan, "Climate and Species Range," *Nature* 382 (1996): 765–766; T. L. Root, J. T. Price, K. R. Hall, S. H. Schneider, and J. A. Pounds, "Fingerprints of Global Warming on Wild Animals and Plants," *Nature* 421 (1996): 57–60.

[11] While double preindustrial levels will be reached before midcentury, the changes in distribution of the sugar maple will take more time, as the species dies back in the southern part and establishes itself north of the current range. A. M. Prasad and L.R. Iverson: http://www.nrs.fs.fed.us/atlas.

[12] Ove Hoegh-Guldberg, "Climate Change and Marine Ecosystems," 256–273 in T. E. Lovejoy and L. Hannah (eds.), *Climate Change and Biodiversity* (Yale University Press, 2005) 418.

[13] E. E. Berg, J. D. Henry, C. L. Fastie, A. D. De Volder, and S. M. Matsuoka, "Spruce Beetle Outbreaks on the Kenai Peninsula, Alaska and Kluane National Park and Reserve, Yukon Territory: Relationship to summer temperatures and regional differences in disturbance regimes," *Forest Ecology and Management* 227 (2006): 219–232.

[14] *The New York Times* June 28, 2009, p.17.

[15] J. A. Kleypas, R. A. Feely, V. J. Fabry, C. Langdon, C. L. Sabine, and L. L. Robbins, "Impacts of Ocean Acidification on Coral Reefs and Other Marine Calcifiers: A guide for future research," Report of a workshop held April 18–20 2005 in

St. Petersburg, Florida, sponsored by the National Science Foundation, the National Oceanic and Atmospheric Administration, and the U.S. Geological Survey (2005) 88.

[16] The Hadley Center in Great Britain is home to work on one of the five major supercomputer global climate models. In contrast to the others, it has feedbacks built in to its modeling, and thus is probably closer to the real-world climate system.

[17] P. M. Cox, R. A. Betts, M. Collins, P. Harris, C. Huntingford, and C. D. Jones, "Amazon Dieback under Climate-Carbon Cycle Projections for the 21st Century," Hadley Centre Technical Note 42 (2005), available at www.metoffice.gov.uk/research/hadleycentre/pubs/HCTN/HCTN_42.pdf.

[18] World Bank, "Assessment of the Risk of Amazon Dieback" (2009) September.

[19] E. Salati and P. B. Vose, "Amazon Basin: A state of equilibrium," *Science* 225 (1984): 129–138.

[20] Preindustrial levels were 280ppm. 450 ppm equates to a 2.0 degree increase in average global temperature but more realistically to a range of temperature both above and below it.

[21] J. Hansen, "Target Atmospheric CO2: Where Should Humanity Aim?" in *The Open Atmospheric Science Journal* (2009). available at http://dx.doi.org/10.2174/1874282300802010217.

[22] D. Beerling, *The Emerald Planet: How Plants Changed Earth's History*. Oxford University Press (2007) pp i-xviii 1-288.

[23] T. E. Lovejoy, "We did it, we can undo it.," *International Herald Tribune* (October 28, 2008) 6.

Chapter 11, "Lessons from Risk Analysis: Terrorism, Natural Disasters, and Technological Accidents"

[1] Preparation of this article was supported by Decision Research, Oregon, and by the U.S. Department of Homeland Security under grant number 2008-GA-T8-K004 (Federal Emergency Management Agency, FEMA, National Preparedness Directorate) to the University of Southern California. Points of view and opinions expressed in this document are solely those of the author and do not necessarily represent the official positions or policies by Decision Research or by FEMA's National Preparedness Directorate or the U.S. Department of Homeland Security.

[2] S. Kaplan and B. J. Garrick, "On the Quantitative Definition of Risk," *Risk Analysis* 1(1) (1981): 11–27.

[3] Unfortunately, the advice by risk analysts did not prevent the subsequent Columbia Shuttle disaster, which was caused by a loss of tiles.

[4] U.S. Nuclear Regulatory Commission, *Reactor Safety Study: An Assessment of Accident Risks in U.S. Commercial Nuclear Power Plants*, WASH 1400, NUREG-75/014. Washington, DC: Nuclear Regulatory Commission (1975).

[5] See, for example, U.S. Nuclear Regulatory Commission, *Severe Accident Risks: An Assessment of Five U.S. Nuclear Power Plants,* NUREG-1150. Washington, DC: Nuclear Regulatory Commission (1989).

[6] See V. Bier and L. Cox Jr., "Probabilistic Risk Analysis for Engineered Systems," in W. Edwards, R. F. Miles, and D. von Winterfeldt, *Advances in Decision Analysis* (Cambridge University Press, 2007): 279–301.

[7] M. E. Pate-Cornell and P. Fischbeck, "Probabilistic Risk Analysis and Risk-Based Priority Scale for the Tiles of the Space Shuttle," *Reliability Engineering and Systems Safety* 40(3) (1993): 221–238; M. E. Pate-Cornell, "The Engineering Risk Analysis Method and Some Applications," in W. Edwards, R. F. Miles, and D. von Winterfeldt, *Advances in Decision Analysis* (Cambridge University Press, 2007) 302–324.

[8] See, for example, L. A. Cox, Jr., "Health Risk Analysis for Risk Management Decision Making," in W. Edwards, R. F. Miles, and D. von Winterfeldt, *Advances in Decision Analysis* (Cambridge University Press (2007): 325–349; National Research Council. (2009). *Science and Decisions*. Washington, DC: National Academy of Sciences Press.

[9] H. Kunreuther, R. Ginsberg, L. Miller, P. Sagi, and P. Slovic, *Disaster Insurance Protection: Public Policy Lessons* (Wiley Interscience, 1978); G. White (ed.) *Natural Hazards: Local, National, Global* (Oxford University Press, 1974).

[10] These tools failed in the recent economic crisis, because of the built-in "normality" assumptions in traditional financial risk models.

[11] From a speech at the University of Southern California, August 17, 2006.

[12] See, for example, National Research Council, *Department of Homeland Security Bioterrorism Risk Assessment: A Call for Change* (National Academy Press, 2008).

[13] See, for example, V. Bier and D. von Winterfeldt, "Terrorism Risk Analysis," Special volume of the Journal *Risk Analysis* 27 (2007): 503–634.

[14] H. H. Willis, A. R. Morral, T. K. Kelly, J. J. Medby, *Estimating Terrorism Risk,* MG-388-RC, RAND Corporation, Santa Monica, CA (2005).

[15] D. von Winterfeldt and T. O'Sullivan, "A Decision Analysis to Evaluate the Cost-Effectiveness of MANPADS Countermeasures," *Decision Analysis* 3 (2006): 63–75.

[16] In 2003, terrorists attacked a DHL plane in Baghdad using a MANPADS weapon. The plane was hit by the missile, but the pilot managed to safely land the plane.

[17] G. Keeney and D. von Winterfeldt, "Identifying and Structuring the Objectives of Terrorists," Technical Report, Center for Risk and Economic Analysis of Terrorism Events, University of Southern California, Los Angeles, CA (2009).

[18] H. Rosoff, *Using Decision and Risk Analysis to Assist in Policy Making about Terrorism,* Ph.D. Thesis, School of Policy, Planning, and Development, University of Southern California, Los Angeles, CA (2009).

[19] P. Gordon, J. E. Moore II, J. Y. Park, and H. W. Richardson, "The Economic Impacts of a Terrorist Attack on the U.S. Commercial Aviation System," *Risk Analysis* 27(3) (2007): 505–512.

[20] Defined as cracking of the containment with releases of radioactive gases; for the context, see R. L. Keeney and D. von Winterfeldt (1991). "Eliciting Probabilities from Experts in Complex Technical Problems," *IEEE Transactions on Engineering Management* 38: 191–201.

[21] For example, P. Gordon, J. E. Moore II, J. Y. Park, and H. W. Richardson, "The Economic Impacts of a Terrorist Attack on the U.S. Commercial Aviation System," *Risk Analysis* 27(3) (2007): 505–512.

[22] J. Y. Park, "The Economic Impacts of a Dirty-Bomb Attack on the Los Angeles and Long Beach Port: Applying Supply Driven NIEMO," *Journal of Homeland Security and Emergency Management* (2009) in press.

Chapter 12, "Turning Danger (危) to Opportunities (机): Reconstructing China's National System for Emergency Management After 2003

[1] Peijun Shi, Jing Liu, Qinghai Yao, Di Tang, Xi Yang; "Integrated Disaster Risk Management of China." OECD: *First Conference on the Financial Management of Large-Scale Catastrophes*, Hyderabad, India, February 26–27 2007, 9, www.oecd.org/dataoecd/52/14/38120232.pdf.

[2] "Flooding in China Summer 1998," http://lwf.ncdc.noaa.gov/oa/reports/chinaflooding/chinaflooding.html.

[3] Thomas Abraham, *Twenty First Century Plague: The Story of SARS* (John Hopkins University Press, 2005).

[4] WHO, "Summary of Probable SARS Cases with Onset of Illness from 1 November 2002 to 31 July 2003 (Revised 26 September 2003)," www.who.int/csr/sars/country/table2003_09_23/en/index.html.

[5] Robert F. Breiman, et al., "Role of China in The Quest to Define and Control Severe Acute Respiratory Syndrome," *Emerging Infectious Diseases* 9(9) (September 2003).

[6] David Fidler, *SARS: Governance and the Globalization of Disease* (Palgrave MacMillan, 2004).

[7] Karl A. Wittfogel, *Oriental Despotism: A Comparative Study of Total Power* (Yale University Press, 1957).

[8] Leonard Herman B. "Dutch" and Arnold M. Howitt, "Against Desperate Peril: High Performance in Emergency Preparation and Response," in Deborah E. Gibbons (ed.), *Communicable Crises Prevention Management and Resolution in an Era of Globalization* (Elsevier, 2007) 1–24.

[9] Maryn McKenna. *Beating Back the Devil: On The Front Lines of the Epidemic Intelligence Service* (Free Press, 2004) 236.

[10] "Guangdong Brings Atypical Pneumonia under Control," *Xinhua News Agency*, February 12, 2003, http://news.xinhuanet.com/english/2003-02/12/content_726479.htm.

[11] Susan M. Puska. "SARS 2002-2003: A Case Study in Crisis Management," in Andrew Scobell and Larry M. Wortzel (eds.), *Chinese National Security Decision Making Under Stress* (Strategic Studies Institute, U.S. Army War College, September 2005) 85–134.

[12] Anne-Marie Brady, "'Treat Insiders and Outsiders Differently': The Use and Control of Foreigners in the PRC," *China Quarterly* 164, (December 2000): 943–964.

[13] "Survey: Half People Got Information from Their Friends and Relatives," *Yang Cheng Evening News*, February 14, 2003.

[14] Zhang Xiaoqun, "Analysis of the Number of the Reports on SARS by State Media," in Hu Aangang (ed.), *See through SARS: Health and Development*, Beijing: Tsinghua University Press (2004): 120–132.

[15] John Pomfret, "Beijing Told Doctors to Hide SARS Victims," *The Washington Post* (April 19, 2003) A10.

[16] Thomas A. Birkland, "Focusing Events, Mobilization, and Agenda Setting," *Journal of Public Policy* 18(1) (January/April, 1998): 53–74.

[17] "Chinese Premier Urges Strengthening Public Health System," *Xinhua News Agency*, http://news.xinhuanet.com/english/2003-06/17/content_923981.htm.

[18] Zhong Kaibin, "National Emergency Management System Construction in China," *Cass Journal of Political Science* 1 (February 2009): 78–88.

[19] "Contigency Plan Issued for Accidental Calamities," *Xinhua News Agency*, http://news.xinhuanet.com/english/2006-01/22/content_4086543.htm.

[20] "Good Planning Helps Cope with Emergencies," *People's Daily*, January 10, 2006.

[21] "Emergency Response Guidelines Announced," *Xinhua News Agency*, January 9, 2006, http://news.xinhuanet.com/english/2006-01/09/content_4026605.htm.

[22] "New Directions in Public, Media Relations," April 5, 2005, www.china.org.cn/english/2005/Apr/124725.htm.

[23] "Natural Disaster Toll No Longer State Secret," *Xinhua News Agency*, September 12, 2005, www.chinadaily.com.cn/english/doc/2005-09/12/content_477122.htm.

[24] "China's First 'International Safe Community' Born in Shandong," *Xinhua News Agency*, March 1, 2006.

[25] "Chronology of China's Constitutional Amendments," *Xinhua News Agency*, March 8, 2004, http://news.xinhuanet.com/english/2004-03/08/content_1352359.htm.

[26] "State of Emergency Law to Set Basic Rights," *China Daily*, April 5, 2004.

[27] "China 'Not Ready' for Snow Crisis," February 2, 2008, http://news.bbc.co.uk/1/hi/world/asia-pacific/7226002.stm.

[28] Leonard Herman B. "Dutch" and Arnold M. Howitt, "Against Desperate Peril: High Performance in Emergency Preparation and Response," in Deborah E. Gibbons (ed.), *Communicable* CrisesPrevention *Management and Resolution in an Era of Globalization* (Elsevier, 2007): 1–24.

[29] Based on Lan Xue's site visits and interviews in Qiannan Autonomous Region in Guizhou Province in September 2008.

[30] Marshall McLuhan, *Understanding Media: The Extension of Man* (McGraw-Hill Book Company, 1964).

[31] Zhong Kaibin, "Crisis Management in China," *China Security* 3(1) (Winter 2007): 90–109.

Chapter 13, "Dealing with Pandemics: Global Security, Risk Analysis, and Science Policy"

[1] L. Saker, K. Lee, B. Cannito, A. Gilmore, and D. Campbell-Lendrum, *Globalization and Infectious Diseases: A review of the linkages* (TDR, 2004).

[2] UNAIDS/WHO, AIDS epidemic update. In UNAIDS and WHO: 2007, http://data.unaids.org/pub/EPISlides/2007/2007_epiupdate_en.pdf.

[3] RBM, World Malaria Report 2005. In Roll Back Malaria Partnership: 2005. www.rollbackmalaria.org/wmr2005/.

[4] R. Arnold, J. de Sa, A. Percy, J. Somers, "A Potential Influenza Pandemic: Possible Macroeconomic Effects and Policy Issues." Congressional Budget Office.(2005), available at http://www.cbo.gov/ftpdocs/69xx/doc6946/12-08-BirdFlu.pdf.

[5] D. Hanna and Y. Huang, "The Impact of SARS on Asian Economies," *Asian Economic Papers* 3(1) (2004): 102–112.

[6] A. Siu and R. Y. C. Wong. "The Impact of SARS on Asian Economies," *Asian Economic Papers* 3(1) (2004): 62–83.

[7] "Dual Use Research of Concern" was defined by a Health and Human Services (HHS) news article HHS Will Lead Government-Wide Effort to Enhance Biosecurity in 'Dual Use' Research," March 4, 2004, available at www.biosecurityboard.gov/NSABB_press_release.pdf.

[8] White House, "The National Security Strategy of the United States of America in 2006."

[9] These three processes are used by bacteria to bring about change to their DNA make-up. In conjugation, two bacteria are joined by a tube called pilus through which DNA from either bacteria can enter the other. In transformation, DNA molecules are taken in wholesale by bacterial cells. Finally in transduction, DNA is transferred from one bacteria to another by means of a virus, which takes a part of its bacterial victim's DNA every time the virus leaves to infect another bacterial cell.

[10] R. J. Kinsella, D. A. Fitzpatrick, C. J. Creevey, and J. O. McInerney, "Fatty Acid Biosynthesis in Mycobacterium Tuberculosis: Lateral gene transfer, adaptive evolution, and gene duplication," *Proceedings of the National Academy of Sciences of the United States of America* 100(18) (2003): 10,320–5.

[11] J. Gamieldien, A. Ptitsyn, and W. Hide, "Eukaryotic Genes in Mycobacterium Tuberculosis Could Have a Role in Pathogenesis and Immunomodulation," *Trends Genet* 18(1) (2002): 5–8. A eukaryotic cell's defining feature is the nucleus, a membrane-enclosed structure containing DNA. Other cells, such as prokaryotes, contain DNA but not enclosed by a membrane.

[12] The term *pleomorphic* when used in microbiology denotes the variability of physical properties of the microbe, often as a result of expressing different sets of genes.

[13] J. Davies, "Inactivation of Antibiotics and the Dissemination of Resistance Genes," *Science* 264(5157) (1994): 375–82.

[14] CDC, Antimicrobial Resistance: A Growing Threat to Public Health. In 2002.

[15] I OM, in Antimicrobial Resistance: Issues and Options, Forum on Emerging Infections, Washington, DC (1998); P. Harrison and J. Lederberg (eds.) (National Academy Press, 1998).

[16] S. R. Palumbi, "Humans as the World's Greatest Evolutionary Force," *Science* 293(5536) (2001): 1,786–90.

[17] DHHS, "The Problem of Antibiotic Resistance: Fact Sheet," www.niaid.nih.gov/factsheets/antimicro.htm.

[18] A. K. Pradhan, J. S. Van Kessel, J. S. Karns, D. R. Wolfgang, E. Hovingh, K. A. Nelen, J. M. Smith, R. H. Whitlock, T. Fyock, S. Ladely, P. J. Fedorka-Cray, and Y. H. Schukken, "Dynamics of Endemic Infectious Diseases of Animal and Human Importance on Three Dairy Herds in the Northeastern United States," *Journal of Dairy Science* 92(4) (2009) 1,811–25.

[19] Escherichia coli 0157:H7 infections in children associated with raw milk and raw colostrum from cows—California, 2006. *MMWR Morbidity and Mortality Weekly Report* (2008), 57(23): 625–8.

[20] A. Clark, S. Morton, P. Wright, J. Corkish, F. J. Bolton, and J. Russell, "A Community Outbreak of Vero Cytotoxin Producing Escherichia Coli O157 Infection Linked to a Small Farm Dairy," *Communicable Disease Report. CDR Review*. 7(13) (1997): R206–11.

[21] M. L. Ackers, S. Schoenfeld, J. Markman, M.G. Smith, M. A. Nicholson, W. DeWitt, D. N. Cameron, P. M. Griffin, L. Slutsker, "An outbreak of Yersinia enterocolitica O:8 infections associated with pasteurized milk." *Journal of Infectious Diseases* (2000), 181, (5), 1834–7.

[22] S. M. Ostroff, G. Kapperud, L. C. Hutwagner, T. Nesbakken, N.H. Bean, J. Lassen, R. V. Tauxe, "Sources of sporadic Yersinia enterocolitica infections in Norway: a prospective case-control study." *Epidemiology and Infection* (1994) 112, (1), 133–41.

[23] R. V. Tauxe, J. Vandepitte, G. Wauters, S. M. Martin, V. Goossens, P. De Mol, R. Van Noyen, G. Thiers, "Yersinia enterocolitica infections and pork: the missing link." *Lancet* (1987) 1, (8542), 1129–32.

[24] P. Much, J. Pichler, S. Kasper, H. Lassnig, C. Kornschober, A. Buchner, C. Konig, F. Allerberger, "A foodborne outbreak of Salmonella Enteritidis phage type 6 in Austria, 2008." *Wien Klin Wochenschr* (2009) 121, (3–4), 132–6.

[25] IOM, EMERGING INFECTIONS: Microbial threats to health in the United States. National Academy Press (1992).

[26] M. K. Glynn, C. Bopp, W. Dewitt, P. Dabney, M. Mokhtar, F. J. Angulo, "Emergence of multidrug-resistant Salmonella enterica serotype typhimurium DT104 infections in the United States." *New England Journal of Medicine* (1998) 338, (19), 1333–8.

[27] C. Scholtissek, E. Naylor, "Fish farming and influenza pandemics." *Nature* (1988) 331, (6153), 215.

[28] T. Nesbakken, T. Iversen, B. Lium, "Pig herds free from human pathogenic Yersinia enterocolitica." *Emerging Infectious Diseases* (2007) 13, (12), 1860–4.

[29] Strategic Plan for NIOSH Nanotechnology Research: Filling the Knowledge Gaps. www.cdc.gov/niosh/topics/nanotech/strat_planB.html.

[30] Terrorism, Congressional Commission on the Prevention of WMD Proliferation and Terrorism, WORLD AT RISK: The Report of the Commission on the Prevention of WMD Proliferation and Terrorism. In Congress, U. S., Ed. 2008.

[31] Information was compiled from published and documentary sources held in the Sussex Harvard Information Bank, University of Sussex, United Kingdom, and printed in: Committee on Advances in Technology and the Prevention of Their Application to Next Generation Biowarfare Threats, N. R. C., Globalization, Biosecurity, and the Future of the Life Sciences. National Academies Press, (2006).

[32] K. E. Jones, N. G. Patel, M. A. Levy, A. Storeygard, D. Balk, J. L. Gittleman, P. Daszak, "Global trends in emerging infectious diseases." *Nature* (2008) 451, (7181), 990–3.

[33] WHO. Cumulative number of confirmed human cases of avian influenza A/(H5N1) reported to WHO; 2006. Available at www.who.int/csr/disease/avian_influenza/country/cases_-table_2007_03_01/en/index.html.

[34] J. H. Epstein, H. E. Field, S. Luby,J. R. Pulliam,P. Daszak, "Nipah virus: impact, origins, and causes of emergence." *Current Infectious Disease Reports* (2006), 8, (1), 59–65.

[35] C. Akoua-Koffi, K. D. Ekra, A. B. Kone, N. S. Dagnan, V. Akran, K. L. Kouadio, Y. G. Loukou, K. Odehouri, J. Tagliante-Saracino, A. Ehouman, "Detection and management of the yellow fever epidemic in the Ivory Coast, 2001". *Med Trop (Mars)* 2002, 62, (3), 305–9.

[36] Hantavirus pulmonary syndrome—five states, 2006. *MMWR Morbidity and Mortality Weekly Report* (2006) 55, (22), 627–9.

[37] L. H. Gould, E. Fikrig, "West Nile virus: a growing concern?" *Journal of Clinical Investigation* (2004) 113, (8), 1102–7.

[38] Outbreak(s) of Ebola hemorrhagic fever, Congo and Gabon, October 2001 to July 2002. *Can Commun Dis Rep* (2003) 29, (15), 129–33.

[39] A. W. Rimoin, N. Kisalu, B. Kebela-Ilunga, T. Mukaba, L. L. Wright, P. Formenty, N. D. Wolfe, R. L. Shongo, F. Tshioko, E. Okitolonda, J. J. Muyembe, R. W. Ryder, H. Meyer, "Endemic human monkeypox, Democratic Republic of Congo, 2001–2004." *Emerging Infectious Diseases* (2007) 13, (6), 934–7.

[40] I. B. Bayer-Garner, "Monkeypox Virus: Histologic, immunohistochemical and electron-microscopic findings," *Journal of Cutaneous Pathology* 32(1) (2005): 28–34.

[41] W. K. Lam, N. S. Zhong, and W. C. Tan, "Overview on SARS in Asia and the World," *Respirology* 8 Suppl (2003): S2–5.

[42] E. S. da Rosa, I. Kotait, T. F. Barbosa, M. L. Carrieri, P. E. Brandao, A. S. Pinheiro, A. L. Begot, M. Y. Wada, R. C. de Oliveira, E. C. Grisard, M. Ferreira, R. J. Lima, L. Montebello, D. B. Medeiros, R. C. Sousa, G. Bensabath, E. H. Carmo, and P. F. Vasconcelos, "Bat-Transmitted Human Rabies Outbreaks, Brazilian Amazon," *Emerging Infectious Diseases* 12(8) (2006): 1,197–202.

[43] X. Tang, M. Luo, S. Zhang, A. R. Fooks, R. Hu, and C. Tu, "Pivotal Role of Dogs in Rabies Transmission," China. *Emerging Infectious Diseases* 11(12) (2005): 1,970–2.

[44] R. Alavi-Naini, A. Moghtaderi, H. R. Koohpayeh, B. Sharifi-Mood, M. Naderi, M. Metanat, and M. Izadi, "Crimean-Congo Hemorrhagic Fever in Southeast of Iran," *Journal of Infection* 52(5) (2006): 378–82.

[45] R. Reintjes, I. Dedushaj, A. Gjini, T. R. Jorgensen, B. Cotter, A. Lieftucht, F. D'Ancona, D. T. Dennis, M. A. Kosoy, G. Mulliqi-Osmani, R. Grunow, A. Kalaveshi, L. Gashi, and I. Humolli, "Tularemia Outbreak Investigation in Kosovo: Case control and environmental studies," *Emerging Infectious Diseases* 8(1) (2002): 69–73.

[46] K. A. Feldman, R. E. Enscore, S. L. Lathrop, B. T. Matyas, M. McGuill, M. E. Schriefer, D. Stiles-Enos, D. T. Dennis, L. R. Petersen, and E. B. Hayes, "An Outbreak of Primary Pneumonic Tularemia on Martha's Vineyard," *New England Journal of Medicine* 345(22) (2001): 1,601–6.

[47] A. Currie, J. MacDonald, A. Ellis, J. Siushansian, L. Chui, M. Charlebois, M. Peermohamed, D. Everett, M. Fehr, and L. K. Ng, "Outbreak of Escherichia coli 0157:H7 Infections Associated with Consumption of Beef Donair," *Journal of Food Protection* 70(6) (2007): 1,483–8.

[48] P. D. Frenzen, A. Drake, F. J. Angulo, "Economic cost of illness due to Escherichia coli O157 infections in the United States." *Journal of Food Protection* (2005) 68, (12), 2623–30.

[49] WHO, "Variant Creutzfeldt-Jakob Disease," www.who.int/mediacentre/factsheets/fs180/en/.

[50] K. E. Jones, N. G. Patel, M. A. Levy, A. Storeygard, D. Balk, J. L. Gittleman, and P. Daszak, "Global Trends in Emerging Infectious Diseases," *Nature* 451(7181) (2008) 990–3.

[51] A. M. Kilpatrick, A. A. Chmura, D. W. Gibbons, R. C. Fleischer, P. P. Marra, and P. Daszak, "Predicting the Global Spread of H5N1 Avian Influenza," *Proceedings of the National Academy of Sciences of the United States of America* 103(51) (2006): 19,368–73.

[52] W. K. Lam, N. S. Zhong, and W. C. Tan, "Overview on SARS in Asia and the World," *Respirology* 8 Suppl (2003): S2–5.

[53] J. Lederberg, R. E. Shope, and S. E. Oaks Jr., "Microbial Threats to Health in the United States," National Academies Press (1992).

[54] "An Alberta Swine Herd Investigated for H1N1 Flu Virus," Canadian Food Inspection Agency, May 2, 2009, www.inspection.gc.ca/english/corpaffr/newcom/2009/20090502e.shtml.

[55] A. Prüss-Üstün, R. Bos, F. Gore, and J. Bartram, "Safer Water, Better Health," in WHO (2008), http://whqlibdoc.who.int/publications/2008/9789241596435_eng.pdf.

[56] A. Goubar, D. Bitar, W. C. Cao, D. Feng, L. Q. Fang, and J. C. Desenclos, "An Approach to Estimate the Number of SARS Cases Imported by International Air Travel," *Epidemiology and Infection* 137(7) (2009): 1,019–31.

[57] We deliberately use the concept of *compact* to avoid the term *treaty* for many of the reasons discussed by Jean-François Rischard in "Global Issues Networks: Desperate Times Deserve Innovative Measures," *Washington Quarterly* 26(1) (Winter 2002–03): 17–33. We expect that the compact will have a structure resembling networked governance as described in Rischard's paper. We also do not rule out on the alternatives, both legal and political.

[58] We use the word *ontology* in a systems sense—it refers to the nature and property of a particular technical entity defined in most part by its relationships with other entities. For instance, a particular computer language word would not necessarily function the same way or use the same set of variables in different information software applications—hence giving rise to their incompatibility when information are shared between different operational software applications.

[59] G. J. Ikenberry and A. Slaughter, "Forging a World of Liberty Under Law: U.S. National Security in the 21st Century," www.wws.princeton.edu/ppns/report/Final Report.pdf.

Chapter 14, "Long-Term Contracts for Reducing Losses from Future Catastrophes"

[1] For a more detailed discussion of the reasons why homeowners do not invest in disaster-mitigation measures, see Chapter 12 in H. Kunreuther and E. Michel-Kerjan, *At War with the Weather: Managing Large-Scale Risks in a New Era of Catastrophes* (MIT Press, 2009).

[2] This example illustrating the concept of interdependent security is discussed in more detail in H. Kunreuther and G. Heal, "Interdependencies within an Organization," in *Organizational Encounters with Risk*, B. Hutter and M. Powers (eds.) (Cambridge University Press, 2005).

[3] Union Carbide was purchased by the Dow Chemical Corporation in 1999.

[4] For more details on the AIG case, see Useem (this volume).

[5] E. H. Bowman and H. Kunreuther, "Post Bhopal Behavior of a Chemical Company," *Journal of Management Studies* 25 (1988): 387–402.

[6] F. Oberholzer-Gee, "Learning to Bear the Unbearable: Toward an Explanation of Risk Ignorance" Mimeo., Wharton School, University of Pennsylvania (1998).

[7] H. Kunreuther and M. Pauly, "Terrorism Losses and All-Perils Insurance," *Journal of Insurance Regulation* 23 (2005): 3.

[8] For more details on the consequences, see Kunreuther and Useem (this volume).

[9] J. D. Cummins and O. Mahul, "Catastrophe Risk Financing in Developing Countries" (The World Bank, Washington DC, 2008).

[10] The example in this section is based on actual data compiled as part of a report prepared for the World Bank by a team from the International Institute of Applied Systems Analysis (IIASA), Risk Management Solutions (RMS), and the Wharton Center for Risk Management and Decision Processes (Wharton Risk Center). IIASA-RMS-Wharton Risk Center (2009). "The Challenges and Importance of Investing in Cost-effective Measures for Reducing Losses From Natural Disasters in Emerging Economies" (The World Bank, Washington DC, 2009).

[11] D. Jaffee, H. Kunreuther, and E. Michel-Kerjan, "Long Term Insurance (LTI) for Addressing Catastrophic Market Failure" National Bureau of Economic Research, NBER working paper 14210 (2008).

[12] For more details on the Turkish insurance program, see H. Kunreuther and E. Michel-Kerjan, "A Framework for Reducing Vulnerability to Natural Disasters: Ex Ante and Ex Post Considerations" (The World Bank, Washington DC, 2008).

[13] H. Kunreuther, W. Sanderson, and R. Vetschera, "A Behavioral Model of the Adoption of Protective Activities," *Journal of Economic Behavior and Organization* 6 (1985): 1–15.

[14] R. Tobin and C. Calfee, "The National Flood Insurance Program's Mandatory Purchase Requirement: Policies, Processes, and Stakeholders" (American Institute for Research, 2005).

[15] The principles that premiums should reflect risk and that subsidies in the form of insurance vouchers be given to those deserving special treatment are discussed at length in Kunreuther and Michel-Kerjan (2009) op. cit. (Chapter 14).

[16] L. Cohen and R. Noll, "The Economics of Building Codes to Resist Seismic Shocks." *Public Policy* (Winter 1981): 1–29.

[17] EPA's Region III office revealed that it had only five auditors for inspecting its many industrial facilities in Delaware, Maryland, Pennsylvania, Virginia, West Virginia, and the District of Columbia. H. Kunreuther, P. McNulty, and Y. Kang, "Improving Environmental Safety through Third Party Inspection," *Risk Analysis* 22 (2002): 309–18.

[18] C. Coglianese and D. Lazer, "Management-Based Regulation: Prescribing Private Management to Achieve Public Goals," *Law and Society Review* 37 (2003): 691–730.

[19] For a more detailed discussion as to how such a process would operate see Kunreuther, McNulty, and Kang (2002) op. cit.

Chapter 15, "Developing Leadership to Avert and Mitigate Disasters"

[1] Michael Useem, *The Go Point: When It Is Time to Decide* (Random House, 2006); Michael Useem, Mark Davidson, and Evan Wittenberg "Leadership Development Beyond the Classroom: The Power of Leadership Ventures to Drive Home the Essence of Decision Making," *International Journal of Leadership Education* (January 1, 2005): 159–178.

[2] Paul J. H. Schoemaker and George S. Day, "How to Make Sense of Weak Signals," *MIT Sloan Management Review* Spring (2009) 50: 81–89; George S. Day and Paul J. H. Schoemaker, *Peripheral Vision: Detecting Weak Signals That Will Make or Break Your Company* (Harvard Business School Press, 2006); Alex Lewis, Safety in Wildland Fire: Leadership and Employee Voice, College of Graduate Studies, University of Idaho (2008); A. C. Edmondson, "Speaking Up in the Operating Room: How Team Leaders Promote Learning in Interdisciplinary Action Teams," *Journal of Management Studies* 40: (2003) 1419–1452; Claus Rerup, "Attention Triangulation: Learning from Unexpected Rare Crisis," Ivey School of Business, University of Western Ontario (2008); W. Ocasio, "Toward an Attention-Based View of the Firm," *Strategic Management Journal* 18 (1997): 187–206; Charles Perrow, *The Next Catastrophe: Reducing Our Vulnerabilities to Natural, Industrial, and Terrorist Disasters* (Princeton University Press, 2007).

[3] Diane Vaughan, *The Challenger Launch Decision: Risky Technology, Culture, and Deviance at NASA* (University of Chicago Press, 1996).

[4] We draw upon several sources, including Ben Levisohn, "AIG's CDS Hoard: The Great Unraveling," *Business Week Online*, April 7, 2009; Carrick Mollenkamp, Serena Ng, Liam Pleven, and Randall Smith, "Behind AIG's Fall, Risk Models Failed to Pass Real-World Test," *Wall Street Journal*, October 31, 2008; Gretchen Morgenson, "Behind Insurer's Crisis, Blind Eye to a Web of Risk," *New York Times*, September 28, 2008; Steve Lohr, "In Modeling Risk, the Human Factor Was Left Out," *New York Times*, November 5, 2008; Eric Dickinson, "Credit Default Swaps: So Dear to Us, So Dangerous," Fordham Law School, November 20, 2008; Donald L. Kohn, Statement to the U.S. Senate Committee on Banking, Housing, and Urban Affairs, March 5, 2009; Eric Dinallo, Testimony to the U.S. Senate Committee on Banking, Housing and Urban Affairs, March 5, 2009; Nell Minow, Testimony to the U.S. House of Representatives Committee on Oversight and Government Reform,

October 7, 2008; Scott M. Polakoff, Statement to the U.S. Senate Committee on Banking, House and Urban Affairs, March 5, 2009; William K. Sjostrom, Jr., "The AIG Bailout," Salmon P. Chase School of Law, Northern Kentucky University, March 10, 2009; American International Group, Inc., *2008 Annual Report*; and Michael Lewis, "The Man Who Crashed the World," *Vanity Fair*, August, 2009.

[5] Dinnalo (2009) op. cit.; Gillian Tett, *Fool's Gold, How Unrestrained Greed Corrupted a Dream, Shattered Markets, and Unleashed a Catastrophe* (Little Brown, 2009) 76.

[6] Morgenson (2008) op. cit.

[7] Morgenson (2008) op. cit.

[8] Mollenkamp et. al. (2008) op. cit.

[9] Levisohn (2009) op. cit.

[10] Personal interviews with Jay Fishman in 2009 on April 14 and June 19 (the latter conducted by Howard Kunreuther).

[11] Morgenson (2008) op. cit.; Lewis (2009) op. cit.

[12] Minow (2008) op. cit.

[13] Polakoff (2009) op. cit.

[14] Itshak Ben-David, John R. Graham, and Campbell R. Harvey, "Managerial Overconfidence and Corporate Policies," Duke University, 2007; William F. Wright, "Mood Effects on Subjective Probability Assessment," *Organizational Behavior and Human Decision Processes* 52 (1992): 276–291; Anand M. Goel and Anjan V. Thakor, "Overconfidence, CEO Selection, and Corporate Governance," *Journal of Finance*, 63 (2008): 2,737–84; Haim Mano, "Risk-Taking, Framing Effects, and Affect," *Organizational Behavior and Human Decision Processes* 57 (1994): 38–58.

[15] The account that follows draws on Michael Useem, *The Leadership Moment: Nine True Stories of Triumph and Disaster and Their Lessons for Us All* (Random House, 1998) (and a number of sources cited therein), and Roy Vagelos and Louis Galambos, *Medicine, Science, and Merck* (Cambridge University Press, 2004).

[16] Vagelos and Galambos, 2004, op. cit., 254.

[17] The company website: www.merckfrosst.ca/mfcl/en/corporate/products/vioxx_withdrawal/vioxx_gen_letter.html (accessed May 29, 2009).

[18] Merck was one of the featured companies in Jim Collins and Jerry I. Porras's account of especially enduring enterprises, *Built to Last: Successful Habits of Visionary Companies* (HarperBusiness, 2004).

[19] See, for instance, Fred Fiedler, *Leadership Experience and Leadership Performance* (U.S. Army Research Institute for the Behavioral and Social Sciences, 1994);

Gary Klein, *Intuition at Work: Why Developing Your Gut Instincts Will Make You Better at What You Do* (Currency Doubleday, 2003).

[20] The account is based on several sources, including Norman Maclean, *Young Men and Fire* (University of Chicago Press, 1990); Karl E. Weick, "The Collapse of Sensemaking in Organizations: The Mann Gulch Disaster," *Administrative Science Quarterly* 38 (1993): 628–652; Useem, 1998, op. cit., Chapter 2; Michael Useem, James Cook, and Larry Sutton, "Developing Leaders for Decision Making Under Duress: Wildland Firefighters in the South Canyon Fire and Its Aftermath," *Academy of Management Learning and Education*, 4 (2005): 461–485; and James N. Maclean, *Fire on the Mountain: The True Story of the South Canyon Fire* (William Morrow & Co., 1999).

[21] Useem, Cook, and Sutton, 2005, op. cit.

[22] See, for instance, Edward Betof, *Leaders as Teachers: Unlock the Teaching Potential of Your Company's Best and Brightest* (American Society for Training and Development, 2009); Jay Conger, *Learning to Lead: The Art of Transforming Managers into Leaders* (Jossey-Bass, 1992).

[23] Max Bazerman, *Judgment in Managerial Decision Making* (Wiley, 2002).

About the Authors

Alan Berger is associate professor of Urban Design and Landscape Architecture in the Department of Urban Studies and Planning at Massachusetts Institute of Technology. He is founding director of P-REX, the Project for Reclamation Excellence, a multidisciplinary design and research lab discovering new ways to see, measure, and act on highly disturbed sites and landscape systems earmarked for adaptive reuse by society.

Case Brown researches large landscapes from the perspective of interdisciplinary design, specializing in the use of digital tools to visualize data-driven futures. He is currently assistant professor at Clemson University, senior research associate at P-REX, and recipient of the Charles Eliot Traveling Fellowship from Harvard University Graduate School of Design.

Seán Cleary is chairman of Strategic Concepts (Pty) Ltd, managing director of the Centre for Advanced Governance, founder and executive vice-chair of the Future World Foundation and chair of the Advisory Board of Abraaj Capital. Between 1970 and 1985, he was a diplomat in Iran, the United States, and Namibia. He lectures on global business strategy, conflict resolution, and risk management at universities and defense colleges in South Africa, is a faculty member of the Parmenides Foundation, and a board member of the International Foundation for Electoral Systems (IFES) and LEAD International.

Arnold M. Howitt is executive director of the Ash Institute for Democratic Governance and Innovation and faculty co-director of the Program on Crisis Leadership at the John F. Kennedy School of Government, Harvard University, where he has been a faculty member and administrator since 1976. He has conducted training and lectured widely on emergency preparedness and response. Among other writings, he is coauthor and coeditor of *Managing Crises: Responses to Large-Scale Emergencies* (CQ Press, 2009) and *Countering Terrorism: Dimensions of Preparedness* (MIT Press, 2004).

Bridget M. Hutter is Professor of Risk Regulation at the London School of Economics and Political Science and director of the ESRC Centre for Analysis of Risk and Regulation. She has an international reputation for her work on compliance, regulatory enforcement, and the impact of risk regulation on organizations. She is the author of numerous publications on these topics. Her forthcoming edited book, *Anticipating Risks and Organizing Risk Regulation*, will be published in 2010 by Cambridge University Press. She is currently examining trends in risk regulation and preparing a research monograph on business responses to regulation.

Michel Jarraud is secretary-general of the World Meteorological Organization, having been reappointed by the Fifteenth World Meteorological Congress to a second four-year term starting January 2008. A research scientist specialized in numerical weather prediction, he has also been in charge of operational weather forecasting in France, including responsibility for national early warnings of extreme events. He is a member of several Meteorological Societies worldwide and also a member of the management oversight board of the UN International Strategy for Disaster Reduction (ISDR).

Carolyn Kousky is a fellow at Resources for the Future. Her research focuses on natural resource management, land use, decision making under uncertainty, and individual and societal responses to natural disaster risk.

Howard Kunreuther is the Cecilia Yen Koo Professor of Decision Sciences and Public Policy at the Wharton School, and Co-Director of the Wharton Risk Management and Decision Processes Center. He has a longstanding interest in ways that society can better manage low-probability, high-consequence events related to technological and natural hazards. He is a member of the OECD's High Level Advisory Board on Financial Management of Large-Scale Catastrophes, a fellow of the American Association for the Advancement of Science (AAAS) and distinguished fellow of the Society for Risk Analysis, receiving the Society's Distinguished Achievement Award in 2001. He is the recipient of the Elizur Wright Award for the publication that makes the most significant contribution to the literature of insurance.

Herman B. "Dutch" Leonard is the George F. Baker Professor of Public Management and the Faculty Co-Director of the Program on Crisis Leadership at the John F. Kennedy School of Government and the Eliot I. Snider and Family Professor of Business Administration at Harvard Business School, Harvard University.

Geoff Love is a former secretary of the Intergovernmental Panel on Climate Change (IPCC), member of the IPCC Bureau and a contributor to the IPCC's Fourth Assessment Report. He is also a former CEO of the Australian Bureau of Meteorology and has served the World Meteorological Organization (WMO) in a variety of capacities over the past thirty years. Dr. Love is currently the WMO's director, Weather and Disaster Risk Reduction Services.

Thomas E. Lovejoy is the biodiversity chair of the H. John Heinz III Center for Science, Economics and the Environment. He served as president of the Heinz Center from 2002-2008. Before coming to the Heinz Center, he was the World Bank's chief biodiversity advisor, lead specialist for Environment for Latin America and the caribbean and senior advisor to the President of the United Nations Foundation, and science advisor to the Secretary of the Interior. He conceived the idea for the Minimum Critical Size of Ecosystems project (a joint project between the Smithsonian and Brazil's INPA), originated the concept of debt-for-nature swaps, and is the founder of the public television series *Nature.*

Michele McNabb has implemented early warning and disaster preparedness programs throughout East and Southern Africa for the past 15 years. She worked closely with the government of Mozambique to strengthen its flood and cyclone early-warning systems and established famine early-warning systems in Kenya, Tanzania, Rwanda, and southern Sudan. She authored the lead chapter in the *2009 World Disasters Report* for the International Federation of the Red Cross and Red Crescent. She currently heads the humanitarian products division of Freeplay Energy, which manufactures solar and windup radios and lights for relief and development activities.

Erwann O. Michel-Kerjan is managing director of the Wharton Risk Management and Decision Processes Center (United

States) and faculty associate at the Ecole Polytechnique (France). He serves as chairman of the OECD Secretary-General High Level Advisory Board on Financial Management of Large-Scale Catastrophes and advises top decision makers around the world on these issues. In 2007, Dr. Michel-Kerjan was named a Young Global Leader by the World Economic Forum, a five-year nomination bestowed to recognize and acknowledge the most extraordinary leaders of the world under the age of forty.

Suzanne Nora Johnson is former vice chairman of The Goldman Sachs Group, Inc. She serves on the boards of American International Group, Inc., Intuit, Inc., Pfizer, Inc., Visa, Inc., The American Red Cross, the Brookings Institution, the Carnegie Institution of Washington, Technoserve, and Women's World Banking. She chairs the investment committees at the University of Southern California and the Markle Foundation. She also serves as co-chair of The Trade Advisory Council for the Mayor of Los Angeles and is chair of the World Economic Forum's Global Agenda Council on Systemic Financial Risk.

Kristine Pearson has served as the CEO of the nonprofit Freeplay Foundation, which provides sustainable access to clean energy technologies, since 1999 and works extensively across sub-Saharan Africa. Previously, she held an executive position at a South African banking group. Kristine is a fellow of the Schwab Foundation of the World Economic Forum and serves on the Women's Leadership Board of the Kennedy School of Government at Harvard. In 2005 she was selected as the James C. Morgan Humanitarian Award and in 2007 by TIME magazine as a Hero of the Environment.

Harvey Rubin is the director of the University of Pennsylvania's Institute for Strategic Analysis and Response (ISTAR) and has spearheaded many preparedness projects on behalf of the university. He was the cochair of the City of Philadelphia's Emergency Preparedness Review Committee (EPRC) and oversaw the extensive operation to improve preparedness procedures throughout the city in 2006. Dr. Rubin holds secondary appointments as professor in the Department of Microbiology, School of Medicine and as professor of Computer and Information Sciences at the University of Pennsylvania School of Engineering and Applied Sciences. He also serves on numerous federal boards in biosecurity such as the National Science Advisory Board for Biosecurity.

Klaus Schwab is executive chairman and founder of the World Economic Forum, a global partnership of leaders committed to improving the state of the world. He is the founder of the Forum of Young Global Leaders (2004) and the Schwab Foundation for Social Entrepreneurship (1998 with his wife Hilde), supporting social innovation around the world. Dr. Schwab's academic activities include Professor of Business Policy, University of Geneva (1971–2003) following studies at the Swiss Federal Institute of Technology in Zurich, the University of Fribourg, and Harvard University. He holds numerous academic distinctions and international and national honors, including an Honorary Knighthood (KCMG), for initiatives undertaken in the spirit of entrepreneurship in the global public interest and for peace and reconciliation efforts in several regions.

Jiah-Shin Teh is the associate director of the University of Pennsylvania's Institute for Strategic Analysis and Response (ISTAR) and has been involved in numerous preparedness projects involving the university. He has helped secure numerous federal preparedness projects, developed curriculum blueprints on all-hazards preparedness, and organized several federal and university workshops as part of ISTAR's portfolio in biosecurity. Dr. Teh possesses degrees in medicine and physiological sciences from the University of Oxford and completed his postdoctoral research fellowship in infectious diseases at the School of Medicine of the University of Pennsylvania in 2005. He has published numerous scientific and policy papers in infectious diseases.

Michael Useem is William and Jacalyn Egan Professor of Management and Director of the Center for Leadership and Change Management at the Wharton School, University of Pennsylvania. He is author of numerous books, including *The Go Point*, *The Leadership Moment*, and *Investor Capitalism.* He has presented programs and seminars on leadership and governance with corporations, government agencies, and non-profit organizations worldwide and has consulted on organizational development and change with the U.S. Agency for International Development, U.N. Food and Agriculture Organization, and companies and other organizations in Latin America, Asia, and Africa.

Detlof von Winterfeldt is the director of the International Institute for Applied Systems Analysis (IIASA) in Laxenburg, Austria. He is on leave from the University of Southern California (USC), where he is a professor of Industrial and Systems Engineering and a professor of Public Policy and Management. In 2003, he cofounded the National Center for Risk and Economic Analysis of Terrorism Events (CREATE), the first university-based center of excellence funded by the U.S. Department of Homeland Security, serving as CREATE's director until 2009. He is a fellow of the Institute for Operations Research and the Management Sciences (INFORMS) and of the Society for Risk Analysis.

Lan Xue is professor and Dean of School of Public Policy and Management (SPPM), Tsinghua University. His current research includes crisis management and S&T policy. He coauthored *Crisis Management in China: The Challenge of Transition* (Beijing: Tsinghua University Press, 2003). He has a Ph.D. in engineering and public policy from Carnegie Mellon University and taught at the George Washington University before moving back to Tsinghua. He is a member of the Expert Committee for Emergency Management of the State Council of China and the founding director of the Center for Crisis Management Research at Tsinghua University.

Richard Zeckhauser is Frank P. Ramsey Professor of Political Economy, Kennedy School, Harvard University. In his research—comprising 12 books and 250 articles—and his life he seeks ways to effectively confront the unknown and the unknowable. He is the author of *2 + 2 = 5: Private Roles for Public Goals* (forthcoming) with John Donahue.

Kaibin Zhong is an assistant professor of Public Management at China National School of Administration. He is the author of *Crisis Decision-making: Explaining the SARS Crisis* (Beijing: Press of China National School of Administration, 2009). He also coauthored *Crisis Management in China: The Challenge of Transition* (Beijing: Tsinghua University Press, 2003). He was a visiting researcher at CRISMART Swedish National Defence College on a project about SARS crisis management from December 2005 to February 2006. His research interests include crisis decision making, risk communication, and social regulation.

World Economic Forum Global Agenda Council on the Mitigation of Natural Disasters

Members, 2008–2009

Sean M. Cleary, Strategic Concepts (Pty) Ltd, South Africa

Arnold Howitt, John F. Kennedy School of Government, Harvard University, United States

Bridget M. Hutter, London School of Economics and Political Science, United Kingdom

Michel Jarraud, World Meteorological Organization (WMO), Switzerland

Howard Kunreuther, The Wharton School, University of Pennsylvania, United States

Herman "Dutch" Leonard, John F. Kennedy School of Government, Harvard University, United States

Thomas E. Lovejoy, The H. John Heinz III Center for Science, Economics and the Environment, United States

Erwann Michel-Kerjan, The Wharton School, University of Pennsylvania, United States

Markku Niskala, International Federation of Red Cross and Red Crescent Societies (IFRC), Switzerland

Kristine Pearson, Freeplay Foundation, United Kingdom

Michael Useem, The Wharton School, University of Pennsylvania, United States

Detlof von Winterfeldt, International Institute for Applied Systems Analysis (IIASA), Austria

Lan Xue, School of Public Policy and Management (SPPM), Tsinghua University, People's Republic of China

Richard Zeckhauser, John F. Kennedy School of Government, Harvard University, United States

Network of Global Agenda Councils

The World Economic Forum has formed Global Agenda Councils on the foremost topics in the global arena. For each of these topics, the Forum has convened the most innovative and relevant leaders to capture the best knowledge on each key issue and integrate it into global collaboration and decision-making processes.

Global Agenda Councils challenge prevailing assumptions, monitor trends, map interrelationships, and address knowledge gaps. Equally important, Global Agenda Councils also propose solutions, devise strategies, and evaluate the effectiveness of actions using measurable benchmarks.

In a global environment marked by short-term orientation and silo-thinking, Global Agenda Councils are designed to foster interdisciplinary and long-range thinking to address the prevailing challenges on the global agenda.

The formation of Global Agenda Councils marks a major milestone in the World Economic Forum's evolution toward becoming the "integrator, manager, and disseminator of the best knowledge available in the world." These Councils build upon a unique strength of the Forum: its extraordinary ability to convene the best of the world's thought leaders.

For more information, visit www.weforum.org/gac.

Global Agenda Council on the Mitigation of Natural Disasters

Major natural disasters can cause great human and material damage and thus set back economic growth in both developed and developing countries. The Council seeks to identify operational and leadership principles for preventing, mitigating, and responding to a host of large-scale risks ranging from natural disasters and climate change to international terrorism and financial crises.

The Council has focused on the following issues:

- **Guiding principles:** These will provide a framework for taking actions to reduce global risks from natural disasters. They should also be relevant to other large-scale risks.
- **Linking pre-disaster measures with post-disaster measures:** The development of early-warning systems, the preservation and effective management of ecosystems, investment in loss reduction measures for property and infrastructure, and provision for financial protection insurance-type mechanisms are needed. Many countries lack the resources to effectively monitor disasters and invest in these measures. What lessons can be learned from developed nations to assist developing countries?
- **Climate change and natural disasters:** We need to better understand what scientists can tell us about the relationship between climate change and future losses from natural disasters and the degree of uncertainty surrounding the models they have developed.
- **Innovative risk management strategies:** Strategies for reducing risks from natural disasters that can be utilized in other contexts through public private partnerships should be proposed and examined. These strategies will be guided by the current institutional arrangements of the country under consideration and the decision processes of the relevant interested parties.
- **Education:** Education on responses to natural disasters can greatly mitigate their damage. How can the experience of countries with effective education programs best be applied to other nations?
- **Emergency management/disaster relief/humanitarian assistance in countries hit by natural disasters:** Large-scale disasters can greatly stretch domestic and international relief organizations. How should countries integrate and coordinate their own efforts with those of donors?
- **Business response to natural disasters:** Natural disasters often force the mass movement of people. Developing

countries may face particularly costly recovery and reconstruction processes. Business firms can play an important role in helping rebuild post-disaster communities by providing expertise and resources to domestic and international organizations.

- **Crisis leadership:** What do public, private, and NGO leaders need to know about risk assessment, behavioral biases, decision-rules, and their personal and organization leadership to prevent, prepare for, and respond to natural disasters?

For more information, visit www.weforum.org/pdf/GAC/issue_descriptions/MitigationofNaturalDisasters.pdf.

INDEX

D

E

F

G

H

I

J–K

L

S

W–Z

Wharton School Publishing

In the face of accelerating turbulence and change, business leaders and policy makers need new ways of thinking to sustain performance and growth.

Wharton School Publishing offers a trusted source for stimulating ideas from thought leaders who provide new mental models to address changes in strategy, management, and finance. We seek out authors from diverse disciplines with a profound understanding of change and its implications. We offer books and tools that help executives respond to the challenge of change.

Every book and management tool we publish meets quality standards set by The Wharton School of the University of Pennsylvania. Each title is reviewed by the Wharton School Publishing Editorial Board before being given Wharton's seal of approval. This ensures that Wharton publications are timely, relevant, important, conceptually sound or empirically based, and implementable.

To fit our readers' learning preferences, Wharton publications are available in multiple formats, including books, audio, and electronic.

To find out more about our books and management tools, visit us at whartonsp.com and Wharton's executive education site, exceed.wharton.upenn.edu.